THE CENTURIONS

ENGLAND'S 100 CLUB • BY HARRY HARRIS

FOREWORD BY SIR BOBBY CHARLTON

EMPIRE
PUBLICATIONS

EMPIRE PUBLICATIONS

1 Newton Street, Manchester M1 1HW

© Harry Harris 2012

ISBN 1901746 968 – 9781901746969

Back cover: *FA Chairman David Bernstein (C) presented (L-R) Babette Wright, daughter of Billy Wright, who won 105 caps, Sir Bobby Charlton (106 caps), Stephanie Moore, the widow of the late Bobby Moore, who won 108 caps, Peter Shilton (125) and David Beckham (115) with their special Uefa '100th caps' awards during the International Friendly match between England and Belgium at Wembley Stadium on June 2, 2012 in London, England. (Getty Images)*

Printed and bound by CPI Group (UK) Ltd, Croydon, CR0 4YY

CONTENTS

FOREWORD BY SIR BOBBY CHARLTON   IX

A SPECIAL MESSAGE FROM STEPHANIE MOORE   XIII

INRODUCTION   XV

BILLY WRIGHT   1

SIR BOBBY CHARLTON   17

BOBBY MOORE   35

PETER SHILTON   62

DAVID BECKHAM   84

BECKHAM PASSES MOORE'S RECORD   114

THE NEXT GENERATION   136

BRITISH AND IRISH CENTURIONS   143

EUROPEAN CENTURIONS   149

WORLD CENTURIONS   213

INDEX   226

STATISTICS: ENGLAND'S CENTURIONS   235

STATISTICS: THE 100 CLUB   244

ABOUT THE AUTHOR

HARRY HARRIS has won a total of 14 journalism awards. A regular analyst on football related matters on all major TV news and sports channels, he has appeared on Richard & Judy, Newsnight, BBC News, ITN News at Ten, Sky and Setanta. He is also a regular on Radio 5 Live, Radio 4, and TalkSport. He has been interviewed on Football Focus and appeared on the original Hold The Back Page and Jimmy Hill's Sunday Supplement on Sky.

Arguably the most prolific writer of best selling football books of his generation, Harry has penned 68 titles including the acclaimed best seller Pele – His Life and Times and George Best's last book, 'Hard Tackles and Dirty Baths'.

Harry has written one of the most influential football columns in the country for three decades and is regarded as one of the best investigative journalists and perhaps the best news gather of his generation. He has worked for the Daily Mail, Daily Mirror, Daily Express, Daily Star and Sunday Express and has nearly 30 years experience as the country's number one football writer. Harry is now Football Correspondent for ESPN Soccernet.

ACKNOWLEDGEMENTS

Special thanks to Sir Bobby Charlton for his extra special foreword. To Stephanie Moore for her wise words on bowel cancer awareness.

To Alex Dixon and Kellie Hazleton at Wembley Stadium

At Empire Publications: John, Ash and Phill.

DEDICATION

To my old friends Sir Bobby Charlton and hopefully soon to be Sir Bobby Moore

FOREWORD
BY SIR BOBBY CHARLTON

REACHING 100 CAPS was a very significant milestone in my life. The first person who spoke to me when I won my 100th cap was Billy Wright, the first Englishman to achieve that honour. He had also been the captain when I won my first cap. At that time Billy was coming toward the end of his illustrious career. I remember training with him at Wembley, not the stadium, but the nearby ground where we used to train. When I won my 100th cap he just said 'congratulations' and 'good luck'. I had a lot of time for Billy Wright. He was a true gentleman.

Bobby Moore was the next to win 100 caps and of course I played many years with Bobby, probably most of my England career, when he was the England captain and we were there, of course, when we won the World Cup in '66. I had a lot of time for his talents. He was a great captain, a great leader.

When we start to talk about players such as Billy Wright and Bobby Moore, it makes me feel privileged to be mentioned in their company and to have, along with them, won 100 caps for my country. When I was a little lad I read up everything about the game, about players such as Stanley Matthews and Tom Finney and foreign greats such as Ferenc

Puskas and it is incredible to think that players such as them with their enormous talents never made it to 100 caps. It increases my pride at having achieved such a milestone. I played another half a dozen games after reaching 100 and when I look back on what I achieved with England I feel very proud and privileged.

Next to reach 100 was Peter Shilton, a great shot stopper, very athletic. More recently he had a word with me and he recalled the day he stopped a shot from me at Old Trafford and he said how proud he was to have stopped one of my shots and how memorable that had been during his career! Well, that is saying something considering how long Peter went on for.

Next was David Beckham and despite all the chit chat about whether he deserved to win 100 caps because of the number of substitutions later in his career, I don't even consider it a controversial issue. It's a fact. He won 100 caps and anyone who plays that long and is so committed to the England cause is to be congratulated, not criticised. Like everybody else who has reached this milestone, he is extremely proud.

I have known David since he was a lad and I know just how much he loves this game. When I started my Soccer Schools, he won our Skills Player of the Year for a few years. Some of the coaches didn't fancy him but I thought he was a certainty to make it. I thought he was just brilliant as a boy when working with him and with a fair wind I knew he would make it, which, of course, he did.

Now we have a new batch of players about to hit 100 caps. The reason? Perhaps it's because of the pitches. They are different to my day, in a far better class by some distance. You leave the pitch these days very much as you found it, in a perfect condition. You feel better at the end of a game when the pitch is in perfect condition. With the pitches flat, the game has changed, the game is played much more on the floor and is no where near as physical as it used to be, its faster but not as demanding physically. In the old days we played in all sorts of weather and conditions, frozen pitches, snow covered pitches, fog. Now there is method and the team shares the work, passing it around.

Ashley Cole is a good player and one would not be considered top quality were they to reach 100 caps. He must also be in top condition because it demands such stamina to play on for so long. So I would wish all those reaching 100 caps 'good luck'

Steven Gerrard is someone whom I would have said right from the word go, was a natural to make it to the very top. I saw him play for Liverpool youth team when they beat Manchester Untied in the youth cup and you could see then that he was another, like Beckham, destined for the top. Frank Lampard is a good midfield player, a prolific goalscorer and for that reason there can be no argument once he reaches 100 caps.

Wayne Rooney has the potential to reach 100 caps and much more. He is a great talent and an automatic choice when we have a shortage of top international talent.

Since the influx of so many foreign players there is a definite shortage of English players from which the England manager can select at the highest level. I feel sorry for the

England manager, whoever he is, as he simply doesn't have enough players to choose from.

Wayne is fine at Old Trafford and it is up to the England manager to find a way of bringing the best out of him at international level and how best to handle him. He is handled very well at Manchester United and I am sure it will evolve with England and if that is the case I feel sure that Wayne is the player most capable of breaking my record of 49 goals which has stood the test of time. Some came close. We all thought Michael Owen would do it and it is a surprise that he didn't. Gary Lineker, of course, came one short. A few have come close but faded away. I must say I am actually quite proud of being England's top goalscorer, perhaps more so now. It's nice when kids come up to me and say 'you're England's top goalscorer'.

If anyone is going to get the record, then its going to be Wayne Rooney, he's good enough and he is still young enough. No matter how much I might like being the top goalscorer, I will be pleased when someone breaks it, particularly if it's Wayne. I would congratulate him. It is certainly a record to treasure.

As for England's future prospects. They haven't got a lot of top quality players to choose from and because of that you must feel it is going to be difficult to win things. You cannot see it happening in Brazil at the next World Cup for instance.

Perhaps, if the right group of players come together and stay together for a while and gelled into a team, with the right manager, then perhaps it might happen, but I have to be honest and say its a way off.

A SPECIAL MESSAGE
FROM STEPHANIE MOORE

I AM ABSOLUTELY DELIGHTED that the publishers are donating £1 from every book sold to the Bobby Moore Fund for Cancer Research UK. Bobby died aged just 51 from bowel cancer, the UK's second highest killing cancer. 44 men and women die every day from this disease in this country. If diagnosed early, 90% of cases would be successfully treated. It is important to drive awareness about bowel cancer and this book will play a vital role.

It goes without saying how honoured Bobby was to reach 100 England caps and I must add how honoured I was that the FA, UEFA and Wembley Stadium made me and the other recipients of the UEFA awards for feeling so much at home.

Billy Wright's daughter brought her young son along, Sir Bobby and Lady Norma Charlton were there, along with David Beckham and Peter Shilton. It was such a lovely day.

It also brought home the huge divide between players now of the status of David Beckham compared to that of Peter Shilton who won a record 125 caps.

Peter Bonetti now works for a taxi company following his illustrious footballing career and when he heard that

Peter Shilton had ordered a taxi to take him to Wembley for the big occasion to receive his award for reaching 100 caps, Peter Bonetti insisted he did the job. There can be no better example of the way the game has gone in recent years. I really cannot imagine that one day David Beckham will need to drive a taxi to earn a living!

INTRODUCTION

WHAT DO PELE, Diego Maradona, Johann Cruyff, Eusebio, Ferenc Puskas and Michel Platini have in common? They all failed to reach 100 caps. Incredibly both Pele (92) and Maradona (91) fell just short, Puskas managed 84, while Platini appeared 71 times for France. Eusebio (64) and Cruyff, the genius Dutchman with the trademark turn, managed a mere 48 – not even half a century of caps.

Pele managed 92 caps for Brazil, with an amazing 97 goals. However there are just over 125 players throughout the history of the entire global game who have surpassed the magical 100 cap mark and here in England we can boast five of them, soon to become eight.

The cap is a symbol representing the first international match, played in 1872 between England and Scotland. For every Englishmen who has ever worn the Three Lions, the cap represents something unique; the prestige, the pride and the passion of representing the country at football. There is no higher honour, no medal that means more than an England cap, not even winning the Champions League, the current pinnacle of the European game. The quest is to win the World Cup or the European Championships in an England shirt and only the Boys of '66 have so far managed it.

The first England international was staged in 1872, but it was not until May 1886 that the FA agreed to award caps. It was originally intended that the caps would be of white silk with a red rose. In fact, they were blue velvet with a red rose. Caps have occasionally been green and a silver tassel has been added with the rose replaced by the Three Lions emblem. At first the caps had the match date embroidered on the peak. Later, the initial letter of the opposition was included, and eventually the full name. To begin with, caps were awarded for every international played. Now one is presented per season for friendly internationals and one single cap for each tournament in which the player has represented England. The cap awarded to Gordon Banks for his six appearances in the 1966 World Cup finals went at auction in 2001 for £27,025.

David Beckham was given a standing ovation when he returned to Wembley to collect his special FIFA award for playing 100 internationals. He sat beside Manchester United legend and World Cup winner Sir Bobby Charlton in the Royal Box to watch England's final Euro 2012 warm-up game against Belgium before Roy Hodgson's squad departed for the European Championships in Poland and Ukraine. Becks and his fellow England Centurions were paraded at half-time to a rousing reception alongside former goalkeeper and 1990 World Cup semi-finalist, Peter Shilton. The widows of both Bobby Moore and Billy Wright were also present to accept the honour on behalf of their late husbands. The celebrated trio then received their medals from European football's governing body UEFA in recognition of surpassing the century milestone of caps. They all received a gold cap encased in a glass presentation case for reaching 100 caps.

The Fab Five who won a century of England caps each epitomised their age.

Billy Wright sprinkled glamour on to a nation desperate to throw off post-war austerity. He married a Beverley Sister, the Spice Girls of his generation, and played at Wolverhampton Wanderers, where they made the first great experiment in European football under floodlights. When he married Joy Beverley in 1959, their wedding stopped the traffic. It received almost as much publicity as the Posh Spice/Becks union 40 years later. Wright was England's captain for three World Cups (1950, 1954, and 1958). Initially a wing-half, Billy moving into central defence for his 60th international, England vs. Switzerland and was a revelation. Wright captained England 90 times on the way to becoming the first footballer to win 100 international caps.

Bobby Moore was the epitome of sixties cool. The image of him walking from the players' exit at Upton Park and tossing a set of keys to a group of boys to unlock his Jaguar will remain a significant memory for me. He seemed as comfortable among the man on the street as he was with movie stars and celebrities. On the pitch there's little doubt he was one of the greats. That iconic moment when he and Pele embraced after their epic World Cup confrontation in the heat of Mexico highlighted the kind of mutual respect Moore had with the very best of his era.

Long after he had retired, Bobby Charlton was still the most recognised English footballer in the world. Now knighted, Sir Bobby is without doubt one of the most famous

English players of all time, synonymous with some of the greatest moments in the English game but also with the highest traditions of sportsmanship and integrity. Unquestionably the greatest player to pull on an England shirt, Sir Bobby still holds the record as England's highest goalscorer.

Peter Shilton kept goal in two of English football's pivotal moments, the defeat by Poland in 1973 and the World Cup semi-final with West Germany 17 years later. He summed up a generation of footballers, in an era where they liked a pint and a bet but who would give everything for a Three Lions shirt. Peter's record is all the more remarkable because of the rich crop of talented goalkeepers about during his time – that he consistently got the nod ahead of the likes of Ray Clemence and Joe Corrigan speaks volumes.

David Beckham represents the 21st century age of celebrity. Yet Becks has stayed true to his roots. The humble lad from Leytonstone might top the global wage earners for his abilities both on the field and his image off it but he still finds time to put something back into English football – using his global image on behalf of the FA and grassroots football. Becks completes the circle from the Billy Wright era, symbolising how the game has irrefutably changed. Footballers didn't earn big money in Wright's era and although Charlton, Moore and Shilton were much better off than the man in the street, they earned nothing like the multi millions that put Beckham into a financial league of his own.

To put it into perspective, David Beckham still earns more in just one week than Billy Wright picked up as a player throughout a 20-year career. Yet, they had a common bond, the love of the game and desire to continue to play it for as long as they could. Just like Beckham, the first England Centurion also rose from humble beginnings to become a folk–hero.

Fabio Capello was Beckham's fifth full–time England manager. Shilton served under four, Moore and Charlton two, while Wright had only Walter Winterbottom as national boss. The national game has followed the rest of football and become a results business with patience and personalities clashing with every England failure.

Now the exclusive club that belongs to just five Englishmen is about to expand. The Fab Five are soon to become the Super Six with Ashley Cole poised to break through the magical 100 barrier. Then it will be the Magnificent Seven, as captain Steven Gerrard hits the ton and beyond as the likes of Frank Lampard and Wayne Rooney notch their 100th international appearances. The latter with the potential to break Sir Bobby Charlton's record of 49 England goals.

'England Centurions' is a personal recollection of the English players who are amongst the most illustrious in the history of the game; those precious few to pull on the shirt with Three Lions for a hundred times or more. Immortalised men who won a century of England caps

I have had the privilege of knowing all five of England Centurions. Not many journalists can boast the honour of actually sharing a dressing room with Sir Bobby Charlton, but I have played alongside him, and once against him, for the England press team in my time. When we ran onto the pitch it was an incredible to think that Bobby looked so fit and trim despite his age. I asked him how he did it. Simple, he replied...warm up properly. "I see so many of these games, and everyone just rushes out and starts running around and chasing the ball, and kicking it as hard as they can, and then they are pulling up with a muscle strain within minutes, the secret is stretching and warming up properly." Sound advice from an old pro. Of course that was many years ago, and I don't think even the enthusiastic Sir Bobby is trying to turn out for charity or press teams anymore. It was also a great pleasure to be able to talk to him in a relaxed atmosphere at the after match meal laid on by our hosts.

Sponsors Adidas would organise a simultaneous football tournament for the mornings before a big match, so when England played in the European Championships and we were paired with Russia, the two press teams turned out on the morning of the big game. On this occasion the Russians only had about a dozen journalists able to cover the entire tournament, so half of their team were travelling from another venue and missed the press team kick-off. The England team 'coach', Michael Hart of the Evening Standard, who was a fairly capable Sunday park footballer, decided that all of the England stragglers, those usually consigned to the bench for a bit part at the end, would make up the numbers in the Russian press team. I played for Russia at left back and I recall lunging into a sliding tackle to stop Bobby Charlton from tearing in on goal! Yes, I stopped the one and only Sir Bobby, one of the all time greats... well, I was a few years younger back then and he had slowed up a touch! Russia were leading 4–1 at half time, in what was turning out to be the shock of the media tournament before the rest of the Russian players turned up in time to take their places in the second half, and I was switched to the England team. England ended up winning the game 6-4. In the England team dressing room at the end, one of the Russian contingent came in and handed me the Russian shirt I had worn in the first half. The reason? I had scored for Russia against England.

As well as playing with and against Bobby Charlton in the same game, I have also hooked up with Sir Bobby at numerous sponsors' functions, once alongside Pele, and have the ball with both of their autographs on it to prove it. What a memento! That's one of the perks of being in my line of work and, as a bit of a collector, I have been able to pick up some fantastic memorabilia. Pele and Sir Bobby are both ambassadors for MasterCard and at a central London hotel, a small, hand-selected cohort of international football writers gathered to interview the two great men over a very informal lunch. Pele was late, very late, as usual, but once he got there, he didn't want to leave, and had to be dragged away by his entourage to ensure he caught his flight.

Pride of place on my office wall at home goes to an England No 7 shirt personally signed "To Harry, Love, David Beckham". The shirt fits in well alongside two Pele shirts, both also personally signed to me, another from George Best, plus several further shirts I have picked up along my travels, including an England shirt signed by Geoff Hurst and Martin Peters. That is most definitely one of the perks of doing my job out in the field and I'm honoured to have been considered a good friend to these legends of the game to have taken the time and trouble to sign memorabilia for me.

After David's shirt arrived, I thanked him for it the next time I bumped into him, which just happened to be at the launch of his autobiography, David Beckham - My Side, in Madrid. I reassured him that I wouldn't be selling the shirt on eBay, unless I could find someone called "Harry"!

I have known David since he first arrived in the England camp with his autograph book searching for the signatures of his heroes such as Alan Shearer, Paul Ince and David Seaman and I have felt that, amidst all the hyperbole and headlines, he has retained that boyish enthusiasm and love for the game which is the reason he has lasted so long at the very top of his profession.

As a football pundit I am asked many times to appear on documentaries to comment about David and the Beckham family, who have dominated the last decade in terms of media profile and been at the centre of moving football from the back to the front pages of newspapers. His life has been lived very much in the spotlight but there's no doubt that his enthusiasm for the game has never diminished.

The argument that great players do not make great managers is certainly true of the five England Centurions. Bobby Moore was briefly in charge at Oxford City and Southend, while Bobby Charlton was boss at Preston and Wigan. Famous players do not fail in management because they have been stars. It is more a question of clubs believing that by appointing a well-known name the process of learning to be a manager can somehow be bypassed.

Of course if the club has the right structure and a tradition of success a novice can survive. Until his abrupt departure from the England job Kevin Keegan, with his successes at Newcastle and Fulham, was a rare star who shone off the field as well as on it. Unlike another former England captain, Billy Wright, who in 1962 arrived as Arsenal's new manager with 105 caps, a Beverley sister as his wife and a golden future in the game. It was fool's gold, as it turned out, Wright leaving Highbury after four fraught years to embark on a successful career in television.

Whatever else they achieved (or didn't) during the rest of their lives, these five England footballers remain legends for their membership of the very select 100 Club. This book is a tribute to them.

BILLY WRIGHT

1946-1959 - 105 CAPS

Billy was the first Englishman to reach 100 caps, the first 59 as a wing-half rather than centre-half, the position usually associated with the legendary England captain. Billy led his country in three World Cup finals, played in 70 successive internationals, all as captain. Ninety of his final total of 105 were as captain, a record equalled later by Bobby Moore.

"It's easy to forget just how idolised he was"

GEORGE BEST

BILLY WRIGHT was lifted onto the shoulders of two team-mates after the home international with Scotland in recognition of his achievement in becoming the first footballer in the world to amass 100 caps. That game on April 11th 1959 at Wembley had not seen Wright's defensive qualities tested severely in a game England dominated and should have won by more than a solitary goal but for some inspired goalkeeping from Spurs 'keeper Bill Brown. Yet his colleagues recognised Billy's achievement.

Fittingly the winner came from Bobby Charlton, who would become the next England player to join the 100 club. At the end Wright was given a standing ovation and the Scotland players shook Wright's hand, momentarily putting aside their disappointment in defeat as he was chaired off the pitch by team-mates.

A blond England star, captain of his country and married to a pop star from an all-girl group, with a contract endorsing hair products, Billy Wright was blazing a celebrity trail almost 50 years before David Beckham. Wright was arguably Britain's first football superstar. He became a household name, for both his exploits in the game and his marriage to Joy Beverley of the chart-topping Beverley Sisters.

"It's easy to forget just how idolised he was," George Best, perhaps British football's first global star, once remarked. "England has had no better or more loyal a servant," commented team-mate Sir Tom Finney, "Billy was as solid as a rock. He was also a nice guy."

Billy started out as an inside-forward, turning professional with Wolverhampton Wanderers during the war. He made his England debut against Northern Ireland in 1946 at the age of 22. After that he missed only three of England's next 107 internationals, including a run of 46 consecutive matches at centre-half. He had been moved into the middle of the defence at the 1954 World Cup in Switzerland, when Walter Winterbottom's side reached the quarter finals for the first time. Bill McGarry was a thoroughly competent right-half, and his selection against Switzerland, in Berne, enabled Wright to move with such success to centre-half, where he would also figure in the 1958 World Cup. He was captain through three unsuccessful World Cup campaigns, but he was the outstanding England defender of his generation – strong, unflappably calm and never booked in 541 League and Cup games, a quite remarkable record for a defender. He scored 19 goals for Wolves. His loyalty, dedication and bravery rightfully made him a legend for both club and country; Wright burst into the Wolves team during the war and in 13 glorious years after peace resumed, he won three League titles and an FA Cup with the Black Country club.

Such was his popularity and star status that at one time Wolves thought he was overdoing the off-field activities. This is what the 1950s magazine *Football Parade* wrote about Wright, "He is a teetotaller, does not smoke, goes to bed early and lives modestly. Because he is such an ideal for youngsters to follow, Billy has many invitations to attend youth clubs, team dinners, the presentation of prizes and similar functions. He's such a good-natured chap that he cheerfully obliged until Wolves found that he was taking too much out of himself and asked him to call a halt."

Wright was described as 'a national treasure' by *The*

Times in 1959. He had became something of an institution in the heart of the England team. Over a period of eight years, starting in 1951, England did not once take the field without Wright in their ranks, a record run of 70 consecutive appearances. Ninety times he led England onto the field as captain, another record at the time.

"Billy had a heart of oak and was the most reliable of men," Walter Winterbottom, the England manager once said. "I considered myself lucky to have him to call on so often." Between 1946 and 1959 Wright experienced defeat with England only 21 times; he went seven years before tasting defeat at Wembley.

Although the enduring image of the 'Ironbridge Rocket' (after the Shropshire town where he was born) is of a no-nonsense centre-half, Wright began as a centre-forward and won his first 60 England caps at right-half, before converting to defence. "Essentially a team player who never tried to seek personal glory, Billy turned simplicity into an art form," Winterbottom said.

After one England international *The Times* wrote, "Billy Wright had a rare day off. He only played like one man."

Footballer of the Year in 1952, Wright was still the captain of both England and Wolves, the First Division champions, when he retired from football seven years later – at the age of 35. An FA Cup winner's medal and two other First Division championship medals completed his collection of honours. Tom Finney referred to his team-mate as 'Mr Dynamo', in tribute to the amount of running he did during a game. "I rate Billy as a challenger for the title of the most consistent centre-half ever to play for England," Finney once said.

Sturdy and competitive, Wright knew his limitations. "I only had two things on my mind as a player: to win the ball and then to give the simplest pass I could to the nearest team-mate," he said.

When, nearing the end of his playing career, he married the glamorous pop singer Joy Beverley in 1958 entering uncharted territory for a footballer: the world of media 'celebrity'. He was already well established as a hero to a generation of aspiring footballers. As a boy Kevin Keegan watched admiringly as Wright led Wolves against crack European club sides in prestigious friendlies played under floodlights at Molineux in the mid-1950s but there were a couple of momentous and historic blemishes on the great man's CV.

The game played at Wembley on 25th November 1953 is game so famous it has its own page on Wikipedia, numerous books and a café named after the infamous scoreline in Budapest.

England 3, Hungary 6

Hungary, the Olympic champions, came to the home of football, where England had never lost to continental opposition and taught them the mother of all lessons. England were flattered by a 6-3 defeat. It was revelatory, revolutionary. Until then almost all teams played in a WM formation, but Hungary patented a fluid 3-1-2-4 that centred around Nandor Hidegkuti baffling opponents with the then unprecedented tactic of roaming all over the pitch. He scored a hat-trick and Ferenc Puskás added two more, the first after a delicious drag-back that fooled the lunging England captain Billy Wright, who was memorably described by *The Times'* Geoffrey Green as playing "like a fire engine going to the wrong fire". That, like the rest of the game, was seared into the psyche of football. "His left foot was like a hand, he could do anything with it" Francisco Gento, Puskas' Real Madrid team-mate, once said.

The outstanding captain of a remarkable Hungarian team labelled "the best team in the world" by Billy Wright, he led Hungary to the World Cup finals of 1954 only for his Magical Magyars to run out of steam against West Germany. Towards the end of his career Puskas looked less footballer and more football but this inside-left was one of the true greats of the game, who helped to rouse English football from a complacency born of insularity and blinkered thinking.

The awakening was rude and embarrassing. In winning 6-3 Puskas's Hungarians not only became the first foreign team to beat England at Wembley; they changed English football thinking forever. Yet for all their conquerors' individual brilliance, the principal lesson for England was that at international level football was becoming a game of movement. As Puskas observed in his autobiography: "The result was determined by the unpreparedness of England's defence for the method of attack adopted by our forwards." Central to this approach was a deep-lying centre-forward, Hidegkuti, whose habit of drifting late into scoring positions confused the English defenders. As Puskas pointed out: "We demonstrated the golden rule of football, and that is: the good player keeps playing even without the ball. All the time he is placing himself so that when the ball comes he is able to make good use of it." This is elementary stuff now but to English eyes back then, it was football from another planet.

Hungary's victory and their even more emphatic 7-1 win against England in Budapest the following summer bred a new generation of English coaches who had been mesmerised by Puskas and his colleagues. Among them was Ron Greenwood, then an attacking centre-half at Chelsea but already set on a career in coaching. Greenwood, like England's defence, was bowled over by Puskas, who he described as "a roly-poly little fellow who looked as if he did most of his training in restaurants". Certainly Puskas was portly but as Greenwood noted, "He was a natural, a grand master of the game. He was entirely left-footed but no matter how the ball came the old left foot went up and his control was instant and precise. It was as if he had glue on the toe of his boot. He seemed to glide rather than run and, a sure sign of a strong personality, he dictated the shape and pace of the game."

The biggest paradox of Puskas's career is that, while his Hungary team ruled the football world in terms of quality, they failed to add the 1954 World Cup to the Olympic title they had won two years earlier. In 1999 he was voted the sixth best player of the 20th century, after Pele, Johan Cruyff, Franz Beckenbauer, Alfredo Di Stefano and Diego Maradona.

With the arguable exception of the 1953 loss at Wembley to Puskas's Hungarians, English football's darkest day was June 29th 1950. Having finally deigned to join in the World Cup, the inventors of the game lost 1-0 to the colonialists from the United States in Belo Horizonte. The England team included Alf Ramsey, Tom Finney and the Wolves trio of Bert Williams, Billy Wright and James Mullen. England were not eliminated from the World Cup until they lost their next match, 1-0 to Spain.

Yet despite his part in these two national disasters, Midlands Today viewers still voted Billy Wright the fourth greatest ever Midlander in a poll that attracted more than 30,000 votes. Meanwhile the Football League officially describes him as 'arguably the greatest club and country servant in the history of the game' – praise indeed for a man with a reputation as a gent both on and off the pitch.

The young William Ambrose Wright had to fight hard to become a professional footballer – and prove a few people wrong along the way. Born in Ironbridge on 6th February 1924, Billy was the son of a talented local footballer who was well-known for terrorising defences. He'd spend hours as a boy kicking a ball up against a door, getting his first football boots at the age of eight as a Christmas present. It was as a pupil of Madeley Wood Modern School that his skills first began to catch the eye – not least when, playing as a centre forward, he scored 10 in one match against Bewdley. Eventually his sports master, Norman Simpson, tipped off Wolverhampton Wanderers and young Billy was given a job on the groundstaff.

He was only 14 years old when he made his debut for Wolves in a B team game against Walsall Wood in the Walsall Minor League after being accepted on an eight month trial. But despite his talent, the then manager, Major Frank Buckley, didn't think the boy would make the grade.

When he first arrived at Molineux, he struggled to make an impression as Major Buckley was initially reluctant to gamble on a youngster who lacked height and was less talented than his peers. Fortunately for Billy, Mr Simpson urged Wolves to reconsider and the Major listened. Billy stayed at Wolves as 'boot boy' and finally got his chance.

His first team debut came just before the outbreak of World War II in a 2–1 victory at Notts County and he signed as a professional when he turned 17, turning out as a guest for Leicester City along with Jimmy Mullen after the worsening war situation prompted the authorities to suspend competitive football. For the Foxes he played as both a forward and a defender before he returned to Molineux in 1942 after breaking his ankle in a cup–tie with West Bromwich Albion. The war interrupted Billy's career and he joined the Army as a physical training instructor in 1943, although he still got to play the odd game for Wolves making over 100 appearances for the club in wartime football.

When peace was restored and football returned to normal, Billy missed only eight games playing in the wing half position of that first post war season in 1946/7. Stan Cullis retired from the playing side of the game at the end of that season and Billy was appointed captain of the club in his place. In the following two seasons he missed only ten games and he picked up his first major honour when Wolves overcame Leicester City in the 1949 FA Cup Final. In 1949/50 the team finished as runners up to Portsmouth on goal average despite a valiant end of season run that saw them win seven of the last ten games - scoring ten goals in the last two

The fortunes of the club then took a downturn and in

the following season Wolves slumped to a disappointing 14th position in the league and also lost out in the semi-final of the FA Cup to Newcastle. In 1951/2 they dropped a further place but by 1952/3 there was a marked improvement with a third place in the final league placings. Wolves finally achieved what they had been threatening to do ever since the war by capturing the League Championship. Billy Wright's captaincy was an inspiration to the team who then set about some of Europe's finest clubs and demolished them in those never to be forgotten floodlit friendlies. The next three years were again to prove almost, but not quite, as the team finished 2nd, 3rd and 6th respectively before in 1957/8 and 1958/9 the championship trophy was again held aloft by Billy. In nine seasons in the fifties he only missed 31 games for Wolves and several of those absences were caused by international call-ups.

Wright played his last league game for Wolves in the penultimate match of 1958/9 when Wolves overcame Leicester 3-0 at Molineux. Shortly after he was awarded the C.B.E. for his services to football and he announced his retirement from the game just before the start of the following season. This came in an age when footballers were often ignored in the Honours List and given today's vogue for handing out knighthoods to the likes of Alex Ferguson, Elton John and Paul McCartney, it's likely that Billy would have been 'Sir Billy' had he been around today. He bid Molineux and its grateful fans farewell in the annual pre-season Colours v Whites game.

On his retirement *The Times* wrote: 'There were more talented and more skilful players, but what he embroidered into the fabric of our lives were the values of loyalty and industry. Billy Wright, the man, is a human being of exemplary character. Billy Wright, the footballer, was a national treasure.'

He became manager of England's youth team, the under 18s, in 1960, before being appointed manager of Arsenal in 1962, replacing George Swindin. Billy became manager of his boyhood heroes. He was manager for four years. Initially Arsenal started strongly under Wright, finishing seventh in 1962–63 and qualifying for Europe for the first time in their history, but failed to build on this. Wright enjoyed mixed success with his signings, who included successes such as Bob Wilson, Joe Baker and Frank McLintock but also less successful players such as Ian Ure. Arsenal were unable to improve on their seventh position in Wright's second season in charge, and their form gradually declined. Wright only won 38% of his matches in charge, the lowest rate for any post-war Arsenal manager (caretaker managers excepted). After a poor 1965–66 season — where Arsenal finished 14th and were knocked out of the FA Cup by Blackburn Rovers (who finished bottom of the First Division — Wright was dismissed by the Arsenal board in the summer of 1966. Football writer Brian Glanville, discussing Wright's time at Arsenal, wrote: "he had neither the guile nor the authority to make things work and he reacted almost childishly to criticism".

After four years he left Highbury and was thereafter associated with sports coverage on ATV in the Midlands. He retired in 1989, and, in May 1990, he delighted Wolves fans young and old, when he returned to Molineux as a director for one of the most popular homecomings of all time. In

September, 1994, at the age of 70, Billy passed away after a fight against cancer. His funeral the following week, bought the centre of Wolverhampton to a standstill as the town bid farewell and paid their respects to its favourite footballing son.

In recognition of his long service to the game the Football Association made him a Life Member. He was the first professional player to be awarded the honour. On the second anniversary of his death, a magnificent statue of the legend was unveiled outside Molineux. And a blue plaque marks the tiny cottage in Ironbridge where he was born.

Old pals paid glowing tributes at the naming of a tram in his honour. The ceremony saw Wright's daughter and granddaughter – Vicky and Kelly Wright – unveil a commemorative name plaque on the Midland Metro system's tram number seven, which has been painted in the new silver and magenta Network West Midlands livery. Among those present for the tram-naming were ex-team mates Malcolm Finlayson, Roy Swinbourne, George Showell and Bobby Mason. Bill Slater, who succeeded Wright as Wolves captain and led the team to victory in the 1960 FA Cup Final, described Wright as "very special".

"This is a well-deserved honour for him today. He was an inspiring figure on the field and had a great international record. He always had time for the younger players. I never once heard him swear," he said. Roy Swinbourne, who starred with Wright in Wolves' famous 3-2 victory over Hungarian champions Honved in 1954, scoring two goals, said: "He was brilliant. He gave 110 per cent all the time, even in training. He loved Wolverhampton and lived for Wolves." The tram naming ceremony began at the Midland Metro depot in Wednesbury and concluded in Wolverhampton. The decision to name the tram after Billy was made after Centro held a public vote and he received 90 per cent of the poll.

One of my most pleasant assignments as a young football reporter was to contact Billy Wright while he was an executive at ATV to check out a story. The thought of speaking to the legendary Billy Wright was a thrill in itself. When I spoke to him on the phone, I was not to be disappointed, when you are sometimes confronted by those you respect and they turn out to be anything other than the image you have of them. I was most impressed by his openness and welcoming tone and he had even told me he had heard of me. I wished all the people I had to check out stories with had treated me with that sort of kindness and respect!

The admiration, affection and recognition of Billy Wright's achievements lives on, as Andy Gray, himself a Wolves legend, explains in graphic detail. Gray scored over 178 goals in 493 matches during a brilliant career beginning in 1970 with Clydebank Strollers, turning professional with Dundee Utd in May 1973 and playing 75 games while also collecting a Scottish Cup runners up medal. In 1975 Aston Villa spent £110,000 bringing him to Villa Park, where he scored 69 goals in 141 matches during his spell with Aston Villa, becoming the first player to win both the PFA Young Footballer and PFA Footballer of the Year award in the same season (1977), a feat only equalled by Cristiano Ronaldo in

2008.

He signed for Wolves on 8th September 1979 for £1.4m becoming the most expensive footballer in Britain. His debut for Wolves was a 3-2 victory over Everton at Goodison Park on the 15th September 1979, in which he scored the first of 38 goals for Wolves. His most treasured but also one of his easiest, came against Nottingham Forest at Wembley in the 1980 League Cup Final, Wolves last major trophy success. Injuries kept him out of a third of the following season's games, before he left Molineux in November 1983 for Everton for £250,000. He scored 14 goals in 49 league appearances and collected winners medals in three different competitions for the Toffees; First Division, FA Cup and European Cup Winners' Cup. He returned to Aston Villa for a second spell for £150,000 in July 1985, before moving on to loan spells at Notts County and West Brom.

He joined his boyhood heroes Glasgow Rangers and helped them to win the Scottish Premier League title and collected a Skol Cup Winners medal. Rangers released him at the end of the 1988-89 season when he joined non-league Cheltenham Town and also began a new career as a sports presenter. Gray also won 20 caps for Scotland, scoring 7 times between 1975 and 1985.

Andy tells me, "When I joined Wolves it was a club steeped in history. When you walked around the old Molineux, you could go all the way around the ground and all it had was history, history, history, and all around the Billy Wright era. Everywhere there were pictures of the achievements of the fifties and sixties; the first floodlit games against the likes of Honved, league championship and FA Cup success and you couldn't help but be aware of Billy Wright and what he did for the club, it was huge in that respect.

"As a player you felt that was something you would try to emulate, even the biggest players that passed through that club such as Derek Dougan, Kenny Hibbitt, and John Richards and that is how I felt. That was the legacy he left to Wolves. If you stopped anyone in the streets of Wolverhampton and asked them to name one Wolves legend, it would be Billy Wright. I am sure no one will ever equal Billy Wright's achievements at Wolves, certainly not in my life time

"But Wolves is a very different club now, we live in a very different era. Everything was much simpler in those days. People played for their club, for their manager, for their team-mates, because they wanted to, because they liked to. Billy Wright did not play for the money, he played for the club, and their managers, he was very aware of the fact that he was playing for the club in the town in which he lived. What he achieved with not just Wolves, but of course England will stand the test of time. No Wolves players now or in the future will ever come close to achieving half of what Billy did.

"For me Billy was right up there at the pinnacle of anybody who ever played for England, yet it was one of his worst games that I would pick out as being one of his most significant. It was Billy's style to launch himself into tackles, but on this occasion, he came up against Hungary and Puskas and the English game was shocked and taken by surprise, as was Bill, when he lunged into that tackle on Puskas, and the great man dragged it away from him. But that actually made Billy learn to adapt, much more than all his caps prior to that game put together.

"He suddenly realised that he had moved to a higher level and had to raise his own game, which he did. He stepped it up and his performances improved and he went on to become as great an England captain as anyone and that includes Bobby Moore.

"The mere fact I mention Billy Wright in the same breath as Bobby Moore shows you how highly I rate Billy Wright, and how much I think of him, not just as a player, a person, but also an ambassador for English football. It is a fitting tribute, I think, to talk about the two in the same breath. Ambassador has become an easy word, especially these days, but Billy Wright, and indeed Bobby Moore, were great ambassadors for their country. The two men are head and shoulders above anyone else who has captained England. They are a class apart."

Billy Wright's record for England was exceptional. He was capped 105 times 90 of them as skipper. He played his first full international against Scotland in 1947, and by the time he made his last appearance 13 years later in the 8–1 thrashing of the United States in Los Angeles he had missed only three games for his country. Of his 105 games, 60 were won, 23 drawn, 21 lost and one game was abandoned. His record of 105 caps was to stand for 20 years until it was broken by Bobby Charlton in 1970.

Billy Wright, captain of Wolves and England, was one of the game's greatest ambassadors.

SIR BOBBY CHARLTON

1958-1970 - 106 CAPS

Bobby is England's record goalscorer with 49 goals. A World Cup winner in 1966, Bobby was substituted in his last international when England led 2-0 in the 1970 World Cup quarter-final, his departure giving West Germany crucial impetus.

"There has never been a more popular footballer. He was as near perfection as man and player as it is possible to be."

SIR MATT BUSBY

SIR BOBBY CHARLTON is without doubt one of the most famous English players of all time. His name is synonymous with some of the greatest moments in the English game but also with the highest traditions of sportsmanship and integrity.

Using his pace from midfield and with a thunderous long range shot, he scored some of the most spectacular goals English football has ever seen. He remains the nation's greatest ever goalscorer with an unsurpassed tally of 49 goals, scoring in 13 successive seasons, in 27 different matches, included four hat-tricks. His greatest strengths were his speed and body swerve. As he flowered as a footballer, he became the fulcrum of the team's attack. An outstanding distributor of the ball, he could spray inch-perfect passes, picking out team-mates with astounding accuracy. He also had a fierce shot that belied his relatively small stature (5 feet 8 inches) and scored almost a goal every other game in an England shirt – no mean feat over the course of 106 internationals. His tally of 49 is one more than that scored by out-and-out striker Gary Lineker, Michael Owen (40) while only goalkeeper Peter Shilton collected more caps.

Having survived the Munich air disaster in February 1958, in April of that year he was handed his first England cap against Scotland at Hampden Park. Then 20 years old, he scored the third goal with a volley in a 4-0 victory watched by a crowd of over 127,000.

As one of the "Busby Babes" to survive the Munich air disaster, he teamed up with Denis Law and George Best in the 1960s to produce some of United's greatest ever football. Charlton remained faithful to United and in his time there from 1956-73, he won the league championship three times, the FA Cup once and the European Cup once, scoring twice as Benfica were beaten 4-1 in a memorable final in 1968 at Wembley. Charlton played more than 750 games for United, scoring 247 goals in all competitions.

He was Footballer of the Year in both England and Europe in 1966, the year in which he won the World Cup with England. His 30-yard 'Bobby Dazzler' against the Mexicans in England's second match in Group 1, helped England towards that famous World Cup triumph. He also scored twice to knock out Portugal in the semi-final. His last international appearance, against West Germany in the 1970 World Cup quarter final in Leon, was his 106th cap and made him England's most-capped player at that time.

The Manchester United captain was given the honour of captaining his country before a full house of 100,000 when he reached his landmark 100th game against Northern Ireland on April 21, 1970 at Wembley. He capped a typically imperious midfield display with a goal, sliding in to beat Pat Jennings at the far post. His United team-mate George Best scored a fine individual goal for the visitors but Martin Peters and Geoff Hurst ensured an England victory as they prepared to go to Mexico to defend the Jules Rimet trophy

Born in Ashington on October 11th 1937. The grammar-school pupil was spotted playing for East Northumberland Schools by legendary Manchester United scout Joe Armstrong in 1953 and signed on June 1, aged 15. After a stint working in an engineering works close to Old Trafford, he signed professional forms aged 17 in 1954 but had to wait for debut until Oct 6, 1956, the month of his 19th birthday. He made his senior debut against Charlton Athletic – and marked the occasion with two goals in a 4-2 win.

United were league champions that season and Charlton, in an outside-left role, played his part with ten goals in 14 matches. The youthful Red Devils also reached the FA Cup final and European Cup semi-final and further glories beckoned but fate was to intervene in tragic fashion. On their way back from a European Cup quarter-final win away to Red Star Belgrade on February 6th 1958, United's plane crashed on take-off after re-fuelling at Munich. Charlton survived but 23 people perished, including eight United team-mates. Busby's side was decimated by the Munich air disaster but Charlton, just 20, was thrown from the plane still strapped to his seat and somehow survived unscathed, although mental scars surely remain from having lost so many contemporaries in such circumstances.

Busby rebuilt his side as best he could and made Charlton the cornerstone. Success returned to Old Trafford in 1963 with an FA Cup triumph, followed by league titles in 1965 and 1967. The crowning glory for Charlton in a United shirt came the following season when, a decade after Munich, he scored twice as they beat Benfica 4-1 at Wembley in the final of the European Cup, becoming the first English winners of the trophy. For captain Charlton, Busby and centre-half Billy Foulkes, the other crash survivor still in the team, it was a deeply emotional moment when Sir Bobby climbed the steps to the Royal Box to collect the famous trophy.

Despite originally making his mark on the left wing, Charlton's international debut came as an inside-forward on 19 April 1958 but, as with his first match for Manchester

United, he celebrated with a goal and a victory, Scotland falling victim to a 4–0 scoreline at Hampden Park. "I can still hear the sound of the ball lashing against the net," Charlton recalls, "after that, all you could hear was the silence." His international introduction at the age of 19 had established the template: a thunderbolt volley from Tom Finney's cross in a four-goal victory, in a forward line that read Douglas-Charlton-Kevan-Haynes-Finney. As team-mate Sir Tom Finney said, it was "a wonderful, unstoppable goal." His performance was enough to merit a call-up for the 1958 World Cup in Sweden but England exited after a first round play-off defeat by the Soviet Union. Charlton did not make a single appearance and manager Walter Winterbottom regretted having selected him, believing he was still suffering from the after-effects of the Munich air disaster. Bobby was made a scapegoat for a 5–0 hammering by Yugoslavia in temperatures of over 100 degrees in Belgrade in the build-up to the tournament for which Charlton was inexplicably omitted throughout the 1958 World Cup finals in Sweden. "He could have been retained – he already had the ability to win us matches" Sir Tom later reflected.

There followed four goals in seven England appearances at inside forward or centre forward in 1958-9. Then, having been switched, against his will, to playing on the wing by Busby, when United were short of wing power following the Munich crash, Charlton also moved to the left flank in a flourishing England front line of Douglas-Greaves-Smith-Haynes-Charlton that ran up 63 goals in 17 matches prior to the Chile World Cup in 1962, 11 coming from Charlton. He recalled that there were days with United "when I died of cold" out on the wing.

By 1962 Charlton was firmly established in the team and he scored his first World Cup goal against Argentina to help England through to the quarter-finals, where they were beaten by eventual winners Brazil. When reflecting on the 1962 World Cup in Chile – where he was voted the tournament's outstanding left winger, he commented: "There was a lot of coaching from Walter Winterbottom, the manager, but I was young and impatient, and I used to think 'just give me the ball and I'll beat them'."

He would continue as an exhilarating England winger, post-Chile, for 40 of his next 42 appearances, although with United, following the emergence of Best, he had more happily returned to midfield freedom at Old Trafford. "Because of his pace, his instant ball control and his passing accuracy, and his ability to attack from midfield, he was so reminiscent of Di Stefano" said Busby, who regarded the Real Madrid legend as the world's No 1. Playing in the hole, as it would be described nowadays, Charlton fashioned tumultuous years together with Paddy Crerand; less a marksman than a provider for Law, Best, Brian Kidd and others.

The ultimate in his evolution with England came with Alf Ramsey's initiation of a wingless 4-3-3 formation in the 2-0 victory over Spain in Madrid in December 1965: Stiles-Charlton-Eastham in midfield, Ball-Baker-Hunt up front, the formula that would win the World Cup, Martin Peters having replaced Eastham and Geoff Hurst moving in for Joe Baker.

On the flight home from Brazil following the England

summer tour in 1964, Ramsey asked Charlton whether he had enjoyed the trip. Yes, he had, Charlton replied, but they had been away from home for more than a month and he had really missed his wife and young daughter. "If I thought that was your attitude," said Ramsey, witheringly, "I wouldn't have brought you." Charlton observed, "It might have been tongue in cheek, or it might not. I still don't know." When Charlton's United team-mate Nobby Stiles wanted a break from the training regime for a few days to be with his wife Kay for the birth of their child, he didn't even dare to ask Ramsey. Sir Bobby admitted Ramsey would have hated the thought of England being led by a foreigner. "Alf would have been insulted without any question. But I can't think of an Englishman I'd really like to see in the job. Having foreign managers won't satisfy everybody but losing is worse."

Ramsey gathered his players together and issued that famous rallying call: "Gentlemen, we will win the World Cup." Sir Bobby talks almost lovingly about the Ramsey era in his book My England Years: The Autobiography. "Alf Ramsey's fervent desire to make his team and his players a family, insulated against everything else in the world – except, perhaps, one of his favourite westerns or James Bond films, to which he led us with great enthusiasm whenever they were available – was, perhaps, a leading reason why few people in the history of English sport have been analysed as relentlessly as the man who delivered the nation's only World Cup. He was the one who, at the moment of triumph, turned his back on the glory, insisting that it belonged solely to the players. It was almost as if he was saying, finally, that if at times he had given us hell, had made decisions we didn't like or perhaps didn't agree with, it was really all for us. We had to take everything he gave to us and then, he had always believed, we would become strong.

"In recent years, I have sometimes wondered about the changes that have come to football, and life, and how they are mirrored in the differences between the England of Ramsey and the one made by Sven-Goran Eriksson nearly three decades later. It was hard not to chuckle, somewhat ruefully of course, when trying to imagine how Ramsey would have dealt with some of the expectations of David Beckham and his generation of England players. He would not have been enthusiastic about the idea of having wives and family installed close to the team hotel for the European Championship in Portugal in 2004, for example. When the England camp disbanded, he would no doubt have blanched at the sight of the bouncy castles being removed. In Germany in 2006, he would have been appalled to know that wives and girlfriends had their own FA official deputed to deal with their needs, which included the demands of the paparazzi.

"By way of historic comparison, I recall Nobby Stiles confessing that he didn't have the nerve to put to Ramsey his wife Kay's request that he break training for a few days to be with her for the birth of their son, Peter. He contented himself with the fleeting visit home allowed all the squad before the last days of World Cup preparation. This is not to make any judgment, just to point out that, apart from anything else, Ramsey was a man of his age who understood that he could push his demands to limits that would not begin to be seen as acceptable today. Even now, nearly a decade after his death, some opinion is still divided over both the man and his football. Some insist he was a tactical revolutionary who showed a genius for getting the best out of the English footballer, a school to which I will always belong, while others claim he set the game back in England with his banishing of wingers and his emphasis on rock-hard defence. Between such extremes there will always be shades of opinion and, if we want to be ultimately precise, the truth probably lies somewhere in the middle.

"Similarly, there is conflict over his character. Selfless and idealistic is one theory, supported perhaps by the fact that he ended his days modestly in the house in Ipswich from where he built his managerial career. Another is that he was quirky, a bigot and an inverted snob – yet this assessment does not begin to take account of so many acts of personal kindness and concern, which I benefited from as much as anybody down the years. Indeed, for me, the greatest strength of the 4-3-3 formation he employed is its power to bring teams together, especially outstanding individuals who are often playing different systems for their clubs. In recent years, when such talented midfielders as Paul Scholes, David Beckham, Steven Gerrard and Frank Lampard have been successful in club football in England, I have been amazed that 4-3-3 was a way of playing almost totally shunned by Sven-Goran Eriksson and his successor, Steve McClaren.'

Ramsey's attitude galvanised the players. Sir Bobby recalled, "During the World Cup in 1966 there was a press conference between two and four on a Thursday afternoon, and that was it. We didn't see any press for the rest of the week. No photographers, nothing. It illustrates that the manager is on the side of the players."

1966 lives in the memory of every Englishman and one which saw the 28-year-old Charlton at the height of his talent. Alongside his brother Jack, who had risen to become a stalwart of the England defence, Bobby was the focal point of the team which triumphed on home soil and received the Jules Rimet Trophy from Queen Elizabeth II on 30 July 1966.

Ramsey's side started badly, with a dour 0–0 draw against Uruguay. Their campaign needed a spark and Charlton was the man to provide it. Thirty-seven minutes into their second group match against Mexico, he collected a loose ball on the halfway line. "I picked up the ball quite deep and I had no intention of shooting at goal," he said in a later interview. "I didn't really expect them to allow me to keep going... so I just banged it." The surging run was rounded off by a net-bursting shot into the top corner and England were up and running. In England's summit year Charlton would remind us of his most stunning asset – a surge from the centre circle past two Mexican defenders and a thrashing drive from beyond the penalty area for England's first goal of the finals. "He has never been surpassed," George Cohen, his right back that day, recalled.

In the semi-final against Portugal, Charlton gave his finest performance. His running kept the Portuguese defence on the back foot, his passing opened up gaps for team-mates to exploit, and when he found himself in front of goal, he let fly. A goal in each half was enough to see England through as narrow 2–1 winners and Charlton scored both of them. The second, in particular, was trademark Bobby Charlton: a first-time shot cannoned into the top corner, which even prompted one opponent to shake his hand.

In the final, West German manager Helmut Schön knew exactly who England's danger man was and assigned the young yet precociously talented Franz Beckenbauer to a man-marking role. When Charlton attacked, Beckenbauer defended, and when Beckenbauer strode forward, Charlton stuck to him. It was an epic struggle between two legendary players, with the final score of 4-2 after extra time indicating that Charlton eventually had the upper hand. As Beckenbauer himself pointed out: "England beat us in 1966 because Bobby Charlton was just a bit better than me."

When England travelled to Mexico four years later to defend their title, Charlton, now 32, remained a central figure. As an inside-right in a team which had evolved from a 2-3-5 at the outset of his international career through 4-4-2 to a 4-3-3 formation, his role had become more defensive, yet no less important. After the group stage had been safely negotiated, England faced West Germany in the quarter-final, in a rematch of the 1966 final. With England 2-1 to the good 20 minutes from time, Ramsey substituted Charlton, preferring to rest him before the semi-final. But an Uwe Seeler equaliser took the game to extra time and Gerd Muller sealed the German's revenge with an extra-time winner. It was to be Charlton's swansong for England as he announced his retirement after the final whistle in Leon, having overtaken Billy Wright's record with his 106th cap. He played another two seasons for United, appearing for the final time in April 1973.

He had a spell at Waterford United, scoring 18 goals in 31 games. Having retired from all football in 1973 he became manager of Preston NE, worked as director of Wigan Athletic in 1976, and was caretaker manager in the 1982–83 season. A coaching career was not for him, though. Instead, Charlton went into business, opening a travel agency in Manchester and also founding a number of football academies for youngsters; Bobby Charlton's Soccer Schools most famous former pupil was David Beckham.

In 1984 he was appointed director of Manchester United. He was awarded a CBE in 1974 and a knighthood in 1994. He is currently working as an ambassador for Manchester United. He was also invited to sit on FIFA's football committee. Since then, he has worked unstintingly for the good of the game in Manchester and England, earning him recognition around the globe as a true ambassador of football. As his friend and manager Busby said of him: "There has never been a more popular footballer. He was as near perfection as man and player as it is possible to be."

He helped promote two Manchester Olympic bids and the 2002 Commonwealth Games and helped England's failed bids for the 2006 and 2016 World Cup and the successful London 2012 Olympics bid.

Jimmy Greaves, regularly his international partner and an equally prolific goalscorer, considers that Charlton gave both United and England an essential element in all great teams. "Most of my caps were alongside Bobby" Greaves recalls, "and he was the mainstay from the day I first played, in Chile in 1959. It wasn't just the skill, it was the stability, and when you have that, you have confidence, which is what helps make successful teams".

David Beckham overtook Sir Bobby's tally of 106 caps

in Belarus with a seven-minute cameo in Minsk. Sir Bobby reacted at the time with typical diplomacy and humility refusing to join the bandwagon of criticism about Beckham's cameos earning precious full caps. Sir Bobby remarked, "Alf never let the press pick his teams, and Capello doesn't either. He wants to see what David Beckham's still got, and if you represent your country 107 times you've got to be a player." Beckham was naturally super proud of reaching the landmark 100 caps, but Sir Bobby stressed, "Well, it was never the most important thing on my agenda. I did like scoring more goals than anybody else, though. I never bothered about it to begin with, but every time Gary Lineker got closer the press used to ask me about it, and eventually I thought 'Hey, this is really important'. I thought Lineker would beat me but here we are still. Mind you, it's hard to compare eras. Dixie Dean scored 60 goals in a season at a time when people were breaking legs every week."

So of all his England goals, which does he recall with most affection? "I suppose the Mexico one. I scored some other terrific goals, but in the context of the game they were not so important."

Charlton captained England three times, all at Wembley, winning one and drawing two. He was substituted in just five of his appearances for England. One of these was in a friendly win over Sweden in 1968, with the other four coming in his last five games, in either warm-ups or World Cup ties in 1970. He scored his 49th and last goal for England in a 1970 World Cup warm-up game in a 4-0 win over Colombia. Charlton is the only England player to be selected for four World Cup squads. He ended his career at Manchester United at the end of the 1972-73 season, his last appearance was against Chelsea. He made 758 appearances for the club while Sir Bobby remains the club's top scorer with 249 goals.

Sir Bobby still retains the affection of United fans, but is one of the few players who has universal appeal, his part in the 1966 World Cup triumph assures him a place in the hearts of all English football supporters. Despite appearing to have a very serious persona, Sir Bobby has a very dry sense of humour, and is very approachable, as I discovered getting to know him over many years. But perhaps a TV commercial for the energy drink Actimel, gave a little insight into Sir Bobby. Responding to a kid who shouts, 'Hey granddad, can we have our ball back?', the footballing knight belts it into the top-right corner. "It took me about 12 goes, before I really connected. It flew in, and the director said 'That's it, we're finished'."

Bryan Robson, a Manchester United ambassador and himself an Old Trafford legend, recalls that commercial with affection for the determination and dedication that Sir Bobby has shown throughout his life. "I was involved in that advert and he kept missing his shot into the top corner, and after a few goes the camera crew suggested that he shouldn't worry, someone else can hit the top corner for him and they will fit it all together. He turned around and just said "no". He told them, "I will do it a few more times and I will get it right", and he did. He may be in his 70s but he was so determined before the cameras that he kept going until he got it right and before the cameras packed up and went away. That's Bobby. I have never seen such a determined person, who wants to make things work, and to do that he is really strong minded. His reputation is that of a gentleman, which, of course, he is, but when he gets onto a football pitch he changes and he becomes driven."

Drive and determination is a common factor throughout the England players who have achieved a century of caps. Robson said, "Shilts was a great professional with whom I played many times. I have never seen a goalkeeper work so hard. He was a world class goalkeeper and at a certain stage in his career, at his peak, I would say he was the greatest ever keeper and that includes Gordon Banks. The main thing that stands out was his sheer determination he was like a beast on the training ground with his routines with England goalkeeping coach Mike Kelly. We would all still be having lunch, we'd finish and Peter would just be coming off the training pitch.

"David Beckham was also a great player and while it is taken for granted his free kicks, he too worked on those – it's a technique he practised endlessly on the training pitch. He was out there practicing, everyday and practice makes perfect, and he had the perfect delivery of those free kicks into the box because of his dedication and determination to perfect his craft. In fact he dedicated his life to football, he loves it and he has come through such a lot of outside pressures in his life after marrying Victoria, so I would say he did terrifically well to play over 100 times for his country. I never played in the first team alongside him at United, but I did turn out a few times in the Lancashire A league when coming back from injury and he was making a name for himself. I played a few times for the reserves as well with David in my final season at United.

"I met Bobby Moore a couple of times and everybody said he was a gentleman and that's how I found him. He was a fantastic reader of the game, his timing was immaculate and his calmness, composure, class and authority must have permutated through the entire team of 66 world cup winning team."

Bryan Robson was dubbed Captain Fantastic when he captained his country and but for a long injury list would easily have been among the elite 100 club. Robson won 90 caps for England, wearing the Three Lions in three World Cups with 26 international goals including a hat-trick against Turkey in 1984, and a strike after just 27 seconds against France in the 1982 World Cup, which was the second-fastest goal of the tournament's final stages. He recalls, "The then press officer Glen Kirton counted up all the games and come to the conclusion I missed 37 internationals through injury. I fell just 10 short of the ton but had terrible injuries especially in two World Cups."

Sir Bobby remains an iconic figure in the English game and is still unarguably the greatest Englishman ever to pull on the Three Lions shirt – a true legend of World Football.

THE TEN GREATEST BOBBY CHARLTON GOALS

• 1956 v Charlton Athletic. First-team debut, turns inside the full-back, shoots from long range.

• 1957 v Real Madrid. European Cup semi-final second leg. First-timer in 5-3 aggregate defeat.

• 1958 v Arsenal. First-timer from cross by Albert Scanlon in a 5-4 victory four days before the Munich crash.

• 1958 v Scotland. Ferocious volley from Tom Finney's cross on international debut at Hampden Park.

• 1962 v Argentina. World Cup first round (Chile). Turns inside right full-back Silvio Marzolini and hammers home a right-foot drive in 3-1 victory.

• 1966 v Mexico. World Cup first round. Runs from the centre circle beating two defenders to blast in from 30 yards.

• 1966 v Portugal. World Cup semi final. Ten minutes from time Geoff Hurst crosses and Charlton drives in his second of match.

• 1968 v Benfica. European Cup final. A rare glancing header gave United a 1-0 lead.

• 1968 v Benfica. European Cup final. Volleys home Brian Kidd's cut back from the line to seal victory.

• 1968 v USSR. European Nations Cup Volley from 25 yards in third-place victory.

BOBBY MOORE

1962-1973 - 108 CAPS

'Mooro' received the Jules Rimet Trophy from HM The Queen as England won the '66 World Cup Final against West Germany on an unforgettable July afternoon at Wembley. Bobby captained England 90 times, sharing the record with Billy Wright and was voted player of the 1966 World Cup. His statue fittingly stands in front of Wembley Stadium.

"Bobby was one of the world's finest defenders and a great sportsman"

Pele

BOBBY MOORE was England's finest captain, a legend who led his country to its greatest triumph. The iconic image of Moore holding the Jules Rimet trophy aloft at Wembley is one that has since been engrained in every English football fan's memory. Arguably he was even better in the 1970 World Cup when he came up against Pele.

Pele said after his death in 1993, "Bobby was one of the world's finest defenders and a great sportsman," adding: "the shirt he wore against me in that 1970 match is my prize possession. The world has lost one of its greatest football players and a great gentlemen." The words of Pele were appropriate. Three years after Moore and Pele took part in that Titanic clash in Guadalajara, the England captain made his last appearance in an England shirt.

He was capped 18 times for England Youth, then a record, and eight times for the Under-23s before Walter Winterbottom gave him his senior bow in a pre-World Cup friendly in Peru in 1962. He impressed enough to be chosen for all four matches in the Chile Finals as England won through to the quarter finals. In the following year, at the age of 22 years 47 days, he became England's youngest ever captain in a friendly in Czechoslovakia, succeeding Jimmy Armfield.

When Alf Ramsey took over from Walter Winterbottom as England manager in 1963, Moore was already the captain and this arrangement suited the new manager. Ramsey used Moore as the fulcrum for his new, tactically innovative side which saw the abandonment of the traditional 'WM' formation in favour of a more modern 4-4-2 style, without dedicated, touchline hugging wingers. This new side, dubbed the 'wingless wonders' quickly made an impact and Moore's, finest hour arrived on Saturday, 30 July 1966 against West Germany in the World Cup Final, which still remains the greatest day in England's football history.

England, playing in unfamiliar red shirts, fell behind early on only for Geoff Hurst to equalise soon after. In the last quarter, Martin Peters put England in front but, just as it seemed England were about to win the match, Wolfgang Weber stole in to level at 2-2. Extra time was to bring controversy, create history and put a memorable sporting phrase into the English language. But before the re-start, Ramsey called his team together and gave them a pep talk. It was Moore who was later to reveal its secrets. According to Moore, this is what Ramsey said: "Look at the Germans. They're flat out. Down on the grass. Having massages. They can't live with you. Not through extra time."

In extra-time two goals from Moore's Upton Park colleague Geoff Hurst secured the match for Ramsey's men. Subsequent slow-motion replays suggest that England were lucky at a crucial moment in the game as Hurst's shot bounced down near the goal line. But the referee had no such high-tech luxuries, only the assistance of a Russian linesman (Tofiq Bahramov – technically not Russian but Azeri). There was an agonising wait as the two officials locked in consultation. Then the goal that knocked the stuffing out of the Germans was given.

With the seconds ticking away, the BBC commentator Kenneth Wolstenholme noticed jubilant spectators coming over the touchline. "Some people are on the pitch," he began. As Wolstenholme measured the words that were to gain immortality, Moore was also measuring an inch-perfect pass. It found Hurst in space, deep in the German half. "They think it's all over," continued Wolstenholme as Hurst raced on goal and shot. The ball hit the back of the net. "It is now," concluded Wolstenholme in a masterpiece of timing. And so the goal that made it 4-2, putting the World Cup beyond doubt and sparking that momentous phrase, had its roots in Moore's pass.

Moore, after climbing the steps to the Royal Box to receive the trophy, was just two yards from the Queen when, ever the gentleman, he realised his hands were dirty with mud and grass stains and wiped them on the velvet draping before shaking Her Majesty's white gloves.

Ramsey knew how great was his debt to Moore. "My captain, my leader, my right-hand man," was how he summed up Moore's assured authority. "He was the spirit and the heartbeat of the team. A cool, calculating footballer I could trust with my life. He was the supreme professional, the best I ever worked with. Without him England would never have won the World Cup."

Moore was predictably modest, preferring to emphasise the collective spirit. "We were more than a team. We were a formidable nation, bonded and held together by our will to win for England."

The squad that flew out to the 1970 World Cup in Mexico as defending champions was in many ways a stronger one than that which had claimed the trophy four years previously. Moore, still playing at something near the peak of his powers, and others in the squad felt that the Three Lions had a good chance of retaining the trophy. With Moore still at the helm, they set off with high hopes to defend their trophy in the heat of Mexico. Trouble was looming on the way, however. In Bogota, Colombian police accused Moore of stealing a £625 emerald-studded gold bracelet from a hotel jewellers. His arrest and imprisonment sent shock waves around the world amid claims of a South American stitch-up back home. Throughout the ordeal, Moore maintained his dignity and his innocence. He was held for four days and underwent a four-hour court hearing at which he was represented by a former Colombian Minister of Justice. After intervention by FA secretary Dennis Follows he was released and flew to join his team in Mexico. But he was not declared innocent until many weeks later and played the World Cup with the charge hanging over him.

That they were knocked out at the quarter-final stage by West Germany was naturally a disappointment but the abiding memories of that World Cup come from the group match against eventual champions Brazil in one of the most brilliant matches England ever took part in. The result may have been a 1-0 defeat but two top class teams played at the heights of their powers under a boiling sun. Gordon Banks' astonishing reflex save that almost defied belief from a downward Pele header and Alan Ball hitting the Brazilian crossbar with two minutes to go are now legendary moments but possibly greater still is the sight of Moore holding the England defence firm, making one brilliant tackle after another and then at the end of the match swapping shirts with the peerless Pele. Their embrace served to underline the poignant mutual respect between these two giants of the game.

England were knocked out of that World Cup by the finalists of 1966, West Germany. A match that England were comfortably winning 2-0 they somehow contrived to lose 3-2 after some slipshod goalkeeping by Bonetti and magnificent striking by Gerd Muller, helped of course by the premature substitution of Bobby Charlton. With Bobby gone, German captain Franz Beckenbauer was given the freedom to roam into midfield as England melted in the Mexican heat.

Moore returned to West Ham after Mexico but he was restless. He wanted a move to one of the glamour clubs, such as Arsenal or Spurs. Brian Clough tried to sign him for Derby, but nothing came of it. It wasn't money that caused Moore's disenchantment, though he claimed: "Footballers all over the First Division were earning more than me." In fact, his pay in 1971 was £200 a week – the amount West Ham fined him for drinking in a Blackpool nightclub with Jimmy Greaves until one o'clock in the morning on the eve of an FA Cup tie which the Hammers lost.

What really mattered to Moore was winning a championship. But it was not to be. His relationship with Greenwood deteriorated and he left Upton Park in 1973 to play out his last three seasons with Fulham. He said of Greenwood: "He respected me, but he didn't like me. I cannot forgive him for my never winning a League championship medal. His man management was bad – he couldn't motivate players. With the right management we could have gone on to dominate the game for a period. It sickens me that we were unsuccessful."

Ice-cool and a master strategist, Bobby continued to play for England until 1973 when he appeared in his last international at the age of 32. England lost 1-0 to Italy in a Wembley friendly and Fabio Capello scored the only goal three minutes from time. On November 14th 1973, Wembley witnessed the end of an era with Moore's 108th and final game for his country. It was a narrow defeat but another bleak moment for England just a few weeks after failing to reach the World Cup finals for the first time. Capello still cherishes the memory of his Wembley winner, the only goal of the game, turned in from a cross by Giorgio Chinaglia. Although he had scored against England in his country's 2-0 victory in Turin five months earlier, it was that goal at Wembley which helped nourish his affection for English football and inspired his determination to manage a national team, "I have very good memories of the old stadium," Capello said, "playing for my country at the home of football was one of the highlights of my career."

Moore played for England 108 times and captained them in ninety matches, a record held jointly with Billy Wright. He won the FA Cup in 1964, the European Cup Winners' Cup 1965 and the World Cup in 1966 – making it three trophies lifted in three successive years at Wembley, a record. He was also the 1964 Footballer of the Year but he enjoyed one of the easiest nights of his international career when he won his 100th cap in a friendly at the start of a year that turned sour for him against Poland in Chorzow that June. Moore, Peters and Ball were the only survivors from the boys of '66 but it was the new guard who did the damage in this

Valentine's Day mauling of Scotland at Hampden Park with Allan Clarke, collecting two goals, Martin Chivers, Mick Channon and an own-goal making up the goal total in an impressive 5-0 victory.

Moore was chosen by football fans nationwide as England's greatest player of the last fifty years, polling 50% of the vote and winning by some distance from his nearest challenger, Lion of Vienna Nat Lofthouse (18%). Third was England's leading scorer of all time, Sir Bobby Charlton (10%), who finished just ahead of the England captain at the time of the vote, David Beckham. Legendary winger Sir Stanley Matthews finished fifth in front of some more modern-day greats - Alan Shearer (6th), Gary Lineker (7th) and Paul Gascoigne (8th). The top ten was completed by 44-goal man Jimmy Greaves and Kevin Keegan, the highest placed player from the 1970s, followed by Michael Owen, Sir Tom Finney, Gordon Banks, Bryan Robson and Tony Adams.

Born in Barking on 12 April 1941, Moore's rise to the top began when he was discovered playing on an East London school ground called Flanders Fields. It was an appropriate place to find him. The spirit of those First World War heroes was to be echoed in his cool courage under pressure. In a game for East Ham against Leyton, he was scouted and he was invited at the age of 16 to join West Ham ground staff on £7-a-week.

Moore made his debut for West Ham United against Manchester United on 8 September 1958, gaining his place at the expense of Malcolm Allison who was suffering from tuberculosis. Football began to attract huge crowds in the post-war years and on his debut the 18-year-old Moore played in front of a crowd of nearly 36,000 fans. His debut was marked by positive praise from legendary Manchester United manger Matt Busby. It was a fantastic season for Moore and West Ham who finished sixth in their first season back in the top league. Just four years later he was playing for his country.

Moore would spend fifteen years at the east London club, making 544 League appearances and scoring 24 goals. He made the No 6 jersey his own but it was at left-half that he appeared for many years, which was some achievement considering his left foot was his weaker. By the 1960s he was one of a triumvirate of Hammers with an almost permanent presence in the England team. Moore, Hurst, Peters... three names always to the fore of manager Alf Ramsey's England team building. West Ham had a reputation for attractive football and none was classier than Moore. He was not the quickest yet, like so many touched by greatness, he always seemed to have time to spare - especially in the tackle.

The respected sports journalist Mike Langley, a one time award-winning colleague of mine on the *Daily Mirror*, wrote of Moore's trademark challenge: "The right leg stretches out and Bobby, echoing the opening batsman Essex so keenly wanted him to be, sinking on his left knee like Denis Compton about to sweep the ball through fine leg. But Moore's knee doesn't touch the ground. Somehow, marvellously, he rises with the ball now completely filched from Charlie Cooke of Chelsea and Scotland. Few, indeed, were the defenders able to steal possession from an opponent as clever as Cooke, yet

Moore did it without bother."

The 1963/64 season was possibly Moore's finest in club football as West Ham won the FA Cup, beating Preston North End 3-2 in a wonderful final. Moore was also named Footballer of the Year that season, receiving his award, as was traditional, on the eve of the Cup Final. He was stung by a snub from the club as his team-mates were not allowed to attend the presentation because of the Cup Final. Neither manager Greenwood nor any West Ham director turned up to see their finest ever player honoured.

By 1965 the Hammers were in a European final. They met Munich 1860 for the Cup Winners' Cup and, skippered by Moore, they triumphed 2-0. In 1967 Moore was awarded an OBE for his services to football.

Such was Moore's link in the popular imagination with the Upton Park club that it came as a huge shock when he asked for a transfer from West Ham in 1973. In 1974, at the age of 34, Moore crossed the capital to join Fulham for £25,000 and he would go on to make another 124 League appearances whilst at Craven Cottage. He took his career to a final high when he led his new team to the FA Cup Final. The opponents, ironically, West Ham. And, although the result didn't go Fulham's way, the match was a great end to Moore's career.

Bobby Campbell was Moore's manager at Craven Cottage, and the vastly experienced Campbell, who also managed George Best during his spell in west London, told me, "I have managed some formidable players in my time; Alan Ball, Liam Brady, Terry Venables, George Best and Bobby Moore.

George Best was the best player I managed but Bobby was the best professional. It was a privilege and an honour to coach Bobby but the truth is that nobody coached Bobby Moore, he didn't need coaching. To be Bobby Moore's manager and mentor for the time that I managed at Fulham, I can safely say that he was the best professional I ever managed. As I said, not the best player, that was George but the best professional in the sense that even if you told him there was a game in Outer Mongolia on Christmas Eve kick off 2 o'clock he would be there at 1 o'clock boots in hand. He was never late.

"Everything he ever did was immaculate, whether that was in training or in a match it didn't matter to him, that's the way he was both on and off the field. He lived in Chigwell, so it must have taken him an hour and a half to drive to the Fulham training ground on the other side of London. Training was from 10 am, I was there every morning at 8.30 and Bobby always turned up around five to nine, he was never late. That kind of thing sticks in the mind. It's not a common place thing among footballers, far from it. His manner and his character were top class and he represented West Ham and England as the ultimate pro. He even wiped his hand before shaking the Queen's hand before he received the World Cup trophy and he dealt with the so called stealing of the watch with such dignity. As for reaching 100 caps, that in itself is such a wonderful milestone and anyone who makes it to 100 caps deserves to have done so, and that includes David Beckham, another great player. Let's face it, David Beckham hasn't done football any harm at all."

Campbell believes that, although Moore was recognised as a footballing genius, he hasn't quite been given the universal credit he deserves, even though a statue of Moore has pride of place at the new Wembley stadium. Campbell argues: "I don't believe that he received the accolade and credit that he deserved. He should have been moved straight to the FA when he finished playing in just the same way the German FA embraced the Kaiser. The German authorities took Franz Beckenbauer straight into their fold and made him a global ambassador for their country and that should have happened to Bobby. He should also have been knighted. Tell me this, if any player captained England to a World Cup triumph in the future, do you think they would be knighted? I am sure that they would. So why wasn't Bobby knighted? In fact, it's not too late. He should be knighted posthumously. So many of the '66 World Cup team have been knighted, but why not Bobby Moore? I really don't know the answer to that."

Moore moved to the States to take part in the formative seasons of the American soccer league with his old Fulham colleagues Rodney Marsh and George Best. But that wasn't the end of Moore's international career. In 1976 he was capped by the USA for a tournament to mark their bicentenary. The match was in Philadelphia and the opponents were England! And who was the forward to whom Moore kept pumping measured passes throughout the match? None other than Pele, his Team America colleague. How fitting that those two old warhorses, who stood for everything that is great about football, should finish their days playing on the same side.

Moore tried his hand at management himself at Oxford and Southend, but with mediocre results. He was never suited to it. His mind was light years ahead of the players he was trying to coax into adopting a football philosophy that, down in the lower divisions, was probably beyond them. Equally, Bobby would have found it difficult to communicate in terms of tactics and motivation the way he did as England's undisputed leader on the pitch for a generation with club and country. The mix wasn't right to coach at the lower end of the footballing spectrum. At the highest level, it might have been vastly different; he had the credentials to be an England coach, but was never given the opportunity in an era where you had to earn the right in management the hard way through the divisions. It puzzled many fans that a man who had given so much to football could not find a job inside it. Bobby should have been an England coach, or an ambassador for the country's national sport, more hands on than, say, Sir Bobby Charlton, who has assumed that role.

Bobby was managing at Roots Hall, with a Southend United club in dire financial straights, so coming up to Christmas one year I thought of a seasonal feature interviewing Bobby about the number of players under his charge on the bread line – and, of course, hardly able to afford the Christmas turkey. Bobby seemed pretty busy as I tried to contact him at Southend and when I eventually got through he sounded totally preoccupied. When I explained to him my idea, he told me that he would speak to me at length later that day but if I thought the players were suffering hard times because of the club's perilous financial position, I should consider the fans, who had been contributing all year to the club's Christmas Saving fund. Thousands of them been queuing overnight to recoup their savings, only to discover that the guy in charge had done a bunk with their money. Well, it did make a good story at Christmas but the time Bobby could spare to discuss the issue with me coincided with a long standing lunch date with none other than Old White Beard himself, chairman Ken Bates, the all powerful owner, at that time, of Chelsea. Now, Ken was one of my closest friends and contacts at the time, and still is, so I knew him well, well enough to know that he didn't and still doesn't, take kindly to anyone turning up for appointments late. So, I was determined to be my punctual self, even if it meant somehow juggling this very important interview with Bobby Moore and a thoroughly good Christmas tale for the *Daily Mirror*.

Over champagne cocktails in the relaxed bar section of the swish Langan's Brasserie, the Stratton Street eatery which was once co-owned by Michael Caine, one of Bobby's celebrity pals, Ken asked his usual opener, "what's happening in the bazaars?" That was Ken's usual reference to what was the inside gossip within Fleet Street, the sort of insiders tittle-tattle he loved. I told him that Southend were facing crippling debts and that the guy in charge had done a runner with the supporter club's Christmas fund, and that I had to speak to Bobby Moore about it, and I hoped he didn't mind too much if I spent just a couple of minutes working, after all, it was a working day, even though it was so close to Christmas. I asked him if he minded if I made a very quick call to Bobby Moore. Ken agreed, but you always knew with the Chelsea chairman that anything that distracted him from his agenda at one of these lunches or interfered with his precious pre-assigned time was putting him out and putting his demeanour at risk, and I suppose he had a point.

Back then, of course, there were no mobile phones. So the only means of communication was a pay phone one floor down from the restaurant area, in the wash rooms adjacent to the loos. Two or three times I made my apologises to Ken and made my way to the loos to place a call through to Southend United football club. Unfortunately, I couldn't get hold of Bobby and it took a couple more tires before I eventually got through to him in his manager's office at Roots Hall and got the interview I wanted. But having now got the full picture, I realised how chronic the finances were, made worse by the missing Christmas funds and the plight of the ordinary fans. Bobby was distraught. There were fans in wheelchairs, families with small children, the elderly mostly, queuing around the ground for hours, waiting in vain to recoup their money. Their Christmas present, the turkeys, even the Christmas trees, would not be affordable without the return of their savings. Bobby said the club would have willingly reimbursed the fans while they sought to find the money, but the club were bust and couldn't pass cash on to their stricken supporters. In fact, the situation was grave, time was running out and Bobby was pleading for some urgent assistance as part of the article I was going to write. Bobby feared the club would soon go under.

Ken Bates might be hard as nails on the outside but inside he has a genuine soft spot – if you can find it. But a worthy cause can trigger that soft spot. However, his mood was pretty dark, after all the enforced absences being used up trying to call Bobby. It reached the stage where I had to make an excuse and say I was actually bursting for the loo!

Once I got the full picture from Bobby Moore, I fleshed out the story over lunch to Ken Bates. The Chelsea chairman was hugely sympathetic, and in fact, was willing to help but not without a startling challenge, which really threw me – no doubt Ken's intention. At this time, for some reason, he was finding it troublesome to contact Robert Maxwell, who had been quite active in Football League affairs and increasingly influential, notably on matters relating to TV rights and their value and he wanted to talk to him, so he found it hugely frustrating that he continued to fail to do so. Hence the challenge. Bates would put up £50,000 in cash, if Maxwell matched him.

"Go on and ring Uncle Bob," he told me. He used to call him 'Uncle Bob' as most people in football would do, when they got to know him. Far from Maxwell's image as being a crook, those who met him found him hugely generous and really interested in football, even if he knew little about it. But he knew his business and was one of the few who came into football who kept his perspective and continued to want to run football clubs along business lines which intrigued those already in the industry.

So back downstairs to the loos I went with yet more coins for the pay phone. I got straight through to Uncle Bob, the only sports journalist, either on his staff or outside, with a direct line to the *Mirror* proprietor before plodding back upstairs to Bates' table to pass on the response. Ken looked surprised I was back so soon. He probably thought I had been given the sort of brush off he'd been experiencing himself of late. Not so. I am not sure Ken Bates realised I had such direct access to Maxwell – now he was to find out just how direct.

I had told 'Uncle Bob' of Southend's plight, my conversations with Bobby Moore, of Ken Bates offer to help and his direct challenge to Maxwell to match his offer of £50k in cash. Maxwell asked my view. I suggested that it would be a fabulous thing to do, it would also make national news and make him a national hero, as well as helping out the football club and their ill-fated fans diddled out of their Christmas cash.

Of course, it wasn't a bad follow-up story for me as well... as the *Mirror* would be breaking a major national news item.

"Yes, it's agreed, now go and tell Ken Bates to get his cash ready and I will have mine ready for tomorrow morning!" Maxwell had said.

When I returned to Ken he had one of those 'you ain't got through' smiles. But that was quickly wiped off his face. In those days £50k was an awful lot of money, probably something like £500k now. The next morning I reported for work as usual at the Mirror HQ in Holborn and I was instantly summoned to Maxwell's Up Pompeii offices complete with marble and pillars where 'Uncle Bob' had his living quarters and offices.

Maxwell was not amused as he informed me that there had been no response to his calls to Bates. Clearly Ken was getting his own back, after weeks of being cold shouldered by Maxwell, he was taking his time in replying now. I assured Maxwell that Bates would come up with his half of the bargain. There was no doubt about it. Maxwell gave me one of those 'you don't know what your talking about' glances but I knew Ken was just playing hard to get. And I couldn't tell Maxwell that or he might just tell Bates where to go.

However, time was soon running out for this game of brinksmanship. Bobby Moore had impressed upon me that the club had until 5pm that evening to raise the £100,000 loan, otherwise Southend would fold there and then. By midday Maxwell's patience was wearing thin. He had had enough of hanging around waiting for Bates to reply to his calls

"Sod Bates", snorted Maxwell as he gave instructions to his security staff to escort me to accounts on one of the lower floors where £100k in £20 notes was awaiting me, and had been ready for some considerable time. My instructions was to make my way to Southend to hand over the cash. A limo was waiting outside the Mirror building with a driver and I was sat in the back with a security guard and a suit case stuffed with £20 notes on my lap. We hot footed it to Southend at around 2.30pm.

When the car pulled up outside Roots Hall it was just starting to get dark and I found Bobby Moore pacing up and down outside the main entrance, with hundreds, perhaps thousands of fans in a queue stretching right around the ground. We had beaten the 5pm deadline by about five minutes.

Maxwell called me up just before we left to issue final instructions. "Take a note book and pencil, and I want you to write down every name of each and every person you hand over the money to – interview them all as well, there will be plenty of space allocated in tomorrow's editions for you."

"Fine," I thought, "but I will need more than one pencil to write down every name and interview them all!"

I was at Roots Hall for most of the night, either writing down names, interviewing as many as I could, or as many who might have something interesting to say at least, and then rushing to the phone to continually 'file' copy to the newspaper copytakers for the next morning's editions. That night the £100k that saved Southend United made the main item on all the late night news bulletins. Next morning Bates money arrived as promised.

Much later I discovered that the reason for the delay on Bates' part, was that Maxwell had insisted on a covenant giving him ownership of Roots Hall if Southend failed to repay his money within a certain time and in all probability Ken had the same 'comfort' that a schedule of repayments had been agreed in a binding contract. That's businessmen for you – they were fully covered for their time, trouble, and of course the hard earned cash.

Not long after that, Bobby Moore's health failed. First he suffered heart problems in 1986. Then in 1991 he was struck by cancer. He fought it for two years before dying on February 24th 1993 at the age of 51. West Ham's first home game after his death was against Wolves and the match became a tribute to Moore, attended by former team-mates including Hurst, Peters and the man who nurtured him to greatness, Ron Greenwood.

The tributes to Moore were immense. The great Franz Beckenbauer, an opponent in that 1966 World Cup Final, said: "Bobby was my football idol. I looked up to him. I was so proud to have played against him." West Ham United officially retired the number 6 shirt that was worn with such distinction for both West Ham and England. To mark the 50th anniversary of Moore's debut in a 3-2 victory over Manchester United on September 8th 1958, the retirement of the No 6 shirt took place on 9th August 2008 at the inaugural Bobby Moore Cup game which was the start of a new collaboration between West Ham United and the Bobby Moore Fund, the cancer charity set up by Stephanie Moore, Bobby's widow. Matthew Upson wore the number 6 shirt for the first half before handing the shirt to Stephanie in a ceremony at the half time break. Upson wore the number 15 shirt for the rest of the season.

Tony Gale followed Bobby Moore's career in more ways than you would imagine. Few have been so intrinsically linked to the man and the player than another Hammers No 6. Tony tells me, "I seem to have followed Bobby everywhere! But the only thing I did better than him was on the radio! I was his boot boy at Fulham when I was a 16-year-old apprentice. When Bobby retired I took his No. 6 shirt. When I moved onto West Ham everybody knew and talked about Bobby Moore. I cleaned his boots, but I couldn't lace them."

That sounded like a very well rehearsed line from the highly popular Tony Gale, who has a gift for after-dinner speaking and is a highly respected radio and TV pundit.

Tony went on, "Bobby was top man, the closest you will ever get to footballing royalty and that includes the likes of David Beckham. Yes, of course David has done a great job for his country after all that he has achieved and done, but Bobby is the true Governor. Perhaps his greatest trait was that he was the same to all men, whether is was a journalist, his team mate, the Prime Minister or the Queen, or even the man in the street and some of his closest friends were just ordinary West Ham fans. I don't know anyone who has a bad word for Bobby. I know people don't speak ill of the dead, but they would say the same thing if he was still living.

"It was sad that toward the end of his life he wasn't treated with the sort of respect that he deserved. For me, the respect that he did deserve was to be taken into the England set up in the same way as the Germans did with Franz Beckenbauer, the FA should have held him in the same esteem as the Germans did with Der Kaiser and Bobby should have been our King of football. I am not saying they should have made him the manager but these days England has so many Ambassadors, he would be have been ideal for that role. Equally it was silly that he was never handed a knighthood, especially when you consider how they hand out knighthoods these days. It wouldn't have changed Bobby even if they had knighted him, he couldn't have changed. He was such an approachable guy.

"When I came into the game as a 15-year-old schoolboy and walked into the training ground at Fulham it was in 1975 with Bobby and Alan Mullery there. My bribe, well, not exactly a bribe, more of an incentive, to sign for Fulham was that I asked for two FA Cup Final tickets when Fulham played against West Ham in a final that was all about Bobby at the time. I also asked for two tickets for the after match ball, and got them, and took my dad along where he got to meet Bobby Moore; it was just unbelievable for my dad. Bobby had time for us, he had time for everybody that is what marked him apart. Needless to say I signed for Fulham."

Bobby Moore moved on from a profession that shunned him and into the media where he became a recognisable face in the country's press boxes and where I got to meet up with him quite a bit. For Tony Gale, it was an opportunity to share the press box with him.

"Let me tell you my favourite after dinner story about Bobby", Tony says with great enthusiasm, "Jonathan Pearce was the commentator for Capital Radio at the time, and working for Capital had become a big part of Bobby's life. Even though Fulham were in the Fourth Division Capital decided they would do a special on the club and brought me along, so there I was on one side of Jonathan Pearce with Bobby Moore on the other in the front row of the press box at the Cottage." Tony makes the point that this area is like sitting in the laps of the fans toward the back of the press box. He continued, "It was a really shit, damp, cloudy grey old evening in a match against Oldham, with precious little happening in the game. We were there to feature Fulham so it was a lot of nostalgia and comment and at one point in a very dull game an Oldham player went down injured and there was even more time to kill. So Jonathan being Jonathan, he starts waxing lyrical as he sometimes does, thinking he is some sort of Shakespeare, and so off he went... 'the clouds are turning from grey to black, the air is becoming damper, the clouds look like ships lost in a vast ocean and remind me of crisps packets blowing in the wind...' Quick as a flash Bobby passes me over a small note. It read, 'cheese and onion or salt and vinegar?'."

Sir Trevor Brooking is in the perfect position to assess and analyse the career of Bobby Moore and the legacy he has left to English football. Currently one of the most prominent individuals within the FA for some time, Sir Trev was just a humble apprentice at Upton Park when he first came across Moore.

"Naturally I was very lucky to know the man and the footballer. It was 1965 when I joined West Ham as a young apprentice. Imagine how a young lad at that kind of age felt when the three World Cup winners walked through the door for training, captain of the World Cup winners Bobby Moore, the man who scored the hat trick in the Final, Geoff Hurst, and the other goalscorer against the Germans, Martin Peters. With three such enormous national heroes at the same club any youngster would have to benefit from their mere presence. Incredibly, Bob told me that after winning the World Cup a few of the lads said to each other 'let's go out to have a bite to eat'. Imagine that happening today. It would be impossible to walk out into the street without being mobbed after achieving such a feat."

But it was vastly different in those days, of course, illustrating how enormously the game has evolved. Bobby Moore hit 'celebrity' status but could still pop out for a quiet West End meal but David Beckham would need a body guard just for himself and an army of security and police if Becks and a victorious England team attempted that, if they had landed the World Cup. Then again, it probably wouldn't be necessary because they would be asked to dine with the

Queen and Prime Minister and would be lining up to receive their knighthoods. Remarkably, Bobby Moore was never knighted. A national disgrace!

Sir Trevor went on, "What I learned as a young apprentice is the sheer dedication of a player like Bob. Often I would report on a Sunday morning for some treatment with the physio Rob Jenkins for a couple of years even before I signed for West Ham. You couldn't help notice and be impressed by the fact that Bobby Moore would turn up on the training pitch on a Sunday morning. He would like to socialise after the match on a Saturday night, as most of the players would traditionally do in those days, but on a Sunday morning he would turn out in all his sweat gear and sweat off any excesses from the night before. Even at that time, and at the highest level, it was important to look after yourself and your fitness and no one recognised that more than Bob who made it a ritual of socialising on Saturday night but sweating it out on Sunday morning. Now that was a good lesson for a youngster to appreciate that you need to keep yourself fit."

As for the football, it was a thrilling time for Trevor to be playing alongside the three World Cup winners. There was rarely a dull moment. "I made my debut in 1967 and Bobby was in the team and we drew 3-3 with Burnley who were formidable in that era under owner Bob Lord with manager Harry Potts. On the day of my debut the goalscorers wither Moore, Hurst and Peters, how fitting. I played quite a few years alongside Bob until he left in the early 70s. Perhaps one of the most memorable series of games was against Stoke in the League Cup semi finals when it went to a fourth game and our keeper 'Fergie' (Bob Ferguson) was concussed and Clyde

Best, who would normally take over in those circumstances, felt he couldn't do so under so much pressure in the game. So Bobby, cool as you like as always, picked up the gloves, and went on to parry a penalty but they scored from the rebound.

"It turned full circle after Bob left and went on to play for Fulham as we played them in the 1975 FA Cup Final at Wembley and of course I played against Alan Mullery and Bob in the Fulham team."

As for Bobby Moore's legacy to West Ham and indeed English football, Sir Trevor spent his entire stroll down Wembley Way to his FA offices answering that one. "His legacy? I suppose local lad done good, or done very good. When you look back its remarkable to think that people at West Ham right at the outset of his career had doubts about him because of his size, he wasn't the biggest for a central defender, but they couldn't help but be impressed by the way he could knock those long range pin point passes up to the feet of the front men. So the way he placed those through balls, the calmness of his game, the reading of the game, were qualities that emerged to mark him out as one of the best. He is a fine example to youngsters in his determination to succeed when many thought it was impossible to make the grade because of his lack of inches for a central defender. Of course as his reputation evolved he became a role model for all youngsters making their way in the game."

Naturally Sir Trevor saw a side of Bobby Moore few were able to glimpse. "He was meticulously tidy. He folded everything up, everything had its pace, nothing was out of place. Frank Lampard roomed with him at first, but after a while nobody wanted to room with Bob because he was too tidy. I never roomed with him but I roomed with Kevin Keegan in our England days and we were the world's worst, everyone thought our room had been ransacked it was too untidy!"

Sir Trevor has memories too of another England captain whose lack of inches were not an issue, Billy Wright. "I watched Wolves in the 50s notably when Wolves played in Europe, and Billy was one of the smallest defenders of that era but just like Bob it was his reading of the game that stood out and marked him out as such a formidable defender with his calmness under pressure again very much like Bob. The football at the time of Billy Wright and Bobby Moore, clubs were seeking six foot plus athletes, but they proved that size doesn't matter, and we are beginning to realise that again when you look at Lionel Messi with Barcelona and the way Spain play, it proves it doesn't matter how big you are, what matters is retaining possession of the ball."

Dignity was Moore's key attribute according to Lord Triesman, the short lived FA Chairman, who hailed England's greatest ever captain. "I watched Bobby Moore play many times and he won because of his talent, ability, sense of fairness and sense of camaraderie. I do admire that kind of dignity in players and in clubs like Liverpool in the Bill Shankly period, United through Matt Busby and Danny Blanchflower's team with their courtesy," added the lifelong Tottenham Hotspur fan. "Some of these values are absolutely intrinsic if football is going to be great to watch and play and also great as part of our social fabric. I don't want kids on Sunday morning feeling they can imitate the very worst things they saw on Match of the Day the night before. This sounds partisan but Teddy Sheringham had phenomenal courtesy and visible respect for the people around him on a pitch. Jurgen Klinsmann did as well – tremendous dignity and sportsmanship. At the risk of great heresy, Tony Adams had a fearsome leadership."

Visitors to the new Wembley are greeted by a statue of Bobby Moore which reminds them of the greatest footballing moment England experienced in the old stadium. At the same time it reflects the serious lack of international icons in the English game. England have never been short of heroes but those heroics have so far won them just one major tournament, when all their matches were played at Wembley.

Moore is a true English hero. There will never be anyone quite like the late, great Bobby Moore.

PETER SHILTON

1970-1990 - 125 CAPS

Peter is England's most-capped player... a total that would have been significantly higher had it not been for fellow legend Ray Clemence, with whom he alternated in the England goal during the 70s and '80s.

"What can you say about Peter Shilton? Peter Shilton is Peter Shilton, and he has been Peter Shilton since the year dot."

BOBBY ROBSON

GORDON BANKS is universally accredited as being the undisputed No. 1 England goalkeeper of all time, and there is a compelling assessment of the goalkeepers virtues by Bob Wilson later in this chapter, but it is clear Banks has an admiration for the man who has run him such a close second, Peter Shilton, and the man who holds the formidable record of England caps.

Shilton is the only goalkeeper who can be compared to Banks. For 10 years, 'Banks Of England' was indisputably the best in the world by virtue of being in the 1966 World Cup winning side and pulling off that wonder save against Pele in the 1970 tournament. But at the very peak of Shilton's powers, he too was, in many eyes, the best in the world, having won the First Division title and two European Cups with Nottingham Forest, while the biggest prizes in club football eluded Banks. Yet, England lost only nine of their 73 matches with Banks in goal; he let in just 57 goals, a miserly average of just 0.78 goals per game, keeping 35 clean sheets. The pinnacle, of course, was England's World Cup victory in 1966. Alf Ramsey's team reached the semi-finals without Banks conceding a goal. Yet Banks, the greatest keeper in the world, who not only became a national hero for his country but won the League Cup for his club having appeared and lost in two FA Cup Finals, was put on the transfer list by his club, Leicester City within a year.

Four years earlier Banks had been watching a schoolboy coaching session after training at Filbert Street. One 13-year-old boy caught his eye. "This lad's a good 'un," he had remarked to the club's trainer George Dewis. "Aye," replied Dewis. "He'll be having you out of the team, too." And so it came to pass in 1967, within 10 months of World Cup victory, that prophetic statement came true. The boy's name was Peter Shilton and Leicester considered him good enough to let Banks go. Shankly's Liverpool were desperate to sign him but Banks joined Stoke for £50,000 in April that year, having played 293 League games for Leicester and won 37 international caps.

Banks looks back on his won remarkable career and how it ran parallel with that of Shilton, who was Banks' understudy early in his career at Leicester. "Peter was agile, had good handling of the ball, made saves that a lot of goalkeepers wouldn't possibly have got to. Yes, Peter was an excellent goalkeeper without any question. I suppose you could say I am very proud of the fact that I helped him a lot. In those days there was no such thing as goalkeeping coaches you have in the modern era. But I had a lot of ideas about how goalkeepers could improve their technique and I passed those onto the goalkeepers at Leicester, and of course, young Peter Shilton was one of them.

"And yes, it was quite a bit of a shock, to say the least, when Leicester got rid of me and chose Peter as their first choice keeper. I did at first read some articles in the papers that Peter wanted first team football or he would leave Leicester City and I laughed it off. I laughed it off because he was just a young man with loads of time on his side and I didn't really take the articles in the papers very seriously. Then I read in the papers that there was a Board meeting to decide what to do about Peter. Next thing I knew the manager said he wanted to see me and told me that they wanted me to leave the football club. So Peter replaced me at Leicester, I moved onto to Stoke, and would you believe it, he also replaced me at Stoke!"

In 1972, Gordon helped Stoke to win the first trophy in their history, the League Cup against Chelsea, and he was voted Footballer of the Year – the first goalkeeper to receive the award since his schoolboy hero Bert Trautmann won it in 1956. Within five months, however, Bank's professional life was in ruins – shattered by a road accident in which he lost the sight in his right eye. He had been to Stoke's Victoria Ground that Sunday for treatment after a 2-1 defeat at Liverpool the day before when his Ford Granada was in collision with a van. Banks fought hard to regain fitness but, perfectionist that he is, realised he could not maintain the high standards he had set himself in League football. Not only was his career over, he was fined £250 for dangerous driving. He had played 510 League games, 194 of them for Stoke. He had won 36 caps for England while at Stoke, one fewer than when he was at Leicester.

The 74-year-old Banks told me, "I am sure I would have got to 100 caps if it hadn't been for the accident, but I don't look back with regret, I enjoyed every moment of playing for my country." Banks added, "I saw Peter when he was playing as a schoolboy, and although I could tell he was good even then, I didn't realise he would go on to play for England, but he worked hard, very hard, and he turned out to be one of the best England have had." I mentioned the fact that most judges put him top. But Gordon added modestly, "Different eras, and goalkeepers have vastly different style, so really difficult to judge."

Peter Shilton was the youngest first-team debutant at 16 and played for England until he was almost 41. Sir Alf Ramsey picked him for his first senior international in 1970, a Wembley friendly against East Germany, England's first match after the Mexico World Cup, a game the home side won 3-1 before 93,000.

"It is something you can only dream about when you start out in this game," Peter tells me, "that one day you will play for your country. To reach 100 caps, you have to be consistent but you also have to be lucky with injuries, and I played for 20 years for England, so I was lucky with injuries. Of course I would have played far more than the 125 times I managed for my country but Don Revie preferred Ray Clemence and Ron Greenwood alternated us and it wasn't until the 1982 World Cup in Spain that Ron opted for me as first choice, so yes, I could have played far more times. Reaching 100 caps, though is a massive milestone in any player's career, and I am very proud of that achievement, but if I had to pick one game that stands out for me throughout my England career, than it would have to be the first one, your debut for your country is always something really special. That first time after the World Cup in Mexico, I was selected to play against the old East German team and it enabled me to complete the set of schoolboy, youth, under-23 and then full international. Even if you only ever played once, you could rightly call yourself a full international and that was so important."

In his 20 years with England Peter featured in three World Cups and two European Championships. Italia 90 was his swansong, appearing in all seven matches, making his last appearance as captain in the third place play off against Italy in Bari; his 23rd consecutive international. "I could carry on but I feel it's a fitting time to bow out," he said at the time. "I want to go out at the top and that's the only way to do it, really."

Shilton has the distinction of starring in the most successful England team since '66, as part of Bobby Robson's side that lost a penalty shoot-out in the semi-finals of the 1990 tournament to West Germany. He tells me: "I will always remember the semi-final against Germany in Italia 90 because we came so close that day to reaching the Final, the team played so well on the day and deserved to have got through. But if I had to chose my greatest game for England, it was against Scotland in 1973 when I made a save from Kenny Dalglish that people still keep talking about. We beat the Scots 1-0 that day and it cemented my place in the England team. In those days it was predominantly British players in the league, so there was intense rivalry whenever we played the Scots. You would go back to your club and everyone would be talking about the game, and the save against Dalglish was something to be proud of."

'Shilts' was a brilliant shot-stopper who bossed his area and was renowned for his dedication to training. His domestic career was littered with honours, most notably at Brian Clough's Nottingham Forest from 1977 to 1982, where he won the League Championship, the League Cup and the European Cup twice. He won the PFA Player of the Year in 1978 and received the MBE and OBE for his services to football. In 1990 after his retirement he was awarded the

Order of merit by the PFA.

During Shilton's long career as England's keeper he kept clean sheets on 65 of his 125 appearances and went six matches in a row on two occasions, just short of Gordon Banks' record of seven in a row. He also holds the joint-record of most World Cup clean sheets (10) with Fabien Barthez. He captained England on 15 occasions and had it not been for the rivalry with Clemence, he may well have reached over 180 caps, and for Clemence, his total would have been around 100 instead of 61 had Shilton not been around. In his 125 national appearances England won 66, conceding only 80.

There were many highs but a couple of notable lows. Shilts suffered his greatest set back with the Diego Maradona 'Hand of God' goal, while he had a game to forget two years later on the occasion of his 100th cap, as England succumbed to Holland in the 1988 European Championships. He bore little responsibility for the Marco van Basten hat-trick that sent England crashing out but manager Bobby Robson dropped Shilton for the final group game, before bouncing back to reclaim No. 1 status and playing a key role in the 1990 World Cup in Italy.

"The Hand of God goal and game will always be remembered but for all the wrong reasons. To be perfectly honest I don't like to be associated with that goal, because it came from such a great player, one of the world's greatest, but he had to cheat this way. I did not like playing against a cheat. But, of course, it will always remain the most famous game I ever played in. People remember that Hand of God goal world wide. But I don't recall it with any great relish or fondness, quite the reverse actually."

Born and brought up in post-war Leicester, Peter's sole ambition was always to be the best goalkeeper in the world, and he achieved this, for many years. From his early spell with his native Leicester City, where he turned professional in 1966, to the twilight of his career in the 1990 World Cup, Shilton was perceived as driven and serious, and to a large extent this was an accurate portrait of the man and the professional. It was this drive, dedication and ambition, coupled with a fair amount of natural talent, that saw Shilton surpass all appearance records, both national and international.

Born on September 8th 1949, Shilton started his career at Leicester City as a schoolboy and by the time he was 16 he was competing for a first team place against quite some man standing in his path, none other than Gordon Banks and very soon, forced the sale of Banks to Stoke City. This was a bold move by the club as this was 1967, only a year after Banks' superb showing in the World Cup winning campaign when he was widely regarded as the best goalkeeper in the world, let alone the UK.

He made his first team debut with Leicester City in 1966 at the age of just sixteen. During his 30-year career he played for eleven clubs, making 1005 league appearances. Six months after his England breakthrough, he helped Leicester City win promotion to the First Division. After a three year spell with Stoke City, Shilton joined newly promoted Nottingham Forest in 1977, who went on to shock the footballing world by winning the league title on their return to the top flight. Even greater success followed as Shilton was a big factor in Forest winning two successive European Cups.

Shilton gained his first cap under Ramsey in 1970.

Although Banks was still the No 1, Ramsey was looking for a new under-study, as a result of Peter Bonetti's disappointing performance in the World Cup quarter-final against West Germany which had seen a 2-0 lead turned into a 2-3 defeat. Shilton steadily gained caps until suddenly the whole situation changed when a car crash in 1973 robbed Banks of the sight in one eye. Ray Clemence, the then Liverpool goalkeeper, had made his England debut two years after Shilton but had quickly established himself as a direct competitor for the reserve keeper slot. With Banks unable to continue playing, a shuttle system was put in place where successive England managers were unable to choose between Shilton and Clemence, and in some cases alternated match-by-match. It was a good job the pair were good friends! Unfortunately this embarrassment of riches between the sticks was largely under-utilised as England suffered their most barren time in international football since winning the World Cup.

From 1978 through until 1982 Shilton and Clemence were played on a rotational basis by Greenwood. It was not until the eve of the opening round of the 1982 World Cup that Shilton was finally told he was to be the undisputed No. 1, surely an unsettling position for the team as a whole. For the next eight years Shilton dominated the England goalkeeping position and would not relinquish his grasp until after the 1990 World Cup, which happened to be his fortieth year.

While Shilton and Clemence vied for top spot, England, who had failed to qualify for the European Championships in 1972 with Banks in position, missed out on the 1974 World Cup. Qualifying came down to the last match against Poland at Wembley and the 1-1 draw was not good enough, Shilton taking stick for not saving the Polish strike, in virtually their only attack of the match, with pundits later claiming that he was trying too hard to make the perfect save and should have just concentrated on keeping the ball out. The run of disappointment continued with failure to qualify for the European Championship in 1976, although at this point the pendulum had swung toward Clemence and as a result Shilton only gained three caps between 1975 and 1977. Shilton withdrew from the England squad in frustration in 1976, only to change his mind a few months later, but Clemence remained first choice throughout the run-up to the next World Cup, 1978, for which again England failed to qualify. By the time England qualified for the 1980 European Championship it was to be their first tournament for a decade. Unfortunately another lack-lustre showing saw the team depart for home at the end of the preliminary rounds. Fortunately for Shilton, this was a time of success outside the international arena as he was now with Brian Clough's legendary Nottingham Forest side and was voted PFA Player of the Year in 1978, the year that they won the First Division.

Finally England managed to qualify for the 1982 World Cup only to be held by hosts Spain and exit the tournament unbeaten under a bizarre arrangement for the second group stage. Shilton had played his part, only conceding one goal, in the opener against France, over the five matches and restricting Clemence, who retired from international football shortly afterward, to the reserve bench throughout. Bobby Robson took over from Greenwood after the 1982 World Cup and Shilton established himself as the first choice for the rest of the eighties, although again, success for the team was sporadic. As far as the European Championship went, England failed to qualify for the 1984 tournament and qualified but crashed out in the first stage in 1988.

There were better performances in the World Cup, with an exit in the quarter final in Mexico to Maradona's Argentina and the famous Hand of God goal, where Shilton was lucky not to have been booked for his understandable protestations that it was Maradona's hand, not head, that put the ball in the net. Maradona then scored the famous individual goal as the diminutive player snaked through the majority of the England side before rounding Shilton to score.

In the run-up to the 1990 World Cup Shilton passed Moore's then record of 108 England caps and did not concede a single goal in the qualifying rounds. At Italia 90 England started with some worrying performances but began to gel together as a team and were unlucky to go out in an epic semi-final against Germany, with the Germans clinical in the execution of their penalties, not missing a single one, after the match had ended at 1-1. The third place play-off, which Italy won 2-1, was Shilton's last match for his country, and he captained the team to take his total number of caps to 125, still a record today, as he announced his retirement from international football.

Shilton's club career was spent predominantly with Forest, Southampton and Derby, but he had very fruitful spells at Stoke City and of course Leicester. It was however with Nottingham Forest, and in particular with Brian Clough, where he achieved his greatest prizes. 'Old Big Head' purchased Shilton as the bedrock of his team, after telling Shilton of his dreams for the club. In the seasons that followed, Shilton inspired Forest to the most successful period of the club's history; they won the League once and the European Cup twice. When Shilton was forty-seven years old he signed for Leyton Orient in Division Three and made his 1000th league appearance in December 1996 in their 2-0 win against Brighton. He went on to make another five appearances for Orient before retiring from football. He finally reached 1005, although he carried on playing after that for number of for non-league clubs. Shilton had a brief spell in management in 1992 with Plymouth Argyle and in April 1995 made one league appearance for Bolton Wonderers at the age of forty six. The following season he spent a short time at Coventry City and West Ham United but did not play a first team match for either. Off the pitch his personal life has been marred by gambling, poor business decisions and accusations of extra-marital affairs.

Finally, Shilton became an outspoken pundit. He questioned the then England manager Fabio Capello's use of David Beckham when the LA Galaxy midfielder Beckham was closing in on Shilton's record caps. The big debate at that time was over the use of 'sympathetic' substitutions, firstly by Sven Goran Eriksson and then by Capello, which devalued caps. Beckham made his 107th appearance for his country when he came on as a late substitute in the World Cup qualifier in Belarus and Shilton forcibly expressed his concerns over Capello's motives. "I didn't think it was justifiable to bring him on with two minutes to go against

Belarus," Shilton said at that time. "I couldn't believe it. It is the first time I thought there wasn't a tactical reason for a Capello substitution. I couldn't understand. That was not right. I'm a fan of David's and I don't think he would want to break my record or anybody else's by being given it."

Later Shilton added, "I felt in the circumstances with him being the player and the position he's in, it was really giving him a cap, in a way. When he came on against Kazakhstan with 15 minutes go to they had done very exceptionally well in terms of battling so Kazakhstan were going to die physically. With his quality of passing and crosses they created a lot more chances, so that was a good tactical move."

Shilton was also ambivalent about whether Beckham deserved to beat Moore's record, "A lot of the caps were for the full 90 minutes for the likes of Bobby Moore and Sir Bobby Charlton, but there's been a lot of substitute appearances. But that's the modern game with the commitments at club level. But I certainly feel David does deserve to be up there with the greats and Sir Bobby Charlton and Bobby Moore were tremendous players. So I think any player that achieves that record with or without a few substitute appearances, you can't take anything away from them."

Beckham needed to be playing during the 2010 World Cup if he had any chance of moving beyond Shilton. In the months preceding the World Cup, Shilton observed, "I feel it is asking a lot for somebody his age and with the commitments he's got to play regularly, especially in the World Cup when you've got six or seven games in quick succession to actually try and win it. It will be difficult for David at 34 to put himself in that situation."

Shilton might have strong views, but his record gives him entitlement to an opinion, especially about England. This man credentials also shows in the stats that he played 1,390 times for eleven clubs.

Chesterfield born Bob Wilson comes from a long line of Chesterfield keepers that includes Gordon Banks, and there are few more qualified to assess the wealth of goalkeeping talent throughout the golden gloves years of England keepers, including Ray Clemence, and of course 'Shilts. Not only did Bob Wilson successfully keep goal for Arsenal as a League and FA Cup double winner and represented Scotland, although born in England he had Scottish parents. Bob became the first English-born player in history to play for Scotland when he was capped against Portugal in 1973. He made his television debut in the same year that Neil Armstrong became the first man to walk on the moon. He became one of the most erudite and much loved television personalities and also became a qualified F.A. Coach, and was a trained school-teacher as well as a footballer. He had a short spell as an amateur with Wolves during his college days, and then in 1963 he made his first visit to Highbury, the home of the famous Gunners' of Arsenal and was shown around by the legendary Billy Wright. Bob signed for Arsenal six months later and made his debut against Nottingham Forest on October 26th 1963, a few days after his 22nd birthday. He was an integral part of the famous Arsenal double-winning side of 1970-71, winning a League Championship medal and an FA Cup Winner's medal as Arsenal beat Liverpool at Wembley on May 8th 1971.

"Had Ray Clemence not been around Peter Shilton could have gone on and won so many caps he would have held a world record that would never have been broken," Bob tells me, "But Ron Greenwood, when he was England manager, couldn't chose between them, and he rotated them, I imagine he wanted to keep them both reasonably happy. But he was coming up to a World Cup and he had to make a choice. I was with the BBC at that time and I was about 20 yards away when Ron Greenwood called both his goalkeepers over for a chat on the training ground, and he told Ray he was not going to select him as first choice for the World Cup and I saw from close range just how disappointed Ray was at that moment.

"I like Peter a lot as a goalkeeper and I have met him in more recent years when he does his Q & As, he can be really, really amusing. I did a little bit of work with Shilts at Southampton and you could never be sure if he really needed my input because here is a man totally driven about his football. In his time he was the best, he was unbelievable, and when as a team you win a league title or indeed the European Cup, I am not boasting, but it's a fact, your goalkeeper has to have a blinding season. When we won the league title at Arsenal, it was my best season and I won Player of the Year, so when you win something like a league title you know your goalkeeper has made a huge contribution.

"Brian Clough once told me a wonderful story about Peter Shilton. Cloughie was a genius as we all know and what he achieved with Nottingham Forest was just phenomenal, winning the league and then the European Cup or the Champions League as we now know it. But he had a problem with Peter Shilton, whom at the time was clearly the best goalkeeper in the world, and his contribution to the Forest team immeasurable. But Cloughie couldn't stop him training, the guy was so driven. Before they played Hamburg in the European Cup Final, Cloughie put his players up in a hotel, and the problem with Shilts, he told me, was that if you didn't stop him, he would be training all day and every day. Cloughie needed to reign him in and wanted his players to relax before the big final, but Shilts was having none of it, so because Cloughie didn't take his players to the training ground, he found Shilts training by himself on a roundabout near the hotel!'

"I played against Shilts when he was recognised as the best in the world. When he wore a white jumper everyone thought here was a very brash footballer, but that did not detract from his terrific talents. Having said that, I'm afraid to say that I don't think Shilts can go down as the best ever England goalkeeper, as that accolade belongs to Gordon Banks. It's very much like the Olympic Games, you might hold the world record, as indeed Shilts does with the number of international caps, but when it comes to winning the gold medal that is the top of the league and for Gordon he holds the gold medal having won the World Cup in 66. Shilts made it to the semi-final in Italia 90, and as an individual deserves to be recognised as one of the world's greatest ever keepers. Yet Leicester City sold Gordon Banks and that was a huge shock at the time, selling the World Cup winning goalkeeper and you don't do that unless you have some outstanding goalkeeper to take his place, and of course they did in Peter Shilton.

"But when it comes to assessing the best keepers, certainly I would put Gordon Banks top with Shilts second but the best ever, well, you have got to look at Pat Jennings, eloquence personified, unbelievable composure, a bit like Peter Schmeichel in that sense. I would still place Banks as the top English keeper of all time purely because he won the World Cup, although of course he never won a league title like Shilts or indeed the European Cup and Shilts was instrumental in Forest winning those trophies.

"Then, of course, there was that save from Pele. It must rank as the greatest ever, it certainly does in my book, and there are four or five I could pick out, such as Jim Montgomery in the FA Cup Final for Sunderland against Leeds, and Dave Seaman's save in the semi-final against Sheffield United, even Peter Schmeichel told me that that is the best he has ever seen. But the Banks save from Pele is my tops. Jarzinho crossed and Gordon had to make up four or five yards with amazing foot work to get back into position and then he had to dive backwards, and Pele headed the ball into the ground which gave him the chance from such close range to somehow conjure the ball over the bar. Yes, the greatest save I've ever seen. Yet there is also one Peter Shilton save that everyone raves about, it was against Coventry, and it was one of those 'Oh My god' saves that you see once in a life time. So, yes it is a close call between Shilts and Banks.

"Pat Jennings I would assess as the most naturally gifted goalkeeper I have ever seen. Then there were crack pots like myself and Bert Trautmann who liked nothing better than to race out and dive at a forward's feet and invariably end up injured, but we were prepared to be injured. But Shilts, and keepers like David Seaman, had that wonderful knack of making the goal look small, of filling the goal even though it is 192 square feet. Pat had a gift of doing that and so too did David Seaman, and Shilts filled the goal. Shilts was not a quiet one, like Pat and David were. I have made a tape of Pat Jennings saves and only once did I ever see him get excited, that was when he saved two penalties on the bounce at Anfield, and after saving the second from Kevin Keegan he clenched both fists and that was really exiting for Pat!

"But keepers like Schmeichel and Shilts always got excited, and sometimes the guys in front of you need that, they need that geeing up and direct approach, although some keepers never blame themselves always blame those ahead of them, but as we know all keepers make mistakes. There is a fine dividing line between letting your defenders know what you think, and sapping their confidence, so you have to be careful how you tear them off a strip; sometimes your defender needs lifting when he has made a bad mistake. Pat emanated confidence to his defence just by his presence alone, and David Seaman was the closest I have seen to that."

There was no more exciting sight than John Barnes in his pomp gliding down the wing. The Jamaican-born winger was the first high-profile black player to grace Anfield back in the 1980s. Barnes, alongside contemporaries such as Lawrie Cunningham, Cyril Regis and Viv Anderson, proved a catalyst for change. He broke down racial barriers following his £900,000 move to Anfield from Watford in June 1987.

His sweet left foot helped Liverpool complete a record-equalling 29-game unbeaten run and, ultimately, clinched a 17th League title. 'Digger' walked away with the 1987-88 Player of the Year accolade but defeat to Wimbledon in the FA Cup final denied him a dream double.

Success in the 1989 FA Cup final against Everton was tainted by the tragic events at Hillsborough in the semi-final. A third successive campaign of breathtaking brilliance from Barnes in 1989-90 helped secure another Championship. He top-scored with 22 league goals and was voted FWA Player of the Year. Critics argued that he failed to replicate his outstanding club form for England at a time when he was regarded at club level as one of the top players in the world but few can forget his brilliant solo effort against Brazil in the Maracana. John played in two World Cups, and many forget the impact he had as a substitute in the Hand of God game where his surging runs down the wing nearly forced the game into extra-time. In Italia 90 Barnes was below his best, his best contribution being perhaps his rapping performance on New Order's 'World in Motion', still regarded as the greatest football song of all time.

"Peter was incredible in so much as he must have made 200 trips with England and if on some of those he had been considered the No 2 to Ray Clemence he might have played 200 times for England. Having watched him close up, I know that this man was a perfectionist. I must be honest and say I thought Ray Clemence was the No. 1 in England and having played with him at Liverpool I was convinced of that, that was until I saw Peter Shilton train. As soon as I saw Peter train I wondered why I ever doubted him. From the very first day I saw him train you could understand that he was driven to reach the very top. No one has ever trained so hard and with such determination, no one. His application was such that I would say he is the hardest trainer I have ever seen.

"He might have even helped England win the World Cup, and couldn't have come much closer. The Hand of God robbed him and us in 1986 and you couldn't possibly blame Peter. Some did, but I believe he would have got to that ball if Diego Maradona hadn't handled, no goalkeeper can legislate for that. And in Italia 90 we came so close again. Over all you would have to say that Peter Shilton was the consummate professional."

With the influx of foreign talent, England mangers have had precious few choices when it has come to the selection of modern international keepers. Joe Hart has cemented his place both at club and country levels, and for Shilton here is a young keeper who, if he continues to work at his game, has enough time on his hands to challenge even the mighty figure of 125 England caps.

Shilton, though, has some sound advice, "Joe Hart has done really well, he is still only young, he is still improving, he needs to continue to improve and he needs to work hard at his game. What I like about him is that he seems to want to improve and wants to work hard at his game, which he will need to do. He has stepped in and stabilised the England goalkeeping situation which has been a little up and down over recent years, and to be fair riddled with inconsistency. I had high hopes of Ben Foster for example but he doesn't seem to have risen to the challenge, but again to be fair it isn't easy stepping up a big level to the England team. But Joe has showed a lot of confidence and has started to grow into the position, and if he does work and continues to improve than he can stay the No. 1 for many years to come. He needs to be pushed, he needs to be kept on his toes, because England are relying on him at a time when there isn't a great deal of strength in depth with England goalkeepers, and to be fair there hasn't been any strength in depth now for many years which has been very worrying for the national team. My feeling is that you have to go back some time to find English goalkeepers in the Premier League with the technical ability, these days it is more about agility and reflexes than technical know how, and that worries me. The techniques, the real art of goalkeeping has disappeared."

Shilton believes that Hart has the talent and application to reach 100 caps but he warned, "Yes, that is possible. It is even possible he can reach my total of caps, but there is an awful long way to go, and I was lucky with injuries and he would have to be the same. Loss of form or injuries are the big hazards ahead of any goalkeeper. But, he is definitely young enough to have a very long international career. You can never tell, but I think he has a very good chance. He is at the right age, and there isn't a lot of challenge to his position at the moment."

As for the England team as a whole, Shilton has deep concerns. "The team did ok in the European championships, but there were obviously a few sides better than England. The hope is that in one or two years time that some good, outstanding young players come through and develop. How well England do in the future largely depends on how well some of the youngsters develop, because the England team has got to improve quite a bit, as England are clearly behind on their techniques still with quite a lot of teams such as Spain, and even Italy we were not quite as good technically. We really do need to improve in the next ten years and I am afraid it could take ten years to get it right. I hope it can be achieved in half that time, but we have got to look at how we are developing the skills and techniques of the nine and ten year olds who might one day make it all the way into the national team. If we do it earlier we have to rely on the likes of young players such as Wilshere, and here is a player I do rate highly but we need more of the same, and it's not going to happen overnight, so yes, it could take ten years

"For the short term, the England team needs a genuine out and out goalscorer. Wayne Rooney is not quite that sort of player, not an out an out goalscorer, such as say Gary Lineker, and goalscoring like that is an art form, and more recently we had Michael Owen, and before him Alan Shearer, they are the players I would call goalscorers, and we are a little light in that department relying far too much on Rooney. I am sure he can still develop for England the way he has for Manchester United, and he is the nearest we have at the moment to a goalscorer. I imagine Roy Hodgson has his work cut out, and he might need a miracle to find an overnight solution, however I think its going to take quite a while for England to be a force to be reckoned with."

DAVID BECKHAM

1996 - 2010 - 115 CAPS

Becks was the fifth to reach 100 caps when he started in France in 2008 in Fabio Capello's second match in charge... he surpassed Bobby Moore's record for an outfield player a year later as a second-half substitute against Slovakia at Wembley. David played in three World Cups

You could tell straight away the quality of his passing and his vision, and along with Paul Scholes it was not difficult to select that kind of talent as soon as I become England manager.'

Glenn Hoddle

D AVID BECKHAM was given a standing ovation when he returned to Wembley to collect his award for playing 100 internationals. He sat beside Manchester United legend Sir Bobby Charlton in the Royal Box to watch England's final Euro 2012 warm-up game against Belgium before Roy Hodgson's squad departed for the European Championships in Poland and Ukraine. Becks and his fellow England Centurions were paraded at half-time to a rousing reception alongside former goalkeeper and 1990 World Cup semi-finalist, Peter Shilton. The widows of Bobby Moore and Billy Wright were also present to accept the honour on behalf of their late husbands. The celebrated trio received their medals from European football's governing body UEFA in recognition of surpassing the century milestone. The awards were presented by FA chairman David Bernstein.

UEFA president Michel Platini introduced the ceremonies to celebrate players who reached 100 national team games, and for Beckham there doesn't come much greater an honour to be recognised for his achievements for his country other than receiving his honour from the Queen, and perhaps, not too far off, his eventual knighthood for his good works including helping to bring the Olympics to London.

Of all the highs, all the incredible adulation as a fashion icon, his global celebrity status, as well as a gifted footballer, few aspects of his professional life come higher than reaching 100 caps for his country.

Beckham now looks very different to the boy who stepped onto the pitch in Moldova in 1996 to make his debut; the innocence has gone, from the boy I can recall turning up at his first England training session with an autograph book in hand and still starry eyed at mixing with many players who were his boyhood idols. The arms are now heavily tattooed, the hair changed, many times, (and there have been almost as many memorable haircuts as goals). But as he stood on 99 games for his country he argued that his game was largely the same. "There are a few more wrinkles but I still feel I can do what I did 10 years ago."

Here, I should declare my bias. I do like David Beckham, and for much of what he stands for. He has a love of cars, particularly when he was young and impressionable and didn't quite know what do with the wealth that was suddenly making him one of the richest sportsmen of all time. But generally, he doesn't flaunt it. He is a big family man as we all know and despite one alleged indiscretion is never happier than when surrounded by his children. Again, apart from some high profile indiscretions on the field, he has conducted himself as a worthy England captain, and despite the enormous adverse reaction to winning 100 caps because a number were seen as 'gratuitous' substitutions, on balance he deserves to be accepted as a genuine England Centurion having actually played 100 England games from the start. I actually got to know 'Becks' whereas many commentators these days happily criticise celebrities they have never met or had the opportunity to get to know.

I can recall David Beckham arriving starry eyed and genuinely in awe of the England players when he was first called up by Glenn Hoddle, although he actually attended a couple of England training sessions prior to being selected in the squad. Pride of place on my office wall at home goes to an England No 7 shirt personally signed 'To Harry, Love,

David Beckham'. The shirt fits in well alongside two Pele shirts, also both personally signed to me and another from George Best, plus several further shirts I have picked up along my long career in journalism. One of those shirts is from a couple of the Boys of 66 who signed the famous red shirt they wore on the day England won the World Cup. That is most definitely one of the perks of doing my job out in the field, in the days when I spent my time travelling the world watching the national team and the leading clubs, to have been considered a good enough 'friend' for those legends of the game to have taken the time and trouble to sign such memorabilia for me.

After David's shirt arrived, I thanked him for it the next time I bumped into him, which just happened to be the launch of his autobiography, 'David Beckham – My Side' in Madrid. I assured him that I wouldn't be selling it on ebay, unless I could find someone called 'Harry'! However, the fact that he remembered he had obliged me with my request for his shirt, he wanted to reassure himself that I wasn't using his brand name for any other purpose, not that he really suspected that I was. But unscrupulous people have copied his signature and reproduce it on a range of merchandise, and the brand name Beckham is one of the most valuable. For those who think David lacks intelligence because of his high pitched squeaky voice, they are badly mistaken.

Despite all the hyperbole and headlines, he has retained that boyish enthusiasm and love of the game. As a football pundit I am asked numerous times to appear on documentaries to comment about David and the Beckhams, who have dominated two decades in terms of media profile and been

at the centre of moving football from the back to the front
and often feature pages of newspapers, plus magazines such as
Time Out, Men's Health, GQ and OK, instead of the usual
Shoot, Match and FourFourTwo.

So, I would hope that expressing an opinion that David
Beckham is genuinely happiest playing for his country or
being with his kids, comes with some personal experience of
the man.

'Becks' century of caps came in the Stade de France in
Paris on March 26, 2008 when England lost a friendly 1-0
to France. Never renowned as one of sports most articulate
characters, the warmth and passion for the sport, nonetheless,
is apparent in everything he has to say about football. When
he reached his England milestone, he commented, "When
I started my England career in Moldova, I never believed I
would reach 100 caps. To be in the same company as greats
like Bobby Moore and Sir Bobby Charlton is an honour. The
game wasn't the best, but I felt a real sense of achievement. I
was pleased to have all my family and friends there who had
been with me through the good and difficult times. I owe
them a lot and this was just as much for them as it was for
me."

Prior to England's friendly against the USA at Wembley
on May 28, 2008, Beckham said in the match day programme
"It's any boys dream to reach 100 matches with your country,
it was one of the proudest moments of my life. I love playing
for my country and to reach that milestone was an incredible
experience for me. You dream about it but can never imagine
it actually happening. As a boy you always dream about
playing for your country but making 100 caps would have

been beyond any expectations. Wembley would have been perfection but just reaching 100 caps means the world to me and I'm so proud to have reached that with all my family and friends there to watch me. Other than Wembley I would have loved to have played it in Paris. The response from the fans and my family made it a very emotional experience for me."

He added, "Even though it's an honour to reach this milestone, I'm not counting every cap. My aim is to play in the World Cup in South Africa and try to win something for my country. As long as I can, I want to keep playing for my country. It's an honour to represent England and I never take it for granted. Our fans are incredible and they travel in their numbers to support us. They care so much for their country and as a player it's important you feel the same passion as they do."

Unfortunately it didn't quite end as Beckham had wished or envisaged, instead his England career, after three World Cups, petered out in injury that robbed him of his final World Cup appearance in South Africa. Despite the so-called Golden Generation, 'Golden Balls' as his wife liked to call him, never won a trophy with his country. Beckham was injured three months before the World Cup in South Africa and went only in a non-playing role as an unofficial coach.

Nevertheless, Beckham established himself as one of the world's biggest stars in terms of personal charisma and celebrity status sprinkling a little stardust on English football along the way. "Throughout my career I've been pretty successful," Beckham said. "I've played for some pretty big teams. I've played for my country quite a few times and for managers without sentiment... I'm very proud of the fact and

I have always found it an honour that people want to buy my shirt, that fans turn up to watch the team I am playing in or to see myself. I've always found that a huge honour."

After beginning his career at Manchester United in 1992, Beckham made his England debut against Moldova on the 1st September 1996 in a World Cup qualifier as a 21-year-old in the Republican Stadium, Chisinau, England winning 3-0. Becks recalls, "As a kid playing football in the park, you dream about putting on the England shirt and this was the realisation of that dream. It was a very proud day for me and my family."

Beckham cannot remember where he was when he took a phone call from Glenn Hoddle that was to lead to his first England cap, though he knew he was at Gary Neville's house when told he was to be made England captain. "I was a big fan of Glenn Hoddle, so to be picked by a man I'd looked up to for many years as a player was something special. Even to be in the same dressing room as people like Paul Ince and Paul Gascoigne was amazing. I was in awe of every player. I have been lucky in my career to have played in a few major championships and to have scored in each World Cup I've played in."

Becks represented England at Youth and Under-21 levels before Hoddle selected him for his first match in charge. His teammates on his England debut make for interesting reading.

Paul Ince – The first black captain of England, Ince

played for seven English clubs and Inter Milan. His career came to an end as Beckham approached his prime.

Andy Hinchcliffe – The least celebrated of the side, Andy played seven times for England, but still had an orchestral work composed in his honour. The former Manchester City full-back inspired Finnish composer Osmo Tapio Räihälä to write Hinchcliffe Thumper in 1993.

Gareth Southgate – Perhaps the most cerebral member of the class of '96, His outstanding contribution may be the description attributed to him of Sven-Göran Eriksson's half-time team talk in the 2002 World Cup quarter-final against Brazil: "When we needed Winston Churchill we got Iain Duncan Smith."

David Seaman – David made 72 England appearances and was at the height of his powers in Moldova but will be remembered by many for failing to stop a mishit shot from Brazil's Ronaldinho that knocked England out of the 2002 World Cup. 'Safe Hands' subsequently enjoyed some success on the reality TV circuit.

Gary Pallister – An Old Trafford teammate, Gary won 20 caps in eight years. He is now a TV and radio pundit.

Paul Gascoigne – The man who rekindled England's love for football with his tears at the 1990 World Cup, Gazza saw his place as England's best-loved player eclipsed by Beckham. Has never filled the hole left by retirement, sectioned under the Mental Health Act.

Stuart Pearce – The Sex Pistols fan nicknamed Psycho was almost a decade into his 12-year international career when Beckham joined him in an England shirt, he subsequently became part-time interpreter for Capello in Becks 100th cap before taking charge of the British team at the 2012 Olympic Games.

Alan Shearer – One of England's most celebrated strikers, Alan is now a regular pundit on BBC's Match of the Day.

Gary Neville – Beckham's best friend and best man has proved almost as durable as the man with whom he shared the right flank for Manchester United and England for over a decade.

Nick Barmby – One of only three who appeared in Moldova and was still playing professionally when Becks won his 100th cap, Barmby scored the first goal of both the Hoddle and Eriksson eras. After spells with Tottenham, Middlesbrough, Everton, Liverpool and Leeds, he returned to home town club Hull City.

Glenn Hoddle – The manager's career has been quite interesting too. Having successfully guided England to the finals in France in 1998, England were beaten on penalties in the round of 16 by Argentina following the dismissal of Beckham for a petulant flick at Diego Simeone. In his post-match comments Hoddle all but blamed Beckham for England's exit. Glenn's reign came to an abrupt end in 1999 following dubious comments about disabled people but he still retains the third best ever stats for an England manager, behind Sir Alf Ramsey and Fabio Capello.

Assessing the merits of Beckham and the England Centurions, Hoddle does not criticise the means by which Beckham reached his 100 caps. "Reaching 100 caps is an outstanding achievement, it epitomises consistency, and it isn't an issue about how David Beckham reached 100 caps or how many times he appeared as a substitute. The rules of the game are out there, and there is nothing in those rules that says David Beckham's appearances can be determined in some other way. In fact, sometimes the substitute can turn out to be the most important person on the football pitch, so in no way should anyone denigrate the worthiness of a substitute.

"It's funny that I gave David Beckham his first game against Moldova and here we are again playing Moldova on the way to the World Cup in Brazil 2014. But it was not a difficult decision to call up players of the calibre of David Beckham and Paul Scholes, they were top quality right from the start. In fact David first came to my attention as an 18-year-old when I was saw him playing for Manchester United when I was Chelsea manager, he came on as a substitute then! You could tell straight away the quality of his passing and his vision, and along with Paul Scholes it was not difficult to select that kind of talent as soon as I become England manager.'

Hoddle also has a lot of time for another east end boy, Bobby Moore. "I never played with or against Bobby, but I did meet him a few times, and obviously saw him on telly. He was way ahead of his time. If you analyse his attributes for a defender, he wasn't 6ft 4in or lightning quick, which might have thrown up some question marks against him when he was a youngster trying to make the grade, but you could see that he had timing. Timing is everything in every sport, whether its cricket, tennis, golf or football and Bobby had immense reading of the game, that would cut across anyone else and because of that he made it look easy. It was like a chess game when he played and he was always two moves ahead of his opponent. He was a composed character, never flustered, a calming influence on the rest of his team."

Hoddle has no concerns about the next generation about to reach 100 caps; Ashley Cole, Steven Gerrard, and Frank Lampard, "In any era, consistency is the key to reaching 100 caps. It doesn't matter how many managers some of these players have had, they all picked them regularly which suggests it isn't just one manager's opinion about their worth. So there can be no doubting their lasting quality. I reached 53 caps and would have loved to have made it to 100 but I am immensely proud to have played for my country and it doesn't matter if it's 100 caps or just one, it is still an honour, a great honour to represent your country, it's the pinnacle for every footballer.

"As we are finding out with the Olympics, it means a lot to players, even to David Beckham being omitted from the GB team. It is something you dream about as a kid and it a momentous feat when it happens. You dream about playing for your favourite club as a boy but your biggest dream is to play for your country and winning the World Cup is unsurpassed in anything you could do in your career and precious few players can boast being a World Cup winner. If you asked the players from '66 what was the best thing they achieved in football, it wouldn't take them long to answer that one, it would eclipse all the trophies in club football. Will England win it again? Well..."

Ironically, Hoddle thought he stood a chance as a player in 1986 in Mexico under Bobby Robson until Diego Maradona's Hand of God, and again as a manager in France, until Beckham was dismissed.

Hoddle has often told me that he held Beckham back in his first World Cup, knowing that he once he integrated him into the World Cup team he could have been the inspiration to have taken England all the way to their first success since '66. For that reason it was such a huge disappointment to Hoddle when Beckham was red carded in the tie with Argentina when it looked as though England were the better team.

That red card against Argentina in the Geoffroy Guichard stadium, Saint Etienne, on June 30, 1998 came at a critical time. England led 2-1 following a frenetic opening during which Michael Owen scored one of the greatest goals in World Cup history. Beckham's dismissal and Zanetti's goal seconds from half-time put a very different slant on Hoddle's half-time speech. There were no further goals in normal time, although Sol Campbell had a header disallowed in extra-time, before (inevitably) England crashed out on penalties 4-3. Most pundits felt England would have won with 11 men. Beckham's reception on his return to England was predictably hostile, with effigies being burnt in the East End and radio pundits calling for his head. Beck's response was typical – he went on to lift an unprecedented treble with Manchester United the following season.

Nevertheless, it proved to be the biggest low of his England career, "I felt in good form in the tournament. I missed the first game, but I came back to score against Colombia and start in the next couple of games. Enough has been written about this game and I have lived this through in my mind for many years. I came through this experience a stronger person and it taught me how to deal with adversity. No person should ever go through what I did."

Redemption came in the World Cup group tie with Argentina in the Sapporo Dome 4 years later. England won 1-0 with a Beckham penalty. "My life has come full circle on many occasions. It had felt like I had been on the bottom and worked my way to the top again. I had achieved a lot of success with Manchester United, particularly winning the treble in 1999, but here was the perfect opportunity to right the wrong of the sending-off. No one else was going to take the penalty but me. When I scored, it felt like the burden had been lifted from my shoulders. I could breathe again."

Peter Taylor, caretaker for one international following Kevin Keegan's dismissal, was the first England manager to see Beck's potential as captain. He handed him the armband for a friendly with Italy. With Hoddle and his successor Kevin Keegan departed, Beckham was stand-in coach Taylor's surprise choice to fill the vacant post of captain. His debut as captain was in the Stadio delle Alpi, Turin, November 15, 2000, a friendly England lost 1-0. "I never expected to get the captain's armband at that time in my career. I couldn't stop smiling. I remember having a battle with Gattuso in the middle of the park." When Becks played on loan with Milan, he remarked, "He (Gattuso) is a nightmare to play against. I'm glad he's in my team now." He was skipper up to and including the 2006 World Cup in Germany, a run of 58 matches.

Sven-Goran Eriksson would reap the rewards of his and Taylor's decision to promote the right winger as skipper the following year, when Beckham dragged England through to the 2002 World Cup finals, notably scoring a last-gasp free-kick against Greece to secure automatic qualification. Beckham was in the form of his life in 2001–02 before he was injured by poor challenge from Deportivo La Coruña's Argentinian hatchet man Duscher in a Champions League tie in April.

Beckham captained the team at the 2002 World Cup under Eriksson despite a metatarsal injury that dominated England's preparations. Short of match fitness, he struggled to recapture his dynamic form and England exited to Brazil in the quarter-finals. While attention focussed on Seaman's horrific error and Eriksson's lack of tactical nous, Beckham was clearly at fault for Brazil's equaliser minutes before half-time.

Beckham's importance to England was brought into question at Euro 2004 when he missed two penalties, one against France in the opening group game and another in the shoot-out against hosts Portugal in the quarter-finals. In October 2005, Beckham's red card against Austria made him the first England captain to be sent off and the first, and only, player to be sent off twice while playing for England. But he captained England for the 50th time in a friendly against Argentina the following month.

More records were broken in Germany 2006 when Beckham scored from a free-kick against Ecuador, becoming the first English player to score in three World Cups - giving England a 1–0 victory and a place in the quarter-finals. Once again England went out on penalties, although Beckham did not get to take a spot-kick this time after being taken off with an injury earlier in the game.

A day after the loss, an emotional Beckham stepped down as England captain, saying he felt it right to pass on the armband under incoming manager Steve McClaren. He was then dropped from the squad by McClaren, who issued his infamous "the door is closed... still ajar" reference to Beckham's exit from his first squad. There was a feeling in the Beckham camp that McClaren had banished him purely to distance himself from Eriksson's regime. McClaren had been the Swede's assistant but no longer wanted to be associated with his regime. Beckham was dropped in August 2006 on 94 caps. Of this period Beckham comments, "I have had a few low points in my time but that phone call was probably the lowest," he reflected. "I was shocked but also hurt and I had a 14-hour flight to think about it. I thought my England career was over. Deep down, I hoped it wasn't but, even deeper, I didn't think I was going to play for my country again. Six months before the World Cup, I made the decision to retire as England captain but I always felt I wouldn't be retiring from football at international level."

Eventually, Becks again earned a dramatic recall after forcing his way back into Fabio Capello's Real Madrid line-up. McClaren was forced to restore Becks in the ultimately unsuccessful 2008 European Championship qualifying campaign but was sacked immediately after England failed to qualify for Euro 2008 and dubbed The Wally With The Brolly following a miserable defeat by Croatia.

Explaining his decisions to drop and then recall Beckham, McClaren commented, "I had to try to freshen things up. I needed to try to find a core of players who would get us by the hurdles which had prevented progress in the past. That meant a new captain and a nucleus of players — the likes of John Terry, Rio Ferdinand, Frank Lampard, Steven Gerrard, Wayne Rooney, Michael Owen and Owen Hargreaves — and also introducing younger players with a bit of pace. I felt this would be an opportunity to start afresh and make a statement that players like Aaron Lennon, David Bentley, Shaun Wright-Phillips and Joe Cole would get opportunities on the right. But the biggest thing was I saw the emergence of Hargreaves during the World Cup as very significant. I envisaged a midfield of Gerrard on the right, Hargreaves, Lampard and Joe Cole, with the younger lads creating healthy competition for places. I also felt it would be insulting to someone of Beckham's stature and reputation to put him on the bench. He had been such a great player he deserved better than that."

Beckham was to have nearly as many comebacks as Frank Sinatra. Yet, at first it didn't look as though there was any way back when Fabio Capello was installed as England manager, mainly due to the fact the pair had history at Real Madrid. Capello dropped had Becks at Real, declaring he would never pick him again, condemning his decision to join Los Angeles Galaxy, but then reinstated him as an integral part of the nucleus of players that snatched the league from Barcelona on the final day of the season. But with Becks it never quite works out as everyone thinks it will. Capello's impact was immediate, as he left the former captain stranded on 99 caps, refusing all sentiment, not even bothering to entertain any commercial reasoning, to simply hand over a 100th cap to someone who had served his country so loyally and enthusiastically. Michael Owen, England's top goalscorer, in sight of Sir Bobby Charlton's record number of goals, was also dropped, and didn't even merit coming off the bench.

Beckham trained at Arsenal in a bid to win his 100th cap against Switzerland — Capello's first game in charge. The momentum built up for Beck's to be handed his 100th cap, a debate that took up so many headlines and column inches. Eriksson's reluctance to drop Beckham was regarded by some as evidence that the captain was too influential. Graham Taylor famously called time on Lineker's international career just one short of Charlton's 49-goal England record and was pilloried for the decision to substitute him for Arsenal's Alan Smith against Sweden in 1992. But Taylor reckoned Becks must be picked, "All of this makes me smile to myself. I brought Gary Lineker off for footballing reasons and I got criticised for it. I made the decision that I wanted someone who could hold the ball up. It was nothing to do with the fact that it was Gary's last game or he was one goal short of Charlton's record. I didn't tell him to retire, I didn't miss the penalty against Brazil when he admits he tried to be a smart-arse. I decided he had to come off for footballing reasons. Having not played politics in taking Lineker off, that damaged me. So why have that at the start of your career when it's not going to do any harm?" Former England striker Jimmy Greaves believed Beckham should win his ton, then "do everyone a favour and announce his international retirement".

Capello accepted debate over Beckham's position within the squad was 'valid' but clearly had no intention of being swayed by Becks popularity or his 99 caps. Former Germany World Cup winner Franz Beckenbauer joined the big debate,

"I don't know what Capello's planning is with regards to England. What I do know is that it's always a nice gesture to give a world-class player, a living legend like Beckham is, a chance to play his 100th cap even if you are planning the future without him."

Beckham did not figure in the initial squad of 30 when Capello named his first England squad after returning from a 24-hour trip to Natal, on the spectacular northeast tip of Brazil, where he was marking the site of his third academy after London and Los Angeles. A week earlier, he made a trip to Sierra Leone on behalf of Unicef. Beckham had not played a competitive game for a while and said at the time: 'I have always said I want to be available. That's what I did when Steve McClaren dropped me. Deep down, I did not think I would ever play for England again. So to be on 99 caps is great. It's more than I dreamt of. If I am not in the squad, I will carry on working hard and trying to get back in. I won't get bitter and twisted because I am old enough and I have got enough respect for the manager to realise that if it does not happen, life goes on. I have been lucky enough in my career to come back from tough times and disappointments. If it doesn't happen, I will come back from it again, in my way. If it does, then great."

Beckham had no intention of calling time on his international career, "I don't want to retire yet and I don't plan on retiring from club or international football. But you never say never. Things might change that might make me feel maybe it is time. Some people might say that if I win 100 caps I should call it a day then and quit on my own terms but that decision can only come from me. I have always said that when I didn't feel I could play at the top level, I would retire. But I still feel I can play at that level." Becks explained just how much reaching the landmark 100 was meant to him. "It would mean the world. Getting picked for your country is always special. The 100th game makes it extra special. Hopefully it will happen. Hopefully I've worked hard enough to get myself fit, but we'll have to see. His [Capello's] approach to football is 'It's my way' — and that's the way it has got to be. He doesn't treat any player in the team or in the squad any differently. He only makes decisions on football, he doesn't care about anything else. If he doesn't think you're fit, he won't play you; if he doesn't think you are good enough, he won't pick you.'

The hard line attitude toward Beckham marked a new approach to friendlies by Capello. Under Eriksson they were reduced to exhibition-game status but Capello's philosophy was to use friendlies as a serious means of building his new team. Ironically, Beckham was in the running to be named England's Player of the Year even though he made only two competitive appearances for his country the previous season. Voting by England fans for the award ended just as Capello was putting the finishing touches to his first squad announcement.

Capello called Beckham the night before he named his squad to inform him that he would not be part of his first England squad, but assured him he could be part of his plans for the future. The Italian told him he wanted his players to be match-fit, and that naming Beckham in his squad to face Switzerland would be unfair on those who have been playing in matches week-in, week-out. He was however been encouraged by his talk with Capello about the future. In the phone call, Beckham was told that there was no reason he would not be picked as long as he was fit enough and playing well for the Galaxy. Capello had no issue with Beckham going to Brazil and Africa. Capello said: "I know there has been a lot of discussion about David Beckham. The reason that David is not in the squad is because he has not had any real match practice since playing in November."

Ex-England captain Terry Butcher commented, "I think it's now unlikely Beckham will ever get to 100 caps. Capello is putting down a very strong marker by saying 'I'm not concerned about people getting 100 caps, I'm more worried about getting my squad right from the word go.' If David had joined the squad he may have actually felt a little embarrassed that he was only there for sentimental reasons. He hasn't played since October and he's not match fit. He's going to go away and play in a league which is out of sight, out of mind and it's very difficult to see whether he will ever get his 100th cap now."

England's most capped player Peter Shilton backed Capello, "Nobody gave me a cap out of the goodness of their heart. I had to earn every single one of my 125. You can't give out caps based on reputation. And it's refreshing after what we saw under Steve McClaren. Capello has clearly made his own mind up about David and not been influenced by anyone at the FA or their marketing department. The manager has made a clear statement with this. Capello was right on this occasion. I for one would love to see David get his 100th cap but Capello has set his stall out. His first priority is to get a squad that's capable of winning the World Cup and he's been known for his strict attitude towards players. It would have looked a bit weak from his point of view to have included David in terms of his preparation for the game. If it had been any other player, I don't even think he would have even considered it.

"Capello has not been intimidated by any outside forces to include David in the squad. He's not completely shut the door but it is going to be very difficult from now on for David. Capello wants to set his own standards. If any player other than David Beckham had had his sort of preparation for this game, he wouldn't even be under consideration. Having 99 caps is special and still a fantastic achievement. But this will hurt. It will be more difficult for him from now on to get back in because the England squad will be moving on under the new manager. David has a life outside football and I admire him for what he's done off the pitch and the life he has created. But playing at the standard he does in America, not playing for such a long time, all this travelling and everything else has a price. He will find it harder where he is based to get back than if he was playing week in, week out in the Premier League."

"I agreed with McClaren when Beckham was dropped. He needed to look forward to a qualifying campaign for Euro 2008. I thought it was a mistake to bring him back. And now we have this situation where Beckham is on 99 caps. I wouldn't like to see him stuck there but there is a reason for it – simply because his preparation hasn't been right to represent England. If anyone is equipped to deal with it, though, it is him. A more 'ordinary' player may find it hard to deal with but Beckham has other things going on in his life to soften the blow. I hope David gets 100 caps. He has been a great player for England."

A day after Beckham was omitted from Capello's first squad he received public support from another figure who had to wait for his ultimate ambition to be fulfilled – Gordon Brown. The then Prime Minister believed that Beckham will remain an exemplary role model regardless of whether he receives a 100th England cap but said he was confident the former England captain would eventually reach a century of appearances. Brown courted Beckham, inviting him for an hour of informal talks at Downing Street and visiting his London football academy. With the prime minister backing England's 2018 World Cup bid there is also every likelihood that Beckham would be asked to play a prominent role in that campaign. Brown praised Beckham's commitment to encouraging young people into sport. "David Beckham has done really well," he said. "I was really impressed by his vision for the future of his academies. He wants to get young people in all areas of the country involved through satellites from his academy in London, and he has set up one in Brazil and in LA."

Beckham agreed it would have been 'unfair' of Capello to select him in his first England squad, "It's always disappointing when you're not included in an England squad. The thing is I half expected it because I know what Fabio Capello is like as a manager and if he thinks you're not fit and ready to play then you won't be in the team. I totally respect that and totally understand that. There are a lot of Premiership players who have played 15 games in the last two months and I haven't played a game since December – so to be called into the squad was probably unfair."

If he joined Shilton, Moore, Charlton and Wright as only the fifth player to pass the century mark for England, Becks reckoned it would be one of the proudest moments of his career. "Reaching 100 games and reaching 100 caps is very special. Being a proud Englishmen, it's something that I've always wanted to do since I was a young boy. I've always wanted to play for my country, I've always wanted to captain my country and I've always wanted to reach 100 games because there's not many players that have done that. It would be a proud moment if I did that but at the moment I'm working hard on my fitness and working hard with the Galaxy and if I get the 100th cap then great."

It wasn't until the Capello's next squad that he was recalled. Former England managers backed Capello's decision. Sven-Goran Eriksson commented, "I am very happy for David, of course. I think he deserves to have his 100th cap - but if he is going to start or come on, I have no idea." Eriksson, then in charge of Manchester City, thought of recruiting an experienced big-name player to help 'fill the stadium' but laughed off any suggestions Beckham could move to Eastlands. Eriksson added: "We haven't talked about that - but I think it would be very difficult to match his salary!" Kevin Keegan, who managed England from 1999 to 2000, confirmed Beckham was called up on merit and not sentiment, "I think all the fans want it, I think all the players who know him would want it, and I think all the managers who have managed him want it. I think at the end of the day it's not nostalgic, if he wins one more cap to get a 100 it will be what he deserves."

Glenn Hoddle suggested Beckham's range of passing and versatility would make him a useful asset to Capello. "If I was England manager now I think there would be even more games for David Beckham. I can see him playing different roles – he can play a deeper role in midfield in international football. And even if the current manager decided to play three at the back, he could step in and play in between the two centre-backs if he switched his mind to defensive mode. I certainly think he has got a few more caps up his sleeve. He can maybe go on and win a few more than the one or two caps people are talking about."

Meanwhile, Steve McClaren admitted Beckham's contribution to football means he is worthy of the milestone. "He has deserved his 100th cap for what he has been through, the kind of person he is, and what he has given to football. David was out the scene then when I brought him back and he was so excited about returning. For what he has given he deserves to get that cap. If he is made captain for the game that would be a big bonus."

Capello understood Beckham's determination to fight back. "The last time we met we were celebrating on the field at the Bernabeu," Beckham said. His last recall by McClaren nearly had that same happy ending as in Madrid. Had Beckham started against Croatia, rather than come on at half-time, it might well have done. "I came back to England [under McClaren] realising that I had to prove again that I deserved to be here. People felt I had it easy because I'd had a good relationship with my previous managers and they were just picking me for my name. I had to prove to people that I deserved to be here. That's always been my motivation; the thing that keeps me going. I started enjoying it more when I came back into the team. I'd seen how it could be taken away from me and I didn't want that to happen again."

Beckham would not celebrate his 100th cap with the captain's armband – as all four of England's previous centurions did. Happy enough with his recall, Beckham did not dispute the arrangement, "As much as reaching 100 is a milestone in an Englishman's career – and there are not too many who have done that – it is important for me to carry on. I am very honoured to be talked about in the same company as Bobby Moore and Bobby Charlton – they are players I have always looked up to. But I want to go beyond that. I want to carry on for quite a few years yet. I'd have turned around and retired if I didn't and I don't feel like doing that now. I wouldn't be here if I didn't feel I could do it physically any more. There are plenty of young players coming through but I feel I can still offer something."

Special golden boots, a shirt embroidered with 100 caps in gold, his family in the stadium, and only a defeat to spoil the occasion. Even so Beckham spoke of his pride at becoming only the fifth player to earn 100 caps for England – and reiterated his desire to continue playing. Beckham reached the milestone playing the opening 63 minutes of the 1-0 defeat in Paris showing Capello that his fitness was up to scratch for international level after a gruelling pre-season with the LA Galaxy. "I enjoyed the hour I played and the most important thing for me tonight was proving my fitness. I felt I did that.

I felt very fresh and a lot better than I thought I would. As much as you work hard in pre-season, nothing is better than playing games. I've played under Fabio Capello before and he knows what I am like as a player. From that point of view I don't have to prove anything – but proving my fitness was the biggest thing."

Capello praised Beckham, who was replaced just after the hour mark by David Bentley. David James brought down Chelsea's Nicolas Anelka to allow Franck Ribery to score the game's only goal from the penalty spot. Capello made four substitutions at half-time, Terry being replaced by Joleon Lescott and Stewart Downing coming on for Joe Cole, Peter Crouch for Gerrard and Owen for Rooney. It was Owen's first action under Capello but he had little opportunity to demonstrate the goalscoring form he has shown recently for Newcastle. He substituted Beckham, who picked up his booking for tugging the shirt of Ribery, only so that he could take a look at Bentley against top-rated opposition.

Alan Hansen commented, "Credit to David Beckham, in an age where players are retiring early he has kept on going and given his all for England. But is he there on merit? Probably not. There is no doubt he deserves 100 caps but maybe he should have had 20 minutes against Switzerland last time round and then you look to the future."

Graham Taylor observed, "As for David Beckham? Everything he did came from a static position and we know he can hit crosses in from those positions like he did. But we are judging him on his 100th game. If Fabio Capello is going to be building a more mobile team I don't think David is going to be the answer – I think the boy David Bentley is going to be."

Beckham remained an ambassador for the FA's bid to bring the World Cup to England in 2018 having played a key role in the successful London 2012 Olympic Bid. Fifa vice-president Jack Warner provided hope to England's bid. "The catalyst of my support for England for the bid for 2018 is because I don't believe any country of England's football pedigree should not have a world cup for almost 50 years," he said at the time. "What England needs is to have somebody like a David Beckham to be its ambassador out there to sell the idea. Beckham is loved by all. Beckham is like Pele and therefore use him to sell the idea. For many people it would bring a legitimacy to the bid." Odd then, that he didn't vote for England when it came to it!

However, back to the main issue of Becks caps, and the controversy refused to subside as he headed towards Bobby Moore's record, making him the second most capped England star behind Shilton. Beckham's loan move to AC Milan was primarily to catch Capello's eye, and to play at a far higher standard than LA Galaxy. He regained much more fitness as a consequence. AC Milan president Galliani said at the time: "Beckham has chosen Milan. He'll stay here in Milan on loan for a few months. Our squad is ultra-competitive and it will remain this way but Beckham is something different and intriguing. David's arrival is a dream that becomes a reality." He joined a stellar squad at Milan, including Brazilians Ronaldinho, Kaka and Alexandre Pato, as well as Italian internationals Andrea Pirlo and Gennaro Gattuso. Coach Carlo Ancelotti welcomed Beckham, "Beckham is a serious athlete, a great professional." Beckham was eligible to play for Milan both domestically and in the UEFA Cup. Real president Ramon Calderon provided an insight into the value Milan derived from signing him. "He is a very well-known player. He is a player who can give a lot to the club he signs for." Beckham spent four seasons at the Bernabeu and Calderon added: "He is a fantastic player, a nice person and we have a lot of good memories. The Real Madrid fans like him very much and he is always welcome at Real Madrid in any sense."

Beckham said: "AC Milan is one of the biggest clubs in the world, I've been lucky enough to play with one of the biggest clubs in England, one of the biggest clubs in Spain and now I'm being given the chance to play with one of the biggest clubs in Italy. I'm very honoured to be given the chance to train and play with the likes of Ronaldinho and Kaka, but it also gives me the chance to keep my fitness up and carry that on for when I come back to the Galaxy for the new MLS season. They've got Kaka, Ronaldinho, Seedorf and also a player with one of the best records in football – Maldini. To be on the pitch or training field and get experience with those players is a big honour for myself. Of course I'd love to carry on playing for my country, but like I've said I'm just taking each game as it comes. If I carry on all the way through to the World Cup then great. I'm enjoying the qualifiers, I'm enjoying the way the team are playing together and bonding."

Capello was instrumental in the move as he wanted Beckham to remain fit and active to stay in the England squad, "Milan have made a good addition," said Capello, who coached the Rossoneri from 1991–96 and 1997–98. "At

Madrid I left him out of the squad because he had signed a contract with Los Angeles but he continued to come on the field and train and I put him back in the team. He is a very serious lad, very sensible, a professional. People think he is a playboy off the field, it's not true at all."

Ronaldinho, who signed for Milan in the summer, commented "He's a great champion. I hope he's happy with us. We'll take turns taking free kicks. I've met him in the past and I have always been struck by his class." Kaka said, "Many people believe Beckham's arrival will be a negative thing, but us players we believe that he can really give a lot to this team and contribute to us winning the Scudetto and the UEFA Cup." Moving to Milan could keep Beckham playing top-class football until he hits 40, according to Gianfranco Zola. He joined one of the oldest squads in world football, a dozen players in their 30s. Zola was confident that if Beckham stays in Italy, Milan's miracle working fitness coaches and doctors will keep him in peak condition for years to come. Of the Milan squad at the time, Paolo Maldini, Pipo Inzaghi, Giuseppe Favalli and goalkeeper Dida were all older than Beckham. Much of the rest of the side - Alessandro Nesta, Clarence Seedorf and former Chelsea man Andriy Shevchenko - were just a year younger.

Peter Shilton remained sceptical that the then 33-year-old would be able to challenge his tally. Beckham needed 19 more caps to pass Shilton's record of 125. England were set to qualify for the 2010 World Cup and if Beckham played every game he could do it in South Africa, but Shilton commented, "I'm proud of my record. I wouldn't like to lose it, but I don't really see David breaking it. The way things are going you can never say never, but I feel he can only break it as a super sub and I don't see that happening. It will be very difficult for him. It's down to the manager and to David if he wants to have that role, but if England are going to do well in the World Cup, they've got to be blooding young players and looking at others."

Victoria and their three sons remained in America during his spell at the San Siro. Beckham explained, "Everyone knows how much I love my wife and my children but at the same time I love football. My children will remain in Los Angeles due to school and Victoria will remain with them. When Victoria comes to Milan she will remain with me for a couple of days." Beckham insisted he did not move to the San Siro purely to stay in Capello's plans. "I didn't join Milan just for that reason. I have never played in Italy and I think it's one of the best leagues in the world. I want to concentrate on working with the team. I am willing to work really hard for my place in the squad. I always try to have no regrets in life, or in my career. I made the decision to go to LA two years ago and I've had a good time there.'

Milan believed that £4.5m would be enough to get an escape clause activated. Victoria, though, was less keen on staying in Italy and did not want to uproot their three sons after their previous spell in a non–English speaking country with Real Madrid. Galliani said Milan would be willing to soften the blow of any loss in earnings if Beckham broke his a highly lucrative deal with Galaxy and MLS. LA Galaxy coach Bruce Arena criticised Milan over the way his club made public their desire to keep Beckham as well as Bayern Munich's plans to keep hold of Landon Donovan.

BECKHAM BREAKS BOBBY MOORE'S RECORD

THE GENERATIONS ARE vastly different. Though Bobby Moore was able to earn reasonable amounts of money from endorsements, David Beckham revolutionised the image of a footballer from the archetypal sweaty athlete to a fashion guru, going well beyond the play boy image of even George Best. Where George chased women, David became a devoted family man, while George drank himself into oblivion, David developed a clean cut image, only briefly questioned with one incident off the field, and the red card against Argentina in the World Cup when he was still very much in the embryonic stages of his illustrious career.

Once he ironed out the glitches he developed into an industry in his own right, a multi-millionaire clothes horse and world icon on a scale Bobby Moore could barely have imagined. For some, the eclipsing of Moore's milestone bordered on sacrilege, given the 1966 World Cup winning captain played in an era when there were fewer internationals and no cheap caps on offer as a substitute. Beckham, though, was selected on merit after proving his worth again in Serie A. Capello said at the time: "I've watched him in Milan and

David's form is okay now. He is fit. Every player in the squad has to play, not just train. He is better than he was six months ago."

Those traditionalists point out Moore first played in the era before substitutes and started and finished all of his 108 England matches, while Beckham started only 99, completing just 54 full games by the time he reached Moore's record, although he did of course go on to establish that he started 100 games for his country.

Beckham insisted at the time that the criticism does not affect him. "To be on the amount of caps is a huge honour. Every time is a bonus. I never expected to make a hundred. Then I made a hundred and people expected me to retire," he said. "Everyone has got their opinions but I'm not looking at [Shilton's] record. Being at AC Milan gives me the chance to play at that higher level I'm enjoying being with the squad at the moment."

In the demanding culture of Serie A, Beckham proved to even the harshest of Italian and English cynics, during his loan spell at AC Milan, to have merited his continued selection for England at that time under Capello. As Milan vice-president Adriano Galliani said at the time: "David has an incredible strength of will. We played in Glasgow, he had a cough and a really bad cold but he didn't want to be substituted. Beckham is polite, he packs his own bags, cleans his shoes on his own, opens and closes the bottle of water and returns it. He's one of the old-school players, the kind I like."

Bobby Moore would have given his blessing to Beckham becoming England's most capped outfield player according to his widow, Stephanie. When Beckham was in line to equal Bobby's 108-cap record for an outfielder in the friendly in Spain, she declared: "He would be the first to congratulate Beckham, shake his hand and say 'Well done, son. Now go out and beat the record'. I don't know David Beckham but he seems still to have that schoolboy passion for football, the way Bobby did. It is an incredible achievement. There are more England games now but it is more physical and the regimes more demanding, so it is an amazing feat."

The West Ham legend died of bowel cancer in February 1993 and the Hammers dedicated the home match with Manchester United to the Bobby Moore Fund For Cancer Research. Stephanie is a leading campaigner in the fight against the disease and addressed fans on the pitch at half-time. She commented: "Each day 44 men and women die of bowel cancer. Yet it is an unfashionable disease and we have to make people aware of it. I am terrified of talking on the pitch to 35,000 people. More nervous than when Bobby walked out for the World Cup final, I reckon, but we have to do something." I have met Stephanie on numerous occasions, and she is delighted that the publishers of England Centurions is making a contribution from the sale of the book to the Bobby Moore foundation.

As for Beckham, Stephanie was delighted to have met him when all the England Centurions were presented with their awards for reaching 100 caps. At one stage it looked highly improbable that Beckham would reach Bobby's milestone. Having been left out of the squad that beat Germany in Berlin, Capello brought him back for the friendly with Spain. "He is a media star and for this reason all the fans spoke about him in this way before he arrived; like a star not a player," Capello said, "but now he has played three games, and every game has been better."

At this time Beckham was tempted by a permanent move to Milan but LA Galaxy turned down a £6.75m bid from AC Milan. Tim Leiweke, chief executive of AEG, the company who own Galaxy, confirmed that the bid was rejected.

Goalkeeping legend Peter Shilton was sure Beckham had done "exceptionally well" to revive his England career at that time and be in line for a record-equalling cap. "At a certain age, as a midfielder lots of things can go wrong stamina-wise," said Shilton at the time, "He went to America thinking his England career was probably over but was thrown a lifeline and took it."

Some of the heroes of '66 had mixed views about Beckham drawing level on the number of caps. Sir Bobby Charlton observed, "You have to be a good player to win 100 caps. David has looked after himself. He is very fit and has a great appetite for the game, and he can go on for quite a while yet. He's been fortunate recently to have been at a good club playing top-level football. They haven't sent him backwards but forwards. There was no similarity between the styles of captaincy of Bobby and David. What I will say is that Bobby was fantastic and anyone who matches his achievements has done well. So that applies to David. He has always loved the game. He has this infectious enthusiasm for the game, which has helped him carry on playing international football into his thirties."

Full-back in the '66 side George Cohen observed, "My

view is that in the four major competitions in which he has played we have been poor and I don't see the necessity now to have him around when we have young players in the squad. People keep telling him he is an impact player but when you have 11 players playing for their country, they should all be impact players. Also, I can't understand why these cameo appearances as a sub should earn a cap. You used to have to play 90 minutes to win a cap. I feel that makes it shambolic. That is not to say that David Beckham has not been a good player for his country or a good captain but eight of his most recent caps have come after he's been brought on as a sub. Bobby was always a great presence in our side but we had a lot of very experienced players all around."

The acidic Jack Charlton commented, "There is no doubt that David is a good player, but what I'd like to know is whether or not the manager wants him in the side. There doesn't seem a lot of point picking him for an odd game and then leaving him out again. It's not the lad's fault. I think the real hallmark is when you reach the 100 caps. He is still only 33 and our kid played until he was 35 and finished his career at the World Cup in 1970. If Capello intends to take him to South Africa and the lad is playing well enough to be picked then that's fine and he has always led from the front, taking the free kicks and penalties. But Bobby Moore was a good captain, though he led by example. He didn't need to say a lot because we had leaders in the side. Just remember that Bobby Moore, my brother and Ray Wilson were all picked in the team of the tournament in 1966."

Ray Wilson added, "David has been a fantastic player or he wouldn't have played so long for all his clubs. But I'm not

FIRST TO 100:

Billy Wright is chaired from the field following England's win over Scotland at Wembley in 1959. The England captain became the first player in the history of the game to reach 100 caps for his country.

Sir Bobby Charlton was the next to 100 caps - reaching the landmark on the 21st April 1970 in a match against Northern Ireland. Sir Bobby went on to reach 106 caps.

Pele and Bobby Moore embrace at the end of England and Brazil's titanic group match in the 1970 World Cup. Bobby went on to his 100th cap against Scotland in 1973.

Peter Shilton won his 100th cap against Holland in the 1988 European Championships. Unfortunately, the game proved a nightmare for Shilts as Marco Van Basten claimed a hat-trick in a 3-1 win to send England out. Although Peter was subsequently dropped for the final group game, he bounced back to win a total of 125 caps before retiring at the 1990 World Cup.

David Beckham is the latest member of the 100 club reaching his century on March 26th 2008, against France at the Stade de France. Becks finished his career with 115 caps, a record for an outfield player.

NEXT GENERATION
With Frank Lampard, Ashley Cole and Steven Gerrard well
past the 90 cap mark and Wayne Rooney in the high 80s,
the 100 club is set to grow in the next few years.

THE MOST CAPPED PLAYERS IN WORLD FOOTBALL

(Far left) Ahmed Hassan, Egypt (184), (top middle) Mohamed Al-Deayea, Saudi Arabia, (178), (top right) Claudio Suarez, Mexico, (178) (below) Hossam Hassan, Egypt, (169), Vitalijs Astafjevs, Latvia, (167).

Overleaf: (top left) Adnan Al-Talyani, UAE, (164), (top right) Cobi Jones, USA, (164), (left) Sami Al-Jaber, Saudi Arabia, (163), (middle) Martin Reim, Estonia, (157), (bottom) Lothar Matthäus, Germany (150)

so sure about when he was playing in America and still got called up to win his 100th. He was effectively playing Third Division football by then. By that token, why don't they call on Geoff Hurst now, put him on the pitch for a minute so that he can win his 50th because he got left stranded on 49 caps. But that's how it is today. Not that I am against using substitutes in general. Too many FA Cup finals were ruined by injuries before the rule came in. Bobby played through all his 108 games. I don't know about David but Bobby was a quiet man who just got on with his own game."

David Beckham equalled Moore's record after coming on as a substitute in the 2-0 defeat in Spain. The number 17 shirt worn by Beckham was auctioned on behalf of The Bobby Moore Fund. "It was a very, very generous gesture," Stephanie Moore said, "that shirt is of great emotional value to David. It was very kind and generous of him to donate it to the charity so we can auction it to raise funds for dedicated bowel cancer research – the disease that killed Bobby so young."

Stephanie was at a loss to explain why some people do not think he is worthy of so many England caps. "How can he not be?" she said. "I don't understand why we're not proud of this man. It baffles me. I know Bobby would have been the first to congratulate him. David has given so much to the sport and continues to so on so many different levels across the world, we should be proud of him. To have achieved 108 caps at this level, whether he goes on for part or all of the match, is considerable. Bobby would have smiled and said well done, congratulations, enjoy the moment and go on and do even better."

"No-one can be compared to Bobby Moore because he's such a legend," Becks commented at the time. "He's a player I'll always look up to. I'm just very honoured to be even be mentioned in the same breath as him. I hope to keep on playing for my country. Of course I do. I have always dreamed of playing for England and to achieve this record is unbelievable. I'm honoured. Bobby Moore won the World Cup with England. He's an icon and a legend. It is very humbling. I don't know what the secret is. I still enjoy my football and, as long as that's the case, I'll keep on going. I've always said I would be honoured to be up there with the likes of Bobby Charlton and Bobby Moore. But the most important thing was the game — and we're disappointed to have lost."

Beckham replaced Middlesbrough's Stewart Downing at the start of the second half with England trailing 1-0 at the Estadio Ramon Sanchez-Pizjuan in Seville. He showed glimpses of his quality with some trademark long passes, but his night was tempered when he was booked for dissent in the closing stages of the match.

Beckham's desire to play for a top club in order to cement his place in the England squad for the 2010 World Cup finals led to him effectively part funding a unique loan deal with AC Milan himself. An LA Galaxy statement confirmed that Beckham had put some of his own money towards the deal which allows him to stay in Italy, saying it "has been funded jointly by Milan and the player himself". "I've been able to help myself stay in Milan, if I can put it that way," said Beckham. "It's never about money, it's always been about the football." Galliani spoke in glowing terms of the financial sacrifice Beckham made. "A lot of players show their affection just with words. David Beckham is one of the very few who has shown it with deeds. I won't cite any numbers, but I can say that the player has made an incredible economic commitment, paying a lot of money from his own pocket."

Garber revealed Milan paid the full $10m pay out they wanted for the extension of Beckham's loan. "We asked for $10 million, we got our $10 million," Garber said. "We don't know where it's coming from, either. There's a lot of different ways it could happen. He cannot get paid from Milan. Milan could pay us. He could pay them. At the end of the day, it doesn't matter." Part of the fee was paid by Milan, the rest by Beckham, who was desperate to stay in European football to keep alive his hopes of playing at a fourth World Cup finals in South Africa.

Capello made it clear at the time that only form, not age, would determine whether Beckham would be picked for future England squads. "I have watched the last few games that David has played for AC Milan and I am very happy with his performances. He's played very well. When I look at it, player age does not come into it. I'm looking for the best players. Italy still pick Fabio Cannavaro and he is 35 years old. I'm looking at other things." Capello was concerned that the standard of soccer in the MLS is not as high as the European leagues. "Beckham made a personal decision. The standard in America is different. In this moment it is important for him to play in Europe – not only Milan but Europe. American football is not at the same level as Italy, Spain, Germany and

England, that's for sure."

Though Beckham played the whole second half in the friendly with Spain, his previous four caps had been won on the back of just 27 minutes. He started just one England game in 16 and has not scored for 26. Perhaps his time was up and time to bring on the younger players. Beckham said: "I think the manager is doing that — even with me still in the squad. That's been one of the exceptional things about Fabio Capello. He's played people like Theo Walcott and I'm not going to complain about that. Theo, Aaron Lennon and Shaun Wright-Phillips have been exceptional for their clubs and to see players with this talent coming through — not only in my position on the right — is important. And, no, I don't feel as if I'm getting in the way. I can help around the squad with my experience but I'd like to think it's more than that. I'd hope that, if I come on in a game, I can set up goals from crosses, free-kicks and corners. And, as I've shown for Milan, the work-rate is still there."

Beckham played all 12 games possible for Milan. He said: "Having always been a confident person, it was important to get that back. When I went there I didn't know whether I was going to play or whether I'd be able to keep up with the pace of some of the players. But I surprised myself. Both form and fitness-wise it's taken me to another level." Beckham continued on the road to a fourth World Cup to draw level with Pele, Diego Maradona, Uwe Seeler, the two Italians Gianni Rivera and Paolo Maldini, Cafu and Polish defender Wladyslaw Zmuda. Beyond them on five are Mexico goalkeeper Antonio Carbajal and Lothar Matthaus — with the former Germany skipper also holding the appearance record of 25. Beckham was on 13.

England warmed up for their qualifier against Ukraine with a comfortable victory over Slovakia as Beckham produced an impressive cameo on his record-breaking 109th appearance for an outfield player. Moore's record of 108 England outfield caps had fallen to another east Londoner. "Obviously it is a very special occasion for myself, to reach this amount of caps and to be up there just above Bobby Moore," commented Beckham, "I am very proud of that, but the most important thing was the way we played and the performance we put in. Overall, it's a good night for myself but a better night for the team."

From high in their own hospitality box, Beckham's wife, Victoria, his three sons and his mother looked down with pride as he strode on proudly for the start of the second half as one of a string of substitutes. The then 33-year-old could not hide his delight at reaching such a personal landmark, and dedicated the achievement to his family, with wife Victoria at Wembley. Beckham demonstrated his industry and quality after coming on as a half-time substitute for Aaron Lennon. In a prime example of Beckham's enduring quality with the ball at his feet, his cross was delivered perfectly for Rooney to rise and direct his header beyond Senecky. Rooney headed a second from Beckham's cross on 70 minutes. "It's what I've done throughout my career," said Beckham, reflecting on his part in the goal. "If I get a chance, there's players like Wayne Rooney, Emile Heskey or Peter Crouch on the end of it. If I can assist in that way, then great."

Becks had captained England at the previous two World Cup finals but he still felt part of the set–up once again, even in the vastly diminished role of impact sub. It emphasised his commitment to the England cause, irrespective of the circumstances. Naturally, Beckham preferred to be in Capello's team from the start but said he believed he could still play a key role off the bench. "Everyone wants to start for England, but at the end of the day, everyone also wants to play for England. Substitutes can be very important. We saw that in 1999 with Teddy Sheringham and Ole Gunnar Solskjaer," harking back to United's spectacular win over Bayern Munich in the Champions League final. He went on, "Sometimes substitutes come on and can help secure a game, or change a game. I was happy with getting on and happy with the assist. If I start, then I start. If I don't, then I am part of the team – a good team which is going forwards. Everybody wants to start for England. The target is just to play, be involved in every game possible. I have already said I'd love to play in another World Cup – or two – but we will have to wait and see. That is a long way away at the moment."

Rooney hailed Beckham's impact and praised his record-breaking feat. "David has set me up for a few goals, so I have to thank him for that," said the Manchester United striker. "It is a great achievement. All of the players are really pleased for him. You could see how much he is loved by everybody, the players and the fans."

The then England captain John Terry added his praise, "He comes on and always makes the difference – that is the quality he brings to the squad. David has determination and fight, and can go on forever. He has given the manager food for thought, that is for sure."

Beckham was again a second half substitute against the Ukraine in England's 2-1 victory in the World Cup qualifier. Capello was thrilled with Becks' displays against Ukraine and Slovakia and reckoned his break at the end of last year did him good. Capello said: "David is in very good form. He did not play until January and for that reason he is fresh. He also played very well in the last game for AC Milan — he was their best player. His corners, free-kicks and crosses are very important. He is still one of the best." Despite his impressive displays, Beckham was widely criticised for picking up 'easy' caps in short cameo roles from the bench. He insisted his 90-minute performance against Andorra proved he still had what it takes. Speaking after his 100th start for the Three Lions, Becks said: "There has been a lot of people talking about me getting easy caps. People can say that but at the end of the day, subs can come on and make a difference in a game. I've done it at times and other players have done it too. But 100 starts is not too bad so I'm happy."

Much fuss, naturally, would have been made if Beckham continued to break England records. Nelson Mandela was to be asked to propose an accolade for Beckham should he become the most capped player in England's history during the World Cup finals, surpassing Shilton's record of 125 caps during the tournament as the hosts wanted to mark the milestone. Beckham could be only a handful of caps short of the record when the tournament started. Danny Jordaan, chief executive officer of the organising committee, said that South Africa would wish to commemorate the occasion.

"He is a great role model and we look forward to having him in our country and I will discuss it [Beckham reaching 126 caps] with Mandela." Jordaan recognised the impact that Beckham has had on previous finals. "I was working for Fifa at the World Cup in Japan when England played against Denmark [in 2002]," Jordaan said. "I organised the ballboys and mascots but Beckham came out of the dressing-room and they were so excited. All my hard work was gone."

Sadly it wasn't to be. Fabio Capello spoke to Beckham to commiserate over the injury that ruled him out of the World Cup after he suffered a major Achilles injury during Milan's Serie A match with Chievo, ending his hopes of featuring in a fourth World Cup for his country in South Africa. Capello and his assistant, Franco Baldini, were on the phone to offer their best wishes for Beckham to make a full recovery, knowing they had to write the 34-year-old out of their plans. Beckham sustained the injury with just two minutes to go without coming into contact with anyone else, limping to the sidelines for treatment in a match Milan went on to win 1-0. He was treated for about five minutes on the touchline before eventually being carried from the arena face down on a stretcher in tears, mouthing, "It's broken, it's broken" to those on the home bench while members of the Rossoneri's backroom staff attempted to comfort him.

Milan's coach, Leonardo, confirmed Beckham's injury after the match. "The joy of Clarence Seedorf's late goal was tempered by Beckham's serious injury," he said.

"Unfortunately it's quite easy to understand when there is the rupture of the tendon. We will wait for tests but it looks very serious. It's a big blow for us. He is an extraordinary guy and his performance in this game proved that yet again. I cannot enjoy this evening considering what has happened to David. But when the tendon goes you feel it straight away and he understood immediately that he had torn it and what that meant." Beckham concentrates on overcoming an injury that threatened the remainder of his career Capello made alternative plans. "He's in a lot of pain," said his Milan teammate, Clarence Seedorf. "This is a really bad injury."

Milan confirmed that Beckham had snapped the tendon in his left leg, with early indications suggesting his rehabilitation could stretch to five or six months. He flew to Finland where the established specialist in this field, Dr Sakari Orava, undertook a two-hour operation to repair the tendon. A leading doctor, the consultant sports physician Dr Tom Crisp, described the prospects of Beckham featuring in England's first Group C game with the United States in Rustenburg on June 12 as "non-existent". He said: "It's remotely possible he may be running in three months, the chances of him being fit to play for England are non-existent."

Beckham – the only man to score for England in three World Cup tournaments – departed the stadium in San Siro on crutches with the reality that, after a spectacular international career that began back in 1996, the likelihood is that he has now played his last game for his country. His last cap came as a substitute in the 3-0 qualifying victory over Belarus at Wembley, although he has been a regular on the bench for Capello throughout the Italian's spell as head coach. Capello had suggested in the wake of the friendly victory over Egypt earlier in the month that the former captain still had a role to play in his squad at the finals despite the emergence of Aaron Lennon, Theo Walcott and Shaun Wright-Phillips on the right of midfield, with the Italian suggesting that Beckham could "play in the middle" if required.

Capello defined Beckham's role as part of England's backroom staff by asking him to act as a liaison between players and management. Beckham was in a unique position because of his experience and the respect he commands within the squad. He was also encouraged to observe players in training throughout the tournament and report back to Capello as a right-hand man to England general manager Franco Baldini, who is Capello's key lieutenant. Capello and Baldini wanted the 35 year-old to have a meaningful role. Beckham, who missed the pre-tournament training camp in Austria, arrived in South Africa on the Football Association's chartered flight, along with the players and staff, and took up his duties immediately, watching the squad undertake a gentle training session in the afternoon. Beckham does not have any qualifications or experience, although he was listed as a member of the technical staff and was much more than a cheerleader. Rio Ferdinand hinted at Beckham's role when the captain said: "He's come with us and got great experience having played in so many major tournaments and if people need to ask questions, he may be the person to go to because he is a little bit out of it and not playing so he can help."

Beckham continued with his duties as an ambassador for England's 2018 World Cup bid and attended functions, while also continuing his rehabilitation from the injury which curtailed his season at AC Milan. Such is the high esteem in which Capello holds the midfielder, who played for him at Real Madrid, that he immediately extended an offer to include him in the party to South Africa even if he could not play. Beckham said he would only go if he had a meaningful role.

Capello might have used Beckham sparingly, but the Italian was always prepared to use him as an impact substitute, and only injury robbed him of a final World Cup appearance, but he was enrolled as an assistant under Capello. Despite returning to fitness after the tournament, Beckham was dismissed by Capello as being too old for a role in team, meaning that his appearance as a second-half substitute against Belarus in October 2009 earned him his 115th and last international cap.

For family reasons Becks rejected a move to big-spending Qatar-backed Paris Saint-Germain when his contract with LA Galaxy expired. Instead he signed a new two year deal in LA. The French club's sporting director Leonardo said that his club had failed to lure Becks to Paris, venue for his 100th England cap, citing "family reasons", bringing to an end months of speculation. New owner, Qatar's Crown Prince Sheikh Tamim bin Hamad al-Thani, and club president Nasser al-Khelaifi offered Becks a fortune, following the close-season purchase of the club by wealthy investors Qatar Sports Investments, headed by the crown prince. There had been rumours in the French press that the deal was as good as done. Beckham finally opted to stay in LA where his boys are settled at school. Beckham also believed that football in America was improving all the time. Becks said, "My boys are playing basketball and ice hockey. I am becoming a big fan of basketball and the LA Lakers. The fans have been amazing, very positive to me and my family. That's why I wanted to be a part of this. It's my passion to help grow the sport here and encourage kids to play the game."

Beckham's focus turned to securing a spot in Britain's team at the London Olympics. He was included in coach Stuart Pearce's shortlist to form Britain's first Olympic squad since 1960, and was eagerly expected to be one of the three players over age 23 allowed on each roster. His dream was to play in an Olympics staged in his old neighbourhood of East London, as he commented shortly before the final selection, "It's been an honour to be part of the process that brought the Olympics not just to England but to the part of London where I grew up. Everyone knows I would love to be part of the GB team. I need to keep myself fit and healthy, be in form, and then hope to get selected. I'd love to perform there."

However it wasn't to be as Pearce left him out and despite being credited with winning the Olympics for London, Beckham was denied his dream of representing Team GB and was 'very disappointed' by the shock snub by manager Stuart Pearce. It was a blow for the 37-year-old, who for so long has been the face of the London Games, which will take place just a short distance from where he grew up in east London. The previous month he flew in from Los Angeles to light the Olympic torch when it landed in Cornwall from Greece, marking the flame's arrival on UK soil.

Beckham was also a key part of the delegation that travelled to Singapore in 2005 and won the Games. The Paris bid had been expected to win but in an amazing turnaround London beat them. He represented Britain at the closing ceremony of the 2008 Beijing Olympics by kicking a golden football.

Micah Richards, Craig Bellamy and Ryan Giggs were picked as the over-23 players. Beckham said: 'Everyone knows how much playing for my country has always meant to me. So I would have been honoured to have been part of this unique Team GB squad. Naturally I am very disappointed, but there will be no bigger supporter of the team than me. And like everyone, I will be hoping they can win the gold. As a Londoner, I will have been really proud to have played a small part in bringing the Olympics to my home town as part of Seb's team, and I can't wait for the games to begin and enjoy every moment along with the rest of Great Britain.'

Pearce called Beckham to inform him of the decision, explaining that he had enough midfield players and he wanted to add experience to his defence. As one of football's biggest stars, Beckham would have been a big pull for fans to come and watch Team GB at the games and get excited about the Olympic football – which is not normally a major draw for spectators. Nevertheless, Beckham still played a role at the opening ceremony.

GB captain Ryan Giggs felt sad that his friend was not one of those selected. "Obviously as a former team-mate and a friend of David I am disappointed for him, but he will take it on the chin and carry on his career. It's one of those things, it was not meant to be. That's Stuart Pearce's job to pick a team that he thinks will win and that's what he's done.

Unfortunately David is not in that 18. I would like to say as a friend I wish he was. But I am sure the lads who are picked will go out and do the best they can."

Harry Redknapp commented, "There is no doubt Stuart will have upset a few in high places. They would have loved to see Beckham in there. I am surprised and sad that he isn't. Stuart can kiss goodbye to a knighthood but credit for being brave. He is the manager and should be allowed to pick who he wants. David is a great credit to the country. You could not wish for a greater role model. There are lots of great over-age players: Rio Ferdinand, Frank Lampard for starters. In the end he's gone for Richards, who couldn't get in the England squad. I'm surprised there isn't a player from each home nation. His biggest problem is sudden 'injuries' – I wouldn't be surprised if clubs get to their players and they develop strange knocks that stop them competing."

Alan Shearer said he was "amazed as I thought he was going to be part of it after all he's done getting the Olympics to London." While former team-mate Paul Scholes added, "It's a shame about Becks. It's surprising as well, after everything David did to help London get the Olympics. That's Stuart Pearce's decision, but I feel sorry for David as I'm sure he'd have loved to have played in it."

Pearce stressed his decision was based purely on football reasoning and that he would not pick any player out of sentiment. "Form plays a big part and I don't think there is a manager around who picks on sentiment. I have to be comfortable when I have made decisions based solely on football grounds alone, nothing else." Pearce also ruled out any possibility of using Beckham in a coaching capacity, "we only have seven passes [for backroom staff]. We have no passes for that," added Pearce. "The players have to be prepared to come through the door on form alone and that happens to be the case with staffing too. They have their role to play."

BOA chef de mission Andy Hunt said it would be "fantastic" to have Beckham involved in some capacity. "We'd be delighted and honoured to have David Beckham related to Team GB more broadly. That would be fantastic."

Pearce said he made it clear when he was appointed that he would only pick players based on merit, and would not have taken the job if he was not in full control over squad selection. "From the outset, when I sat down with the [Football Association] chairman David Bernstein, some time before Christmas, he offered me the opportunity to pick the squad. If at that stage he had said to me that certain individuals would have to be included I certainly wouldn't do that job. I don't know any manager worth their salt who would have. Right through this process I have had carte blanche to pick whatever players I regard as best. I do enough hours watching matches and I think I've done due diligence on all the players here." The Team GB squad was made up of 13 Englishmen and five Welsh players, with no representatives from either Scotland or Northern Ireland. "I've got a list of names written down now, who I think ability-wise are good enough to do a job," said Pearce. "I didn't pick on personality, I didn't pick on ticket sales and I certainly wasn't picking on nationality."

The London 2012 chairman, Lord Coe was disappointed, although he respected the coach's right to make decisions without outside interference, "Personally I would have loved to have seen him in the football team, but I'm not the coach and you always have to accept the decision that coaches and selectors make. They're horrible decisions to have to make. Of course I'd loved to have seen him there."

Coe found Beckham a role at the Games, as he deserved recognition for helping to bring the Olympics to London. Coe gave another indication that the 37-year-old's omission from the football squad had taken him and the British Olympic Association by surprise, "He's always been a part of our team and he was with us when we poked our heads above the parapet and said this was a good idea, he was there when we handed the documentation over. He was there with us in Singapore and he's devoted a lot of time to helping us, so he'll always be a part of the team. We're still looking at what he might be involved with and clearly a lot of David's plans changed anyway once he heard he wasn't in the final squad, so he will be with us at the Games and we're still working through that. He's a part of our team."

Beckham has huge regrets about not playing in the Olympics and wanted to play with his old United mate Giggs, "Ryan obviously has had such an amazing career with Manchester United and also with the Welsh team and he deserves to be there. He deserves to play in a big competition like this. It would have been great to have been there with him because we have a lot of great memories from playing for Manchester United." David was determined to enjoy the occasion as a supporter of the games if not a participant, "I am going to be just proud just to be there as a fan more than anything. In a part of London where I grew up playing soccer over the fields that have been changed now. As a fan and an Englishman I am going to be very proud."

Asked what kind of person he wants to be remembered as, Becks responded, "I've always wanted to be known as a hard worker on the field and successful. I believe I've always worked hard in every game and every training session that I take part in."

THE NEXT GENERATION

ASHLEY COLE

STEVEN GERRARD

FRANK LAMPARD

WAYNE ROONEY

DAVID BECKHAM REMARKED THAT he would be "ecstatic" on the eve of breaking Bobby Moore's record, but he expected some of his contemporaries to break his record. "It is special," said Beckham of his illustrious career. "It's great to be up there with the best and biggest icons. But I hope the player that breaks it is one of these players from within this squad."

Rio Ferdinand, Gary Neville, Steven Gerrard, Frank Lampard, Ashley Cole and Wayne Rooney were the most likely candidates. Which goes to illustrate how tough it is to break into that exclusive 100 Club, despite Becks optimism that his own records would be smashed.

Rio suffered a couple of seasons of injury problems and failed to make the squad for European Championships in Ukraine and Poland under new manager Roy Hodgson in the most controversial of circumstances. Lampard cruelly missed out through injury. Neville retired and moved smoothly into the Sky studios, and then back as Hodgson's right hand man at the Euros.

The man recognised as the best left back in the world made steady but sure progress toward becoming No. 6 in English football history to make it to the ton, Ashley Cole. Cole, though, was more in the headlines for his off the field activities, marriage then divorce from Cheryl, to accidentally shooting a Chelsea work experience student with an air rifle. He was even been booed by England fans, but has also won back his popularity, despite being nicknamed 'Cashley' when talks over a new £55,000-a-week contract broke down at Arsenal because he thought he had been promised another £5k a week. He was later caught red handed talking to Jose

Mourinho and all and sundry were fined.

Yet, such is his on field record that he can justifiably be recognised as one of the games all time greats. He set an all-time individual record of seven FA Cup wins and then completed a clean sweep of major club honours by helping Chelsea to win the Champions League. He became the most capped England international at a major international tournament, surpassing the record that was jointly held by Peter Shilton and David Beckham when he turned out for his 97th cap against co-hosts Ukraine in the Euros, in a match that saw England top the group with a 1-0 win and Cole's consistency during his long England career is extraordinary as he has only appeared on the losing team 13 times in those 97 internationals, spanning 11 years. Cole has played in all but 16 minutes of every international tournament match for England since his debut in 2001.

The 31-year-old made his international debut in a World Cup qualifier against Albania back in 2001. Current manager Roy Hodgson paid tribute to his qualities. "He misses very few games, either for his national team or his club team, and he always plays to a very high level. It's great to hear that he's got this record to beat when he plays against Ukraine. I'm delighted for him. I think it would be wrong to take him for granted and I don't think any of us do. We are very much aware of his qualities and very much aware how much we need him down that left side.'

Chris Powell, Phil Neville, Wayne Bridge, Paul Konchesky, Nicky Shorey, Stephen Warnock, Leighton Baines and Kieran Gibbs have all tried and failed to dislodge Cole. At only 31, still clearly at his peak, it is far from inconceivable that will go on to overhaul Shilton's all-time England appearance record of 125.

Danny Mills, Radio 5 analyst, remarked, "Cole very rarely has a bad game for England, and he has worked hard at his game down the years. On the pitch, he rarely does anything wrong. He also turns up for his country in every match, he never pulls out of squads. It would be fitting if he won his 100th cap in the final of Euro 2012."

At the age of 31 he had played in every major tournament for England over the last decade, but never progressed beyond the quarter-finals. As he prepared for the Euro quarter final with Italy, he commented, "There is unfinished business, I have been lucky enough to play 97 times for England and hopefully I will get 100 in the final. I have never had the joy of winning for my country and I am not getting too far ahead of myself or the team but so far it is going well. This is my fourth quarter-final now and I have bad memories of the others, so I want to look back at those and think about what I did and what could help me for this one. It is a different game against a great team but the spirits are high and the lads are buzzing for the game, I am confident. We know it will be a tough game on Sunday but they say dreams come true and hopefully this can be one of my dreams."

Cole and his team-mates were determined to give their all when on the pitch. "We are like 11 bulldogs who never give up and basically will die on the pitch for each other. So far it seems to be working." That bulldog spirit was epitomised in his team-mate John Terry. "He has been a great servant for Chelsea and whatever has gone on in his life he has always put that to the back of his mind and done his job in a very professional way. When it comes down to it he would put his body on the line for any team and any players who he plays with and he is a joy to play with."

But the penalty shoot out hoodoo struck again. With England holding a 2-1 penalty shoot-out lead over Italy, Ashley Young smashed his effort against the crossbar before Ashley Cole had his low but none too convincing effort smothered by goalkeeper Gianluigi Buffon. "The two Ashleys are strong enough lads to come back from this and the lads will be with them," said Theo Walcott. "They are two of the most experienced players in that dressing room and they will bounce back from this even better players. I do not worry about that at all. From the next tournament we will be better, they will be stronger. It's a very cruel way to go out in any competition. Luck did not go our way tonight. I don't know how to answer why we cannot win penalties shoot-outs. It can go either way. Anyone can win. I think penalties is always down to luck. It is a lottery. It is just the way it goes in football. You can practice and practice as much as you want but when it comes to the occasion, the big stage, it is always difficult. I hate watching it. I feel for every single player. It is not one of those scenarios you want to be involved in when you are on a losing side. It is a sad way for the players, the supporters, friends and family."

Whilst Cole was assured on reaching his England ton, Gerrard was retained as captain so he too could become No. 7 on the list, and the debate raged on as usual whether

Lampard and Gerrard gel in midfield together with the Liverpool man outstanding in the tournament in Lampard's absence. However, Lampard would be retained by Hodgson with every chance of clawing his way to the 100 caps.

Prior to being relieved of his role as Liverpool manager, and before Gerrard starred in the Euros, Kenny Dalglish held out the prospect of Gerrard winning 100 caps. Despite Steven's struggles with injury which had restricted his appearances in the previous 18 months, Kenny believed he would make the century mark. "He obviously must enjoy representing his country if he's done it 90 times," Dalglish said. "I was a bit older than Steven when I retired from international duty and we never played as many matches. Mind you, we did qualify for four straight World Cups. I only went to three. But to get 100 caps for your country is a proud achievement. To represent the football club you have supported all your life is an equally proud achievement as well. If he's got a decision to make he's got a decision to make but I couldn't say one way or the other. It's up to the individual. They've also got the European Championships coming up this summer and that is an attraction as well."

Wayne Rooney failed again in a major tournament but John Terry has long held the belief that Rooney will beat Shilton's record. Terry was still England captain and Rooney was still only 23 when he scored twice in the 4-0 win against Slovakia, and was set for his 50th cap against Ukraine. Terry also reached that landmark himself while Beckham became England's most capped outfield player with his 109th appearance. Terry commented back then, "Wayne's potential is frightening. I was saying to him he could possibly get to 150 caps. It is a reachable target – and certainly 100. Wayne has probably missed 20 games through injuries and suspensions, but he is very young, very talented and one of the best in the world that is for sure."

On his own achievements in reaching 50 caps, Terry, then 28, reflected: "When you first come in the squad you aim to get to 50, and now I am there I can hopefully kick on and get many more. Now I really want to push on for 100 and that means staying fit for Chelsea and playing as many games as possible for my country." Rooney took his tally to seven goals in his previous four appearances for England with his double against Slovakia, the first England international to do that since Gary Lineker in 1986.

It's clear that with these four players on the verge of breaking the 100 barrier for their country in the next few years, the exclusive centurion club is set for rapid expansion.

BRITISH AND IRISH CENTURIONS

PAT JENNINGS APPEARED in six World Cup qualifying tournaments, ended his playing days at the 1986 finals in Mexico, winning his last cap on his 41st birthday in a 3-0 loss to Brazil. Jennings became the first living player to receive a commemorative cap and medal from UEFA to mark his century of international appearances

Kenny Dalglish was the first to win 100 caps for Scotland and played in three World Cups – West Germany '74, Argentina '78 and Spain '82. On 26th March 1986 Dalglish became the first Scot to make 100 international appearances, as he captained the national side to a 3-0 win over Romania at Hampden. Kenny was presented with a special trophy by German legend Franz Beckenbauer to mark the occasion. Against Romania, manager Alex Ferguson gave the armband to Dalglish, his seventh and last time captaining the national team. Scotland's starting XI included nine future managers, including two - Dalglish and midfielder Graeme Souness - who would manage Liverpool. Dalglish also managed Celtic during his career, as did another team–mate of his that day, midfielder Gordon Strachan. Strachan opened the day's scoring in the 18th minute and was followed shortly by defender Richard Gough (27'). Gough's partner in defence, Roy Aitken, added the third in the 81st minute, his only goal in 57 appearances for Scotland.

The Celtic and Liverpool star made his international debut in 1971, coming on as a substitute in Scotland's Euro '72 qualifier against Belgium. A year later he scored his first goal as Scotland defeated Denmark 2-0 in a World Cup qualifier at Hampden Park. Kenny made the squad for the 1974 World Cup in West Germany but, although Scotland remained undefeated, they were still eliminated at the end of the group stages on goal difference. Kenny also played in the ill-fated 1978 campaign that ended despite a 3-2 defeat to eventual finalists Holland. In Spain in 1982 Scotland exited at the first stage yet again. It was to be Dalglish's last appearance in the World Cup Finals.

With 30 goals, Dalglish holds the scoring record for his country jointly with Denis Law who won just 55 caps. Dalglish earned a record 102 international caps for Scotland. His last goal came against Spain in 1984 and he finished playing for Scotland two years later.

Pat Jennings, the former Northern Ireland goalkeeper, having appeared in six World Cup qualifying tournaments, ended his playing days at the 1986 finals in Mexico, winning the last of his 119 caps on his 41st birthday in a 3-0 loss to Brazil. Jennings became the first living player to receive a commemorative cap and medal from UEFA to mark his century of international appearances on Friday 2nd September, before Northern Ireland's Euro 2012 qualifier against Serbia. "It was always an honour to play for Northern Ireland and the reception I received was very special," said Jennings. "When I was a player I always looked forward to getting selected for the international team. Playing for Northern Ireland for over 22 years provided me with memories I will never forget." Irish Football Association president Jim Shaw, who presented Jennings with his honour, added: "Pat is not only a Northern Ireland legend, he is also one of football's greats. The Irish FA congratulates him on this very special occasion."

After concentrating on Gaelic football in his early teens, Jennings joined home-town club Newry Town as a 16-year-old and was snapped up by Third Division English side Watford in May 1963. He enjoyed a successful maiden season with Watford, making his Northern Ireland debut alongside fellow newcomer George Best against Wales in April 1964 – the first of a national record 119 appearances for his country. He signed for Tottenham that summer and went on to make 472 league appearances for the club, celebrating domestic cup success by lifting the FA Cup in 1967 and the League Cup in 1971 and 1973; Pat also scored from inside his own area past Manchester United's Alex Stepney in the 1967 FA Charity Shield. He helped Spurs win the inaugural edition of the UEFA Cup in 1971/72, the north London outfit advancing unbeaten through the competition before dispatching Wolves 3-2 on aggregate in the final.

Famed for his one-handed catches, positional sense and one-on-one prowess, Jennings was named the Football Writers' Association Footballer of the Year in 1973 and PFA Player of the Year in 1976. Yet he was sold to fierce rivals Arsenal in 1977 as Spurs manager Keith Burkinshaw suspected his best days were behind him, but Pat proved his enduring quality by making nearly 400 appearances for the Gunners before ending his club career with a brief second spell at White Hart Lane. He featured in three successive FA Cup finals for Arsenal from 1978 to 1980, beating Manchester United in the 1979 showpiece; he also finished runner-up in the 1979/80 Cup Winners' Cup after losing to Valencia on penalties following a goalless draw.

Damien Duff led the Republic of Ireland in their final Euro 2012 fixture against Italy to mark his 100th cáp. The 33-year-old was handed the armband by usual skipper Robbie Keane in recognition of the achievement of becoming just the fifth man to complete a century for the country. With Ireland losing both of their opening games to Croatia and Spain, he spent his big night attempting to secure a first point of the tournament. Duff said: "It's obviously an awfully proud moment, but I would take three points ahead of 100 caps at the minute. I know how much it means to myself and my family and what have you, but I am not trying to make a big deal out of it. I just want to get on with the game and hopefully do the business."

Duff has never been one of the more talkative members of the squad and his appearance on the stage alongside Keane and manager Giovanni Trapattoni at the pre-match press conference in Poznan was something of a rarity. He joked: "I was dragged here kicking and screaming, to be fair. I'm never one to make big a thing out of anything in life. It's something that I will probably look back on maybe next week, maybe next year. It's a feat, but at the minute, I just want to get a good performance and a good result."

Keane had no qualms over passing on his duties for the night to a man he holds in the highest esteem both on and off the pitch. The striker said: "He's been obviously a massive, massive player since he made his debut. We made ours together and we have been through a hell of a lot together. As we all know, he's a top-class player and the respect that he has around the dressing room from every player and how people speak so highly of him. When you are around him, he is great company. We have been very good friends since we made our debuts and it was only right for me to make this gesture because he has been an absolute credit to his country and will go down as probably one of the best players that we have ever produced."

Duff is one of a series of thirty-somethings in Trapattoni's squad who called it a day after the finals. The Fulham midfielder admitted he had made his decision in his own mind, but was not about to go public as he contemplated playing on into his mid-30s. Duff said: "I think I have made my mind up what I'm going to do, but it's probably not the right time to be letting anyone know. I am sure the rest of the lads know what they are going to do as well. With regards to playing on well into my 30s, I don't think it should be a problem. I look after myself and feel as good as ever at the minute, so I don't see why not."

Shay Given made his debut in Mick McCarthy's first game in charge, a 4–2 pasting against Russia at Lansdowne Road. The Lifford-born stopper, then a raw recruit at Blackburn following an impressive loan spell at Sunderland, took to the international stage immediately in his quest to follow in the gloves of his boyhood hero Packie Bonner. But he could never have envisaged he would take the great man's appearance record and truly establish himself as Ireland's No 1.

As he reached his 100th cap, Given said: "Growing up in Ireland and supporting the Irish team as a kid with my dad we used to go to the hotel and get autographs off the team, that was special enough for me. If someone had said you'll play for your country one day, I'd think 'no chance, I'm from Lifford, Donegal, it won't happen'. To make 100 caps, I'd never have imagined it. It will be a special occasion for me and my family. I'm looking forward to it but, all that aside, there's massive points at stake and it's not just a friendly when you can relax and take in the occasion. I'll try to do that a bit but it's a massive game for qualification." Given and close friend Kevin Kilbane, were on the point of reaching the century of caps together.

No Welshman has ever reached 100 caps for his country. The current leader is Neville Southall (92), while the active player with the highest number of caps is Craig Bellamy on 70. Ryan Giggs has a mere 64.

EUROPEAN CENTURIONS

GERMANY'S LUKAS PODOLSKI, not long after celebrating his 27th birthday and signing for Arsenal, became the youngest European to win his 100th cap when he played and scored against Denmark as his country qualified for the knock out stages of the European Championships. He is the seventh youngest player in history to achieve the milestone.

With 108 caps and nearly 50 goals, Jurgen Klinsmann is one of the legends in German football. Born on July 30th 1964 in Göppingen, he started his career in the second division club Stuttgart Kickers in 1982. When he became top scorer in the division two years later, the big club in the city, Vfb Stuttgart signed him. He would spend his next five seasons there and achieved much success, both personally and with the team. 1988 was his first big year. He was top scorer in the Bundesliga and was voted "German Player of the Year". The only set-back was the defeat to Holland on his home ground in the European Championship. In the summer of 1989 Klinsmann signed for Inter Milan joining fellow countrymen Lothar Matthäus and Andreas Brehme in a great team that mopped up the Seric A title in their first season. Klinsmann easily adapted to new cultures, playing top level football in England, Italy, Germany and France. In 1990 he, along Brehme and Matthaus, won the World Cup playing five of the games on his home ground in Milan which made the triumph even more special.

France was Jurgen's next destination when he signed for Monaco in 1992. Klinsmann was now established as one of the greatest strikers in world football and after two seasons in France without winning any major trophies, it was time to defend Germany's title in the World Cup in America. "Klinsi" was now 30 years old and at the peak of his career. He scored five goals and had a great tournament personally even if the rest of the German heroes from 1990 had become too old and failed to reach the standards required of winning a World Cup losing 2-1 to Bulgaria in the quarterfinals. Klinsmann's tears after the game summed up his frustration. His journey through Europe continued and Tottenham Hotspur was next stop. He became an instant hit at White Hart Lane, and was voted Football Writers' Player of the Year in 1995. A year later he won the European Championship with Germany at Wembley. He captained the winning side, despite being injured and missing some games. After only one season at Tottenham he joined Bayern Munich, and later Sampdoria, before returning to Spurs to help save them from relegation in 1998. Klinsmann announced he would retire after the World Cup in France 1998. He had been criticised in the German press for being "over the hill" but in the World Cup he scored three goals as Germany once again bowed out in the quarter finals, this time to Croatia.

Miroslav Klose won his 100th Germany cap against Argentina in the 2010 World Cup quarter-finals, having scored his 50th goal for Germany in the 4-1 rout of England in the Round of 16, putting him third in the list of Germany's all-time goal-scorers. The then 32-year-old, who scored five at each of the previous two finals, had already scored 12 in three World Cup Finals, the same as Brazilian legend Pele, and was eager to break Ronaldo's record of 15 at all finals. His century of appearances made him the joint-seventh most capped player to appear for Germany, although he still has a long way to go to beat Lothar Matthaus' record of 150 caps. "If someone has 100 caps, that is self-explanatory," said coach Joachim Low. "We can't praise him enough as he has scored 50 goals in the process, so he scores in every second game. Miroslav has recovered well in the last few years even, after he has had a bad patch for his club. You may sometimes think he is dithering and being self-critical, but he knows himself very well, he knows precisely what his level of fitness is and he is very modest, which I really appreciate about him. No matter what the victory is, he remains down to earth and handles things in a modest way. Even after 100 caps he is still very hungry and ambitious for more success."

Polish-born Klose arrived at the World Cup on the back of a season spent warming the bench at Bayern Munich where he scored just three Bundesliga goals, but, having scored against England and Australia, he wanted to play on and help his country at the Euro 2012 tournament in Poland and the Ukraine. "My main goal is to play at Euro 2012," said Klose. "I was born in Poland, have relatives there and love the country and the people. It would be nice to play a big tournament there once again." Of course, he reached his goal, and scored yet again.

Franz Beckenbauer is without doubt one of the greatest players and coaches of all time. He redefined the role of libero, lifted the World Cup as captain in 1974, before repeating the feat as a manager in 1990. In total, he made 103 appearances for his country, becoming the first ever German player to break through the 100-cap barrier. The son of a general manager of a postal depot, he began his career at the age of nine in the youth team of SC Munchen 06, before joining Bayern in 1958. He made his debut for Bayern on the left wing, against FC St. Pauli on 6 June 1964. In only his first season in the regional league, he helped the club achieve promotion to the Bundesliga. Franz celebrated his first international cap on 26 September 1965, aged 20, and went on to play in three World Cups. He made his first finals appearance in 1966, scoring two goals in a 5-0 victory over Switzerland in his first game. Although West Germany lost in that legendary Final at Wembley, more than 30 years later, Beckenbauer can reflect positively on events: "Being a runner-up in the World Cup isn't too bad for a young player". His second tournament in Mexico in 1970 was also memorable as he played in the semi-final against Italy with a dislocated shoulder, carrying his injured arm in a sling. However, his dedication went unrewarded with the Azzurri running out 4-3 winners, leaving the Germans to settle for third place.

Nevertheless, Beckenbauer still has fond memories of Mexico. "1970 was a magnificent tournament. The fans were fanatical and stadium security wasn't quite so intense in those days. You could still do pretty much what you wanted to. There was just one armed policeman who sat outside the entrance and watched the whole ground. Obviously, that would be unthinkable today. Back then, it was simply more relaxed. The games in Mexico were colourful. The country laughed and football danced."

Then in 1974 came Beckenbauer's finest hour. By now, he was playing in the position he revolutionised - as a libero behind the defence. He organised the team from the back, but also advanced when his side were on the attack. It was in his nature to go forward; he simply could not stop himself. The tournament in Germany was something extra-special for Beckenbauer and his team. From the first whistle, the home fans demanded nothing less than victory. The high expectations were something the captain was all too aware of: "When you are hosts, there is obviously twice the pressure, because everybody expects you to win". Collectively, Beckenbauer, Sepp Maier, Paul Breitner, Wolfgang Overath, Gerd Muller and the rest of the team withstood the pressure to make West Germany champions for the second time. After their 2-1 victory over the Netherlands, Beckenbauer became the first captain to lift the brand new World Cup trophy after Brazil had retained the Jules Rimet trophy in 1970.

Franz supplemented success with his nation by leading Bayern on a trophy laden run that included 4 Bundesliga titles, the Intercontinental Cup, 3 European Cups, the Cup Winners' Cup and 4 German Cup triumphs between 1967 and 1976. In 1977, Beckenbauer left Bayern to join the New York Cosmos. He hoped to find a new challenge in the USA's professional league, as well as earn a good living. From a sporting point of view, however, the switch stateside did not further his development: "Football-wise it was a non-starter," he said. The move across the Atlantic also brought an end to his international career. Since he was plying his trade abroad, he was no longer considered for selection by West Germany.

In 1982, he made his comeback in the Bundesliga at 35, playing for one season with Hamburg. He retired from playing in 1983 after another spell with the New York Cosmos. In July 1984, after the failure of Jupp Derwall at that year's European Championship, Beckenbauer was installed as West Germany's head coach. His first major success from the dugout was at Mexico 1986, where he led his team to the Final. Although Argentina won the trophy, Beckenbauer had come of age as a coach. Four years later, West Germany became undefeated world champions, and when Andreas Brehme converted the only goal from the penalty spot in the Final against Argentina, Beckenbauer secured his place in the record books as the first man to win the World Cup as captain and as coach. Winning the trophy as coach remains the pinnacle of Beckenbauer's football career: "I would say 1990 in Italy was the most important to me, it doesn't come any better than managing a side to victory." Beckenbauer was the president of Bayern until 1998, when he was made the vice-president of the German Football Association. And after helping to return the sport's showpiece event to his homeland, he successfully oversaw the 2006 FIFA World Cup as the chairman of its Organising Committee.

More than 100 European players have surpassed the 100 caps mark, and to recognise their achievements, UEFA announced plans back in August 2011 to present all European players who reached the 100-cap mark with a special award comprising a commemorative cap and medal. Michel Platini welcomed the introduction of the new award. "I think it is a fantastic idea," the UEFA President said. "Any player who has played 100 or more times for his or her country definitely deserves recognition by the football fraternity. Presenting the player with a cap and medal at forthcoming national team matches will highlight their achievement, while helping to refocus public attention on the importance of national team football."

Germany's most capped player, having made 150 international appearances is Lothar Matthäus who won the 1980 European Championship and the World Cup ten years later. Matthäus received a commemorative cap and medal from UEFA to mark his century of international appearances on 11 October 2011, before Germany's 3-1 victory against Belgium in European Championship qualifying. "It's really nice that these players, who are no longer centre stage, return as the focal point," he said.

Named the European Footballer of the Year in 1990 Matthaus became the first World Player of the Year 12 months later. He also enjoyed a glittering club career, winning seven league titles, two German Cups and the 1996 UEFA Cup during two spells at Bayern. During five seasons with Inter, he won a Serie A title and another UEFA Cup in 1991. He narrowly failed to add the European Cup to his list of honours, as he was twice a loser in the final with Bayern, against Porto in 1987 and against Manchester United 12 years later. In both games the German side went ahead only to lose the match in the closing stages.

He took his first coaching post at Rapid Vienna in September 2001 but lasted just a season. He enjoyed more success on his appointment at Partizan Belgrade in December

2002, leading them to the league title six months later and into the Champions League group stage at the start of 2003/04.

In charge of Hungary for 2006 World Cup qualifying he had brief spells at Paranaense of Brazil, Salzburg in Austria and Maccabi Netanya of Israel. In September 2010 Matthäus signed a 12-month deal with the option of two further years with the Bulgarian national team, replacing Stanimir Stoilov following the latter's resignation. His contract was not renewed in September 2011.

Considered one of the most accomplished German central defenders of all time, Jurgen Kohler won the World Cup with West Germany in 1990 and enjoyed a sparkling club career at Bayern, Juventus and Borussia Dortmund. He won his first senior international cap in September 1986 and played all four matches for West Germany at the 1988 European Championship, where he began his long-standing personal duel with Netherlands striker Marco van Basten. He sustained a tournament–ending injury in the opening minutes of Germany's triumphant Euro '96 campaign but won his 100th cap on the eve of the 1998 World Cup, where he called time on his international career, with 105 caps, two goals and six successive major tournament appearances.

Kohler received a commemorative cap and medal from UEFA alongside Matthaus before Germany's 3-1 home win against Belgium in European Championship qualifying. "I like the idea of being part of this tribute," he said. "This is another example that UEFA, under Michel Platini, and the DFB are opening themselves up to the outside."

He started out with Waldhof Mannheim, making his

Bundesliga debut on 7 April 1984 and remaining with club until 1987, when he transferred to Köln. He joined Bayern in 1989 and won the Bundesliga in his first season, to which he added a triumphant World Cup with his country at Italia '90, starting all four knockout matches, including the final. After two seasons at Bayern, he joined the exodus of Germany's leading players to Italy, signing for Juventus, where he spent four seasons, lifting the UEFA Cup in 1993 and ending his spell in Turin by winning a Serie A and Coppa Italia double under coach Marcello Lippi. He returned to Germany and joined Dortmund, with whom he claimed the Bundesliga title in 1996 and the Champions League in 1997, overcoming Juve in the Munich final; Kohler was recognised for his efforts with the 1997 German footballer of the year award. He concluded his career in 2002 with another Bundesliga title and a red card in the UEFA Cup final defeat by Feyenoord (3-2).

When it comes to goalkeepers you can expect longevity, and Peter Schmeichel comes into that category with 121 caps. The Great Dane is Denmark's most capped player of all time. He quickly cemented his place as the nation's No.1 following his debut in 1988 and four years later was a vital part of the European Championship-winning side, where he saved a penalty from Marco van Basten in a semi final shoot-out win over the Netherlands. He represented Denmark in four European Championships and the 1998 World Cup. Schmikes was named the World Goalkeeper of the Year in 1992 and 1993. Thomas Sorensen has recently reached 100 caps for Denmark, but was ruled out of the 2012 Euros with a back-injury and was replaced by Kasper Schmeichel. Meanwhile former Charlton Athletic striker Dennis Rommedahl continues to edge towards Peter Schmeichel's Danish record of 129 caps.

Esteemed football journalist Brian Glanville summed up what we expect from our best playmakers: "an attacker of tremendous, fluent gifts but slightly suspect temperament". The player he was describing? Danish genius and La Liga legend Michael Laudrup. After a mixed period in Italy where, despite winning Serie A with Juventus in 1986 and starring in the fabulous Danish side at Mexico 86, he never showed his true potential, Laudrup's career took off following his 1989 move to Barcelona and a link up with the man who saw something of himself in the Dane, Johan Cruyff. Laudrup came to personify the character and aspiration of Barcelona's 'Dream Team'. The team won four consecutive La Liga championships from 1991 to 1994 as well as the 1991-92 European Cup, with Laudrup twice elected Spanish football's Player of the Year. The arrival of Brazilian star Romario in 1994 caused problems though, with Barca having to rotate their foreign stars. When Laudrup was left out of the humiliating 4-0 European Cup defeat to AC Milan, he moved to Real Madrid. Romario described Laudrup as 'the fifth best player in the history of the game' (behind Pelé, Maradona, himself and Zidane) as he was able to 'create and score goals almost at will'. At Real, Ivan Zamorano dubbed him "El Genio" (the genius) with Raul describing him as "the best player I've ever played with" and Figo proclaiming him "the best player I ever played against." Jose Mourinho was moved to say " He was phenomenal. He was a fantastic player whom I would love to have on my team today." Real won the 1995 La Liga title, Laudrup becoming the first player to win the Spanish league five times in a row with two different clubs and, despite only playing two seasons at the Bernabeu, Laudrup was voted the 12th best player in the club's history in a survey by Marca.

Laudrup made his international debut as an 18 year old in 1982 and four years later was a central part of one the World Cup's most memorable and eye-catching teams. Best remember for his mazy dribble and finish in the incredible 6-1 defeat of Uruguay. However by the time of Denmark's greatest success in winning the 1992 European Championship he had fallen out with coach Richard Moller Nielson and quit the national team along with his brother Brian. By the time of the 1998 World Cup in France the Laudrups were back, with Michael captaining Denmark's finest team for over a decade. In the Danes' second round game against Nigeria his skill and vision virtually destroyed the Africans single-handedly. Denmark were eventually eliminated by Brazil, in a fantastic match which ended 3-2 to the eventual finalists. It took a superb goal from Rivaldo to finally kill off Danish resistance. That was to be Michael's last game in action for Denmark in a career which saw him score 37 goals in a total of 104 games for his country, a figure which, as Michel Platini pointed out, could have been much higher, "Michael had everything except one thing: he wasn't selfish enough". In an emotional farewell, little brother Brian also announced he would retire from international football and eventually retire from football all together due to persistent injuries.

The playmaker king of the Nineties later became manager of Swansea when Michael Laudrup was unveiled as Brendan

Rodgers' replacement at Swansea City. The south Wales side had been a revelation under Rodgers in their debut season in the Premier League, inflicting shock defeats on Manchester City, Arsenal and Liverpool with a game based on possession and intense pressing. But their somewhat measly tally of 44 goals was the sixth lowest in the top flight. "I like possession," Laudrup said, "I admit I am a big fan of Spain, of Barcelona. But it is not possession for possession's sake. You can always improve. I am used to playing like that, trying to keep possession, having people who are not afraid to have the ball, even against the bigger sides. But at the end of the day you have to score goals, you have to win games. Even if you have the ball 65 per cent of the time but lose 2-0, it is not any good. It is a style I like, the way they have done it. If it had been more kick and rush it probably wouldn't be me sitting here right now."

Brian Laudrup won the Danish Footballer of the Year award a record four times. Pele rated him one of the top 125 greatest living footballers at the FIFA 100 ceremony in March 2004, alongside his older brother Michael.

Gheorghe Hagi managed 125 Rumanian caps as one of the world's most exciting players in the 1990s. Known as 'The Maradona of the Carpathians' Hagi is best remembered for performances at the 1994 World Cup. He captained the side to the quarter-finals, beating Argentina en route - Hagi's sublime skill earned him a move to Barcelona that summer. Born in Sacele, his outstanding talent was discovered quickly and after playing for Farul Constanza and Sportul Bucharest and he was soon snapped up by Steaua Bucharest in 1987. With Romania's premier club he won the league and cup double three years in a row.

Hagi was a very skilful and creative player yet often unpredictable. He played in his first World Cup in Italy in 1990, displaying flashes of brilliance in some games, but Romania bowed out in the second round after losing to Ireland on penalties. Hagi was at his peak four years later in America and was regarded as one of players of the tournament alongside Romario, Hristo Stoichkov and Roberto Baggio. He scored three times in that World Cup with one of them being a wonderful 40 yard lob against Colombia. However, once again penalties stood between Romania and further glory as Sweden won the quarter-final shoot-out.

Hagi played for Real Madrid, Barcelona and Brescia with variable success and never quite unleashed his true potential at club level abroad. He struggled with disciplinary problems on the field and was suspended several times. When Romania qualified for the World Cup in 1998, he said it would be his last tournament. Romania reached the second round and lost 1-0 to Croatia. Hagi made another come-back prior to Euro 2000 and got sent off in his 125th and last match for Romania in the quarter-final against Italy. He spent the final stages of his career in the Turkish league at Galatasaray where he won the UEFA Cup and played some of his best soccer at club level.

In Austria, Andreas Herzog, celebrated his century of caps in November 2002 but Norway gatecrashed the fiesta winning 0–1 thanks to a Pa-Modou Kah goal.

Ole Thorbjørn Svenssen holds the Norwegian record, having been capped 104 times, 93 as captain. Svenssen won his 100th cap against Denmark on 17 September 1961. At the time, he was only the second player in history to reach the milestone, after England's Billy Wright. Svenssen's 104th and final outing came in a 2–1 win against the Netherlands on 16 May 1962. He never scored for Norway. The former centre-half died in 2011 so his cap and medal was accepted by his family. "He was one of the best players in our history. In the 1950s he was seen as one of Europe's best centre-halves," said Per Ravn Omdal, former Football Association of Norway (NFF) president and a member of the UEFA Executive Committee.

Born in 1924, Svenssen played youth football for Hegna before signing for Sandefjord, his home-town club in 1945. As a youngster, Svenssen excelled at ski jumping, speed skating and bandy, but football was always his priority. He soon made his name as a solid and dependable centre-back who was almost unbeatable in the air and hard but fair in the tackle. Over time he became known as Klippen (the Rock). Svenssen made his international debut in a 3–1 win against Poland in 1947 and was named as captain for the first time on his 12th international outing, against Egypt on Christmas Eve 1948. In total, he skippered his country on 93 occasions.

At club level, Svenssen played 237 league games over 22 seasons for Sandefjord but never won any major trophies. He came closest when Sandefjord finished league runners-up in

1955/56, and when they lost the Norwegian Cup final in 1957 and 1959. His son, Torgny Svenssen, won the league with IK Start in 1978. Svenssen retired from football in 1965 due to injury, at the age of 41. He took on coaching duties at Sandefjord, and later with Norway's Under-21 and junior teams. He died of a stroke in January 2011, aged 86.

Former Manchester United and Blackburn defender Henning Berg's international career for Norway spanned 12 years and brought him exactly 100 caps. The versatile defender's main claim to fame at club level was as the first player to win the Premier League with two different clubs. Born in Eidsvoll, he started out with Oslo club Vålerenga before moving on to Lillestrøm in 1992, the same year in which he made his international debut on 13 May in a home friendly against the Faroe Islands. Berg left Lillestrøm after one season to join Blackburn midway through the inaugural Premier League campaign, becoming a pivotal member of the expensively-assembled Rovers side that won the title in 1994/95, starting 40 of the club's 42 matches. Berg departed for United in 1997 and helped the club win the treble of Premier League, FA Cup and Champions League in 1998/99 but missed the finals of both knockout competitions through injury. A fixture in Egil Olsen's Norway team during the 1990s, he represented his country at the FIFA World Cups of 1994 and 1998, starting every game in both tournaments; also played under Nils Johan Semb at Euro 2000 but his participation was ended by an injury sustained in the opening game against Spain.

Berg rejoined Blackburn from United in September 2000, initially on loan, and helped the club to victory in the

2002 League Cup, lifting the trophy as captain. He finished his career in Scotland with Rangers, retiring at the end of the 2003/04 season, when he also made his 100th and last appearance for Norway – in an Oslo friendly against Wales. He went straight into coaching and led Lyn for three and a half years before returning to Lillestrøm for the start of the 2009 season.

John Arne Riise earned his 100th cap for Norway on 12 November 2011 in a 4-1 defeat by Wales in a Cardiff friendly. "I'm really honoured to receive such an award," said the left-back. "I hope to keep playing until Euro 2016 and my total may be hard to beat for any Norwegian by then!"

Aged 17, Riise left local club Aalesund after just one season to launch his career abroad at Monaco, winning the 1999/00 French title before moving to Liverpool in 2001. He made a favourable early impression, winning the FA Community Shield against Manchester United on his debut and scored in the 3-2 Super Cup victory against Bayern. Riise won his first senior cap for Norway in January 2000 and scored his first international goal the following month and was selected for the Euro 2000 squad, aged 19, though he did not play; Riise spent the subsequent decade as his country's regular left-back. Seven seasons at Anfield peaked with a Champions League triumph in 2005, to which he was a major contributor (though he missed his penalty in the final shoot-out against AC Milan); he also won two domestic cups, scoring the decisive spot kick in the 2006 FA Cup final shoot-out against West Ham United FC, and accumulated 234 Premier League appearances for the club, scoring 21 goals. John left Liverpool for Roma in 2008 and played a prominent part in helping the

Giallorossi to second place in both Serie A and the Coppa Italia in 2009/10. Later he also linked up with his brother, Bjørn Helge, for the first time at club level when he signed a three-year deal with Fulham in July 2011.

Patrick Vieira spoke of his pride at becoming only the fifth player to reach 100 caps for France after helping Les Bleus to a 1-0 victory against Greece in November 2006. The then France captain Patrick Vieira had two reasons to celebrate at the Stade de France as Les Bleus beat Greece 1-0 and the friendly marked the 30-year-old's 100th cap. Vieira was only the fifth Frenchman to reach that mark, following exalted quartet Lilian Thuram, (125), Marcel Desailly (116), Zinédine Zidane (108) and Didier Deschamps (103). Appropriately, the game was preceded by a ceremony paying tribute to the 1998 World Cup and Euro 2000 winners. Vieira, a member of both squads, did not produce his most spectacular performance, yet still came close to scoring his seventh international goal, first with a header from a Willy Sangol free-kick, then a strike that hit the side-netting. How did Vieira handle his emotions as he stood for the Marseillaise for the 100th time, since first taking the field for France in a 2-1 victory against the Netherlands on 26 February 1997. "I tried to forget about my century when the game started but it was not easy as there was a festive atmosphere caused by the pre-match ceremony," the then Inter midfielder said. "But it's true, I'm proud of this number, not many of us have achieved it. It's extraordinary."

Only Vieira and Thuram remained of the 1998 World

Cup final side, but it was the European success two years later that the former Arsenal skipper cherishes most. "What will leave the deepest mark is probably when we sat with the trophy on the Rotterdam pitch after the Euro 2000 final win. There was 'Liza' [Bixente Lizarazu], Lilian, 'Titi' [Thierry Henry] and a few others. We were talking calmly and thinking, 'Wow, after 1998 now this!'."

Raymond Domenech made Vieira his captain on his appointment in July 2004, and though the armband was selflessly passed to Zidane a year later, the France coach never made any secret of his respect for the Senegal-born player. "One hundred caps, it means ten years at the highest level which deserves great respect," Domenech said. "He will beat all longevity records," Deschamps predicted in 1998. But Vieira promised, "I'll stop at just the right time"

Few players can boast an international career as glorious and dramatic as Zidane's, including incredible highs and desperate lows. The crowning glory in the gifted playmaker's 108 matches was the 1998 World Cup final win, where he scored twice as France beat reigning champions Brazil. The worst moment also came in a World Cup final in which he scored, this time the 2006 showpiece event. Against Italy in Berlin's Olympiastadion stadium, Les Bleus lost a penalty shoot-out to Italy after Zizou was sent off for head butting Marco Materazzi.

After announcing himself on the international stage with two well taken goals against the Czech Republic in 1994, Zidane also won the European Championship in 2000 and retired from the national team after they exited Euro 2004, only to come back for that incredible 2006 World Cup finale.

He finished his international career with an impressive 31 goals, including five in 12 World Cup games.

In November 2011, Iker Casillas broke Spain's all-time appearance record by winning his 127th cap. "Every time I join up with the national team I do so as if it were my last," said Casillas at that time. Spain's captain made history during his side's 2-2 friendly draw against Costa Rica, his 127th cap eclipsing iconic goalkeeper Andoni Zubizarreta's mark as his country's all-time leading appearance holder. Both men – along with Xavi Hernández – were present at a special awards ceremony in which they collected commemorative caps and medals from UEFA for having reached 100 caps for Spain. It was at that event in Madrid where Zubizarreta paid tribute to the new record holder. "I see it as absolutely normal that Casillas moves ahead of me on the all-time list," said the former Athletic Bilbao, Barcelona and Valencia goalkeeper. "Iker is a great keeper and one who has always been ahead of his time because when he started all those years ago he did things that we saw as normal but that, in reality, were not. He's a goalkeeper who has grown, matured and has known how to live through the bad times. I think that he has a point of maturity that when he is between the posts he looks unbeatable."

Xavi, whom Zubizarreta added would "more than likely" also overtake his appearance tally, also had words of praise for his international skipper. "Casillas is a friend of mine; we have a great friendship," said the Barcelona midfielder, who has himself been capped 107 times. "He is a fantastic person among the group and a great captain. He likes to talk to all of his team-mates – be they youngsters or veterans – before making a decision. He's a guy who unites the dressing room and who is always there to help you. He is also very funny and has been so all his life; he's never changed. He's a normal, simple person as are all of the players in the national team. The good vibes he brings are contagious."

Having participated in 92 wins, 22 draws and 13 defeats for Spain, Casillas said it was hard to believe he had moved ahead of the renowned figure of Zubizarreta. "When I started out playing as a kid I never thought I would reach such figures but now that I have I'm obviously very happy," said the then 30-year-old Real Madrid captain. Casillas – whose name is forever etched into Spain's football folklore after lifting the Henri Delaunay Cup in 2008 and the World Cup two years later – made his international bow against Sweden on 3 June 2000. He featured in three World Cups, three UEFA European Championships and one FIFA Confederations Cup. "The only thing I have clear in my mind is that it has been a real pleasure to play for Spain for the past 11 years."

The first Spanish player to reach the 100 caps record was Zubizarreta, from 1985 to 1998, playing 4 World Cups and 2 Euros, while playing for Bilbao, Barcelona and Valencia. In his speech, Zubizarreta made his personal tribute on players who also deserved to reach these 100 games, but never did it, like "Iribar, Arconada, Hierro or Camacho".

The 30-year-old former Liverpool midfield ace Xabi Alonso delivered the goods on his 100th international appearance with a header and a penalty to see off France in their Euro 2012 quarter-final. "There's a lot of personal satisfaction in getting to 100 caps and of course getting on the scoresheet," said Alonso after the Spanish booked a semi-final showdown with Portugal in Donetsk where he crossed swords with Real Madrid team-mates Cristiano Ronaldo and Pepe. "We're through to the semi-finals, which was the main thing. We're pleased about that. The 100 caps is just an extra. It's in these matches that we have to show what we're about. We controlled it from start to finish. The team made things easy. I was happy about my 100th game and the goals. We know every game is difficult now but we're in the semi-finals and we're going to give it everything. We controlled the match, though we knew it wouldn't be easy against opponents that were defending deep. It became easier after the goal. It was a big quarter-final game and you have to know how to play them."

There was criticism of the Spanish after they drew to begin with in their pool opener against Italy and then just crept past Croatia while Del Bosque was happy to keep Torres in reserve when it suits the former's game plan. But the plan worked once again with Alonso stepping into the goalscoring breach. Del Bosque himself dismissed the critics, telling journalists that "the debate is more yours than ours." Alonso dismissed the earlier brickbats, "I'm not bothered about the criticism. We have to work for it as today in football there's not very much between the teams. The most important step is the next one," said Alonso, who went off clutching the shirt of another Real Madrid colleague Karim Benzema having became just the fifth member of the Furia Roja's ton-up club.

An integral part of Spain's domination of European and World football, Xavi Hernandez enjoyed a landmark night and a 2-1 victory in the March Euro 2012 qualifier against the Czech Republic. Given his debut ten years and four months earlier under then coach Jose Antonio Camacho, this landmark encounter was the Catalan playmaker's 100th appearance for La Selección. At that point a magnificent international career featured 76 wins, 16 draws and just eight defeats, spanning three World Cups and two Euro campaigns.

At the age of 31, he was welcomed into that select band of players to have made 100 or more appearances for Spain. So for how much longer did Xavi intend to continue gracing the international scene? "I don't know, give me 100 more games and I'll step aside, ok? Seriously though, I'll be available for as long as I'm wanted. That works for me. At the moment I'm only looking as far as the Euro but maybe I'll get to Brazil (2014) too. That wouldn't be bad would it?" added La Máquina.

In April 1999, Xavi was part of the side that won the Under-20 World Cup in Nigeria after a 4-0 final win over Japan. Scorer of two goals at that competition, a year later in the final of the Olympic Tournament in Sydney, he put Spain in front after two minutes against Cameroon, though the two sides were deadlocked at 2-2 after extra time. And although the Barça star converted his spot-kick, a faultless penalty-taking display from Cameroon and Ivan Amaya's failure to convert his kick handed victory and the gold medal to the Indomitable Lions. Spain manager Camacho gave him a chance with the senior national team in the friendly against the Netherlands in Seville in November 2000. Ten years later against the same side he tasted World Cup triumph.

After a 44-year major trophy drought, La Roja were crowned European champions at Vienna's Ernst Happel stadium after sinking Germany through Fernando Torres' solitary strike. Xavi was subsequently voted the player of the tournament. La Selección went on to lift the World Cup for the first time following victory over the Netherlands in the Final of South Africa 2010. He made 669 passes during the course of South Africa 2010, a stat which underlines his vision and metronomic ability to bring his team-mates into play. Having played more passes than any other player at the competition, he finished with an impressive 81 per cent success rate.

A double tribute awaited for Xavi Hernández, who also got the gold medal of the RFEF, alongside the already mentioned UEFA cap. Surrounded by two special coaches for him, Luis Aragonés and Vicente Del Bosque, Xavi said that he felt "privileged to live from football, achieving so many things of a sport that I love and adore". The Catalan midfielder, who made his debut in the year 2000, made some memory and recalled that, in this team, "we lived in not so good eras, like nowadays, but with all this recognition and these victories, I am enjoying like a kid". Xavi also got a particular tribute in the words of Del Bosque and Aragonés. The current coach of the Spanish team used him as an example by stating that Xavi "represents the modern player in and out of the pitch, a singular player, gathering too much football in his boots, a very complete player". Luis Aragonés, who Xavi himself labelled as the coach who made him reach a new level, highlighted the "virtues of this player and his extraordinary quality" to raise the importance of this player in the current scheme by assuring that "the influence of the coach is not that high, the example is Xavi for his way to live and play".

In the summer of 2006, Luis Aragonés' Spanish team had failed in the World Cup played in Germany. The more experienced French team had knocked out a team that mixed veteran players Michel Salgado, David Albelda, Santi Cañizares and Raúl González with the core of young players that nowadays form the golden generation of the Spanish football. This failure had a bitter taste and there were rumours of rebellion inside the Spanish team, led by the veterans. Salgado, Albelda and Cañizares disappeared from the team for good, but Raúl was the captain. In the following match, already in the qualifiers of the Euro 2008, Spain visited Belfast to face Northern Ireland. Spain failed in a miserable 3-2 defeat. The press exploded and Aragonés was targeted. At that moment, Aragonés took a decisive decision, dropping Raúl from the national team to give a new role to the young generation led by Xavi as the reference of the new style.

This seismic decision meant Aragonés had to deal with uncomfortable questions about Raúl in every press conference. The pressure rose as Euro 2008 got closer, while Raúl's form improved. In the 2006/2007 season, Raúl scored 23 goals and, in the following season, 24 goals. In these two seasons, he also won two La Liga titles. Despite the huge pressure of a section of the press and the constant "Raúl, yes; Raúl no" debate, Aragonés backed the new system and the new generation, leaving Raúl out of Euro 2008. Raúl didn't criticise the decision in public and Aragonés didn't close the door to a possible return but admitted that "there was a point when the national team was too big for Raúl and we had to think of the team and not one player". Aragonés always defended the new model of team around the midfielders, mainly Xavi. The Catalan midfielder and Aragonés designed the team that has given Spain the highest achievements of its history and Raúl did not fit in this new concept.

Borislav Mihaylov and Grzegorz Lato received their UEFA award in September 2011. Former Bulgaria goalkeeper Mihaylov and ex-Poland striker Lato each received the award of a commemorative cap and medal from Platini during a ceremony in Limassol, Cyprus, witnessed by the presidents and general secretaries of all 53 of UEFA's member national associations. The presentations took place ahead of the UEFA Executive Committee meeting in the Cypriot city. Mihaylov appeared 102 times for Bulgaria, most notably captaining his nation to the 1994 World Cup semi-finals, their best ever performance. He is now a member of the UEFA Executive Committee, having been president of the Bulgarian Football Union since 2005. "It was 15 years of my life, to be goalkeeper of the national team and play 102 matches, and it was a great honour to receive the award from Michel Platini in front of all the presidents of the 53 associations," Mihaylov said. "It was a great emotion for me. I feel very proud to be among a group of players who have reached 100 matches – because there are not many! I remember two matches in particular, against France [a World Cup qualifier in 1993] when we won in the last minutes to go to the World Cup where we [came fourth], and the [last-16] match at that World Cup against Mexico where I saved two penalties [in a shoot-out].''

Lato was the first Poland player to be capped 100 times, his record of exactly that mark has only being surpassed by Michał Zewłakow in 2005. He scored 45 goals and finished third at the World Cups of 1974 and 1982. Since 2008 Lato has been president of the Polish Football Federation, overseeing preparations for co-hosting Euro 2012.

Defender Michał Zewłakow, who earned the last of his 102 Poland caps in March this year, said: "A big thank you to UEFA for honouring me this way. I felt again, if only for a few seconds, what it means to be part of the national team. I played 102 games, which means I did not waste my career – I achieved something. It was also moving to be handed the prize by [Polish Football Federation president] Grzegorz Lato, who has 100 caps himself and is a real legend. This way of honouring 100-cap players is a fantastic idea.'

"I will cherish it for the rest of my life," Levan Kobiashvili said of his UEFA award for becoming the first Georgian to win 100 caps – but his international career was far from over. At Tbilisi's Mikheil Meskhi stadium, the midfielder – who played more than 300 Bundesliga games for Freiburg, Schalke and current club Hertha Berlin – was 34 yet remained hungry for more despite having started 99 matches from that century of appearances. "Every game for Georgia is a special occasion and a great responsibility for me. Despite my age, I'm always ready for action and have the same will to win. It doesn't always end this way, but I feel happy just to have been part of the national team for so long. In the future I will tell my children about this period. It has had its difficulties and sad moments, but you can't avoid things like that."

Former Metalurgi Rustavi and Dinamo Tbilisi prospect Kobiashvili was a Georgian youth international in 1994, before making his senior bow two years later. He can look back on "many notable moments – my goals, the pain of defeat, the joy we gave our fans". However, it was "the victory against Croatia in the [recent Euro 2012] qualifying round that stands out," he said, citing Georgia's 1-0 win over Group F's second-placed finishers – a game settled by Kobiashvili's 90th-minute goal. "I hope there will be many more great matches. I still feel fit and well, I play in the Bundesliga, so I hope to be of use to my country for a while yet. I remember my first match, a friendly against Norway in Oslo in 1996. I didn't even expect to be in the squad, but coach Aleksandr Chivadze put me in the starting line-up. We played well only to concede from the spot and it was me who gave away the penalty. However, I got enormous support from everyone in the dressing room." A year later he helped Georgia register a goalless home draw with Italy in World Cup qualifying. "I almost lost my mind when I first faced Italy," Kobiashvili said. "Instead of warming up like usual, I just stared at our opponents, all their legendary players. But when the game started there was no mercy from me. They had to be satisfied with a point in Tbilisi. When I started playing I didn't think about personal records. I dreamt of representing my country at a major tournament, but unfortunately it wasn't to be. Recently I said that I'll have this honour as a coach, but it was a joke – coaching is extremely tough and I don't fancy becoming one. Football is my life and I'll probably stay in it, though I'm not sure in what role." Kobiashvili added: "On

Tuesday, before the Greece match, I fully understood the feelings of those players who have received or will receive this award. My family and I were really happy and it wasn't an everyday emotion. I will cherish it for the rest of my life. But it's not just my achievement – I owe this award to all the people I have worked and played with for the last 15 years. They all played their part and I want to thank them."

Georgia were not in the running to qualify for Poland and Ukraine yet there was some cause for celebration as Kobiashvili earned his 100th cap against Greece. "If UEFA think I deserve this honour for my career, then I accept it with great pleasure," said the then 34-year-old. "I'm not a player who thinks I am better than others. "There were certainly better players than me in the national team; I've been lucky to play 100 times for Georgia"."

Dino Zoff is the only Italian to have won a European Championship and a World Cup. A rock; a workaholic; a perfectionist: Zoff was one of the greatest ever goalkeepers. The son of farming stock he once said, "All that I have, I have earned through hard work." Zoff received a commemorative cap and medal from UEFA to mark his century of international appearances on 11 October 2011, before Italy's 3–0 win against Northern Ireland in European Championship qualifying. "I'm happy to be here today," he said. "This is certainly a good moment for the Italian national team. I'm sure they are among the best four teams in Europe."

One of the game's most celebrated goalkeepers, Zoff

achieved his career high at the age of 40 when he captained Italy to victory at the 1982 World Cup. He also won countless honours at club level during a glorious 11-year spell with Juventus. When he was rejected by Inter Milan and Juventus as a 14-year-old for being too small, Zoff's grandmother Adelaide fed him up on eggs. Five years on and Zoff's displays for his village team, Marianese, gave scouts at nearby Udinese food for thought. He had grown 33 centimetres to 1.82 metres. Soon Zoff was leaving his job as a motor mechanic to sign professional forms. He let in five goals on his debut at Fiorentina on 24 September 1961 in the year the club were relegated. Zoff had made just four appearances for the Friuli club when Mantova restored him to the top flight the next season. Here his career really did take off. By 1966, he was being considered for Italy's World Cup squad alongside Enrico Albertosi, Roberto Anzolin and Pierluigi Pizzaballa. In the event, Azzurri coach Edmondo Fabbri selected that trio because, as Zoff explained, "he did not want to be accused of favouritism being a Mantova man himself". In 1967 Napoli welcomed him to the south of Italy in exchange for 130 million lire and goalkeeper Bandoni. The Naples club succeeded where AC Milan, ever reluctant to meet Mantova's price, had failed. "I have great memories of my time there," Zoff said. "It is such a lively city."

At the end of his first season with Napoli, he made his debut for Italy in a 2-0 win against Bulgaria at the 1968 European Championship and helped the Azzurri win the title, earning only his fourth cap in the replayed final against Yugoslavia. A worthy start to an international career that the great Paolo Maldini would repeat three decades on. Yet not even Maldini made the front cover of Newsweek magazine. That particular honour fell to Zoff in 1982, as he bowed out of international football with a winner's medal.

Moving to Juventus he won Serie A in his debut campaign and followed it up with five further titles, two Coppa Italia triumphs and, in 1976/77, the UEFA Cup. In 11 years at Juventus he did not miss a single Serie A match, running up 330 consecutive appearances, which contributed to an all-time league record of 570 that took 22 years and was only eclipsed by AC Milan's Paolo Maldini.

Zoff was part of four World Cup squads, playing in three and emerging a champion at Spain in 1982. He also appeared in goal for the Azzurri at the 1980 European Championship and went through the entire tournament without conceding a goal – until a long-range strike from Czechoslovakia's Ladislav Jurkemík flew past him in the third-place play-off. Two years later he became the oldest World Cup winner. He carried on for another year, ending up with a then Italian record of 112 caps (with just 84 goals conceded and 61 clean sheets, including a world-record 12 in succession – 1,142 minutes to be precise – between 1972 and 1974).

He retired to become a goalkeeping coach at Juventus. But it was not enough. "As far as I was concerned it was a dead-end job," he said. He took the post of coach to Italy's Olympic team ahead of the Seoul Games - and impressed sufficiently to be offered the manager's job back at Juventus in 1988. Victories in the Italian and UEFA Cups, plus a third-place finish in the league, ensured the club would not regret their choice, although the arrangement lasted only a year. Next stop was Lazio. In Rome, Zoff had four campaigns as coach then assumed the role of president and enjoyed a brief spell as caretaker coach in 1997. His next appointment was arguably the pinnacle: replacing Cesare Maldini as Italy trainer after the poor showing of the Azzurri at France 1998. And but for David Trezeguet's golden goal in the Euro 2000 final, he might well have been the man responsible for the country's first international success since Spain 1982. Yet according to the Italian press, second place was for losers. Stung by the criticism, Zoff retired and returned to Lazio, again as coach. He took them to third position and the Champions League, yet could not satisfy fans who had feasted on a league and cup double a year earlier.

Gianluigi Buffon lined up alongside Zoff and defensive luminaries Paolo Maldini and Fabio Cannavaro as UEFA continued its series of presentations. "I feel I'm entering the football nobility today and I'm happy to celebrate this milestone while still playing," said Buffon, first-choice goalkeeper for Juventus and Italy over the past decade. Buffon equalled Zoff's record of 112 appearances in goal for the Azzurri in November 2011. The 2006 World Cup winner would have won many more caps but for injury, one of which restricted him to just 45 minutes at the 2010 World Cup in South Africa.

Born in Carrara, Tuscany, Buffon joined the youth system at Parma in 1991 and by 17 had made his Serie A debut in a 0-0 draw with AC Milan on 19 November 1995. His father was a shot-putter, his mother a discus thrower, and his two sisters are volleyball players. His grandfather's cousin, Lorenzo Buffon, played in goal for Milan. A participant at the 1996 Olympics, Buffon made his senior debut for Italy aged 19 as an emergency substitute for the injured Gianluca Pagliuca in a 1998 World Cup qualifying play-off against Russia. He replaced Pagliuca as the Azzurri No. 1 during Euro 2000 qualification but missed the final tournament with an injured hand. A UEFA Cup winner with Parma in 1999 against Olympique de Marseille in the Moscow final, he became the world's costliest keeper when he joined Juventus for £32.6m two years later. He saved two penalties in the 2003 Champions League final shoot-out against Milan at Old Trafford but still ended up on the losing side. Luca started all of Italy's matches at the 2002 and 2006 World Cups, and Euro 2004 and conceded only two goals in seven matches during Italy's triumph in Germany – an own-goal and a penalty – yet made no saves in the final shoot-out victory over France.

Buffon celebrated his 100th outing for the Azzurri by keeping a clean sheet as Italy drew 0-0 with the Netherlands in a Pescara friendly on 14 November 2009. He started the opening match at the 2010 World Cup but was substituted at half-time against Paraguay with a sciatic nerve problem, from which he would not return until the following January. He remained with Juventus after their enforced relegation to Serie B in 2006 and missed just three matches in the second tier as the Bianconeri made an immediate return to Italy's top division – passing 300 league appearances for La Vecchia Signora during the 2011/12 season in which unbeaten Juventus won their 28th Italian championship.

Paolo Maldini also received a commemorative cap and medal to mark his century of international appearances before Italy's win against Northern Ireland. Maldini commented, "It's a great pleasure to be here. I'm the only one of the four who hasn't won a World Cup but I had the joy of playing in four of them. I've had so much from life that I cannot regret anything".

The son of Italian international Cesare Maldini, Paolo joined Milan as a schoolboy and made his Serie A debut at the age of 16; he would go on to break all appearance records – both for the club and Serie A – before retiring aged 40 in 2009. He won his first Serie A title in 1988 – the same year he made his major tournament debut for Italy, at the European Championship in West Germany; there would be six more Italian championships for the Rossoneri during the course of his career, including five during the 1990s. He won back-to-back European Cups in 1989 and 1990, adding further Champions League triumphs in 1994, 2003 (in which he was man of the match in the final against Juventus) and 2007; he was also a runner-up three times.

He overtook Dino Zoff to become Italy's most capped international by making 126 appearances between 1988 and 2002, a sequence which brought participation at three European Championships and four World Cups, but no major trophies – he was a runner-up in the 1994 World Cup and Euro 2000. He switched from left-back to the centre of the defence later in his career and bowed out in 2009 with more Serie A appearances (647) than any other player in history; he also set a club record of 902 appearances in all competitions for Milan, including a record 168 in UEFA club matches

Fabio Cannavaro was Italy's captain when they lifted a fourth world title in 2006. Cannavaro also received a commemorative cap and medal from UEFA to mark his century of international appearances before Italy's win against

Northern Ireland. "I'm very proud to have reached this milestone with Italy, the most successful team in the World Cup after Brazil," he said. "I'm only starting to realise now that I'm retired what I achieved at international level. Now I hope that my friend [Gianluca] Zambrotta will join us in the club. He is still 34 and needs just two more caps – I was 33 when I won the Ballon d'Or after all."

Born in Naples, Cannavaro was a ball boy at the Stadio San Paolo during Napoli's glory years of the late 1980s before graduating through the club's youth academy and making his Serie A debut in March 1993. He left for Parma in 1995 and became a staunch favourite for his new club, performing with unerring consistency over the next seven seasons, during which he appeared regularly in European competition, won the UEFA Cup – against Olympique de Marseille in the final – and two Italian Cups and became a regular for Italy.

Blooded by the Azzurri in 1997 after twice becoming European U21 champion, he starred at the 1998 World Cup and Euro 2000 but was suspended for Italy's defeat by South Korea at the 2002 World Cup and also for the final group game against Bulgaria at Euro 2004. He reached his career pinnacle at the 2006 World Cup as he brilliantly captained his country to victory in Germany, earning his 100th cap in the final versus France. He claimed the World Player of the Year and Ballon d'Or double at the end of 2006, by which time he had left Juventus for Madrid, where he won the Liga title in each of his two seasons. He returned to Juventus after missing Euro 2008 through an injury sustained on the eve of the tournament. He captained Italy at the 2010 World Cup but announced his international retirement after the team's shock first-round exit, having represented his country a record 136 times; also left Italy that summer to conclude his career in Dubai.

He announced his retirement in July 2011 – five years to the day since lifting the World Cup due to a persistent knee injury, but will continue working for Al-Ahli as a technical adviser. "I find working for this club exciting," he said. "I wanted to play on for another season, but it wouldn't have been fair."

Joachim Streich made the most appearances and scored the most goals for East Germany. Streich received a commemorative cap and medal from UEFA to mark his century of international appearances on 11 October 2011, before Germany's 3-1 win against Belgium in European Championship qualifying. "It's something special to part of a circle of players like Zidane, Raúl, Laudrup, Luís Figo and Shevchenko, not to mention our top German players. This honours great individual performance, combined with necessary consistency." A prolific goalscorer for the German Democratic Republic over a 15-year period that included participation at the 1974 World Cup, Streich was the first player from the former East Germany to reach a century of caps. With 55 goals, he scored 30 more than any other GDR international.

Born in Wismar, he joined Rostock in 1967 at the age of 16, making his Oberliga debut on 23 August 1969 against SG Dynamo Dresden. During an eight-year spell with the Baltic Sea club, he scored 58 goals in 141 Oberliga matches; he was transferred to Magdeburg in 1975 following Rostock's relegation. First capped by the GDR at 19 in a December 1969 friendly against Iraq, his first goal came in a September 1971 friendly against Czechoslovakia in Berlin. He won a bronze medal with the GDR at the 1972 Olympics in Munich and scored twice in four games at the 1974 World Cup two years later. Streich finished as Oberliga top scorer four times during his ten-year spell with Magdeburg, which also brought him three domestic cup wins (in 1978, 1979 and 1983); he scored 216 goals for the club, including 17 in European competition. He was voted GDR Footballer of the Year in 1979 and 1983 and won his 100th international cap on 12 September 1984 in a friendly against England at Wembley, with his 102nd and final appearance coming the following month in Leipzig in a World Cup qualifier against Yugoslavia.

In 1999, FIFA reduced his cap total to 98, subtracting the four games at the 1972 Olympics, but the German FA (DFB) continues to recognise him as a bona fide member of the 100 club. His final tally of 55 international goals included one hat-trick, scored in a 9-0 win against Malta on 29 October 1977. At the end of his playing career, he turned to coaching, leading Magdeburg from 1985-90 and again in 1991/92 after a short spell at TSV Eintracht Braunschweig.

A versatile defender, predominantly a sweeper, who won exactly 100 international caps for East Germany from 1969-85, 'Dixie' Dörner was an Olympic gold medallist in 1976 and spent his entire career at Dynamo Dresden, captaining the team from 1977 through to his retirement. A GDR international before making his Oberliga debut for Dresden, his first senior cap arrived on 22 June 1969 in a friendly against Chile in Magdeburg. Dörner won the domestic double with Dresden in 1971 and a further Oberliga title in 1973 as he established himself as a regular in the team. Although he missed the 1974 World Cup through injury he proved to be an inspirational figure in helping the GDR win gold at the 1976 Olympics in Montreal. Dörner took over as captain of Dresden and the GDR national side, skippering the latter in 60 of his 100 international appearances, the last of which came on 18 May 1985 against Luxembourg. The GDR footballer of the year in 1977 – the year Dresden won another Oberliga/DDR-Pokal double – Dörner captured the award twice more in 1984 and 1985 at the tail-end of his career. He won a total of five domestic titles and five domestic cups with Dresden, appearing in a club-record 442 Oberliga matches and scoring 65 goals; he also played in 68 European encounters for the club, scoring six times, and skippered Dresden to five continental quarter-finals. Dörner took up coaching after hanging up his boots and led the GDR for five years before taking charge of Bundesliga club SV Werder Bremen from January 1996 to August 1997.

A pacy right winger turned central striker, Ulf Kirsten played for just two clubs – Dresden and Leverkusen – and also two countries, dividing his 100 international caps almost equally between East Germany and the unified German national team. Four times a substitute at the 1998 World Cup, his only start at a major tournament came against England at Euro 2000; he made his 100th and last international appearance as a substitute three days later against Portugal.

Born in Riesa, he made his senior debut for Dresden at 18, becoming a key figure as the club won back-to-back Oberliga titles in 1988/89 and 1989/90, the second coming in a season in which he was recognised as East Germany's footballer of the year. In addition to his 57 goals in 154 Oberliga games, he scored eight in 21 European appearances and helped the club reach the 1988/89 UEFA Cup semi-finals, only to be suspended for the last-four tie against VfB Stuttgart. Capped 49 times by the GDR, he found the net 14 times, his last three goals all coming in the same match – a friendly against the United States in Berlin in March 1990. Ulf joined Leverkusen after reunification, posting double-figure goal tallies in each of his first five seasons, including a joint top-scoring haul of 20 in 1992/93, when he also struck the winning effort in the German Cup final. He returned to the international fold with Germany in October 1992, making his debut against Mexico in his former stomping ground of Dresden; an unused squad member at the FIFA World Cup, he had to wait until France '98 before making his major tournament debut.

He found the target 181 times for Leverkusen in 350 Bundesliga matches during his 13-year spell, putting him fifth in the club's all-time rankings. A runner-up with Leverkusen in three competitions in 2001/02 – Bundesliga, German Cup and UEFA Champions League – he retired the following year, aged 37; he subsequently served the Rhineland outfit in a coaching capacity.

Malta played for pride against Israel but for the country's four national-team centurions the final Euro 2012 qualifier proved an emotional occasion nonetheless. David Carabott, Gilbert Agius, Carmel Busuttil and Joe Brincat took the field before kick-off at the Ta' Qali National Stadium to receive the commemorative caps and medals issued by UEFA for players who have reached a century of international appearances.

The 119-cap Agius, still playing at 37 for Valletta, said that emotions were "running high" for the quartet. "Playing over 100 times for my country is already in itself a wonderful achievement – being recognised in such a manner by Europe's governing body even more so." The Valletta captain, Aguis served his home-town team for the whole of his career save for a short spell in Italy with then Serie C club Pisa in the first half of the 2001/02 season. The striker helped Valletta to seven Maltese Premier League titles and as many domestic cups since making his debut for the club in 1990/91. Agius skippered his team to victory in two one-off competitions in Maltese football – the Centenary Cup in December of 2000 and the National League 100 Anniversary Cup ten years later. The former trophy was one of six he and Valletta collected in a famous 2000/01 campaign The only player to have been crowned Maltese footballer of the year on three occasions, having won the award in 1996/97, 2000/01 and 2006/07. Agius collected the first of his 121 caps for Malta, a total which places him second on the country's all-time list behind Carabott, when he played 45 minutes of a 2-1 friendly victory against Gabon on 7 November 1993. He scored his maiden international goal when Malta lost 2-1 to Iceland in a friendly in Reykjavik on 14 August 1996. His eighth and final goal for the national side earned a 1-1 draw with Austria, also in a friendly, on 7 February 2007. Aguis's last goal came four months before he reached a century of international appearances, his 100th cap being won in a 4-0 defeat by Norway in a UEFA EURO 2008 qualifier.

Carabott, Malta's record appearance-maker with 122 outings spanning 18 years, thanked UEFA for the "special" accolade. The 43-year-old said: "It really came as a surprise to me and I did not expect anything like this. It's an amazing initiative which shows the respect that UEFA has not only for the players active in the game but also for those who have participated in European football history." Carabott also received a commemorative cap and medal before Malta's 2-0 home defeat by Israel in European Championship qualifying. Malta's record appearance maker, Carabott lifted the Maltese Premier League title with three clubs – Hibernians (1993/94, 1994-95), Valletta (2000/01) and Sliema Wanderers (2003/04). He won the Maltese Cup on two occasions, with Hibernians in 1997/98 and in 2000/01 while at Valletta, one of six trophies Valletta won in 2000/01, including the one-off Centenary Cup in December of that season. Since hanging up his boots, Carabott dedicated his time to managing the football school he founded in 2006, Sock Kids. Carabott made the first of his 122 appearances for Malta on 15 November 1987 in a European Championship qualifier against Switzerland, which finished 1-1. He brought up his century of caps on 15 August 2001 when Malta lost 2-0 to Bosnia-Herzegovina in a friendly in Sarajevo. Though a defender, Carabott scored an impressive 12 goals for Malta during his long international career, the first of which was in a 1-1 draw with Cyprus on 23 November 1988.

Now Malta's assistant coach, the 47-year-old Busuttil was equally appreciative. "It is a big honour being recognised by Europe's highest football authority. Credit to UEFA for their recognition of all the centurions in European football.

It rewards all those footballers who have gone past the mark of playing 100 times for their country for the big sacrifices we make," said the first man to achieve a century of Malta caps, who was also named his nation's Golden Player in UEFA's golden jubilee year of 2004. Regarded as his country's greatest player, 'Buzu' started out in 1979 as a 16-year-old with home-town club Rabat Ajax, and was instrumental in helping them secure two league titles and one Maltese Trophy. These victories led to appearances in the European Champion Clubs' Cup against Porto and AŠK Inter Bratislava. In 1987, Busuttil moved to Italian semi-professional outfit Verbania, and the following year to Genk, becoming the first Maltese to play for and captain a top-flight club in Europe. After joining Sliema in 1994 he enjoyed further success, winning a championship medal and a Maltese Trophy – and went on to play 669 games for the club, scoring 236 goals, before retiring in 2001. Buzu represented his country 113 times between 1988 and 2000, hitting 23 goals. His great ball skills, an amazing turn of pace, a goalscorer's instinct and admirable dedication brought him two Maltese footballer of the year awards. In 2000 Busuttil received the prestigious Order of Merit of the Republic from the then president of Malta, Professor Guido de Marco, for his contribution to Maltese sport. After retiring he established his own football school, then served as assistant to Malta coach Horst Heese until July 2005. Busuttil subsequently took up his first head coach's post with Pietà Hotspurs in November 2006 and stayed there until 2008. The following year he accepted the role of assistant national coach, working under his former Maltese international colleague John Buttigieg.

Joe Brincat played 103 times for Malta, scoring five goals.

He made his debut in October 1987 in a 2-0 friendly defeat by England B and received a commemorative cap and medal on 11 October 2011, before Malta's 2-0 home defeat by Israel in European Championship qualifying. "It's a reward for all the sacrifices you put into the game," he said. "It also proves your consistency as a footballer over the years because playing over 100 times for your country is such a memorable and honourable achievement."

A talented midfielder, dubbed as the 'Platini' of local football due to his knack of scoring free-kicks, Brincat was part of the famous Hamrun Spartans squad which took Maltese football by storm during the 1980s, winning the double twice. He also won the league and cup with Sliema Wanderers in 2003/04. In total, Brincat won the Maltese Premier League title on seven occasions –with Hamrun Spartans (1986/87, 1987/88, 1990/91), Birkirkara (1999/2000) and Sliema Wanderers (2002/03, 2003/04, 2004/05). Brincat scored a free-kick in added time of a 3-1 second-leg loss to FC Skonto Riga which sent Sliema Wanderers through on away goals to the 2003/04 UEFA Champions League second qualifying round. After retiring in 2006/07, Brincat turned to coaching with lowly San Gwann, before signing a two-year contract with second-tier Vittoriosa Stars in the summer of 2011.

Switzerland's Stéphane Chapuisat, having won his 100th cap in a Basel friendly against Germany on 2 June 2004, ended his international career at the Euro 2004 finals in Portugal. A technically gifted left-footed striker/winger, he made a name for himself in Germany with Dortmund, where he won two Bundesliga titles and the UEFA Champions League in the mid-1990s. The leading Swiss footballer of his generation, he won 103 international caps, scoring 21 goals, between 1989 and 2004. Son of Pierre-Albert 'Gabet' Chapuisat, a former Swiss international defender, he began his career with local club Lausanne, scoring 36 goals in 104 league games before he was transferred to German side Uerdingen.

Given his international debut in June 1989 – a week before his 20th birthday – in a friendly against Brazil, he scored his first goal in a Euro '92 qualifier against San Marino on 14 November 1990. Moved to Dortmund, where he enjoyed a spectacularly successful debut season, scoring 20 Bundesliga goals as the club narrowly missed out on the title to VfB Stuttgart. He struck six times in Switzerland's qualification for the 1994 World Cup and added another goal – against Romania – at the finals, where he was an ever-present in Roy Hodgson's team; Stephane also played at Euro '96, earning his 50th cap in the team's final group game against Scotland and he was at his best as Dormund won the Champions League in 1997, beating Juventus 3-1 in the Munich final. He ended his seven-year stint at the Westfalenstadion with 102 Bundesliga goals in 218 games, returning home to Switzerland aged 30 to join Grasshoppers, winning the Swiss title in his second season at the Zurich club and topping the scoring chart with 21 goals. He left Grasshoppers for Young Boys in 2002 and continued to thrive, winning the golden shoe once again, in 2003/04, with 23 goals.

Russia's Viktor Onopko is the only player to appear more than 100 times for Russia. A fixture in defence for 12

years following his debut for the then Commonwealth of Independent States (CIS) in a 2-2 draw against England on 29 April 1992, he represented the CIS at the 1992 European Championship. Onopko turned out for Russia at Euro '96 four years later and at the 1994 and 2002 World Cups. Onopko won his 100th cap during the 2002 World Cup in Korea and Japan, in a 3-2 group stage defeat by Belgium. In total, he played in 113 matches for his country, scoring seven goals and he received a commemorative cap and medal on 11 October, before Russia's 6-0 victory against Andorra in European Championship qualifying. "I don't want to highlight just one or two matches from my international career because it has been a huge part — a very positive part — of my life for 12 years," he said. "I remember the disappointment of drawing with Ukraine to miss out on Euro 2000, but I also remember good matches, like when we beat Wales in the play-off to qualify for Euro 2004."

Born in Luhansk, now in Ukraine, Russia's most capped player started his professional career with Shakhtar. From there he moved in 1992 to Spartak, where in the space of four seasons he would become captain and win three league titles and the Russian Cup. Onopko was also named Russian footballer of the year in 1992 and 1993. Onopko spent much of his career in Spain with Oviedo, whom he represented for seven seasons and Vallecano. Upon returning to Russia in 2003, Onopko signed for Alania, where he retired from playing two years later. After retiring as a player, he worked for the Russian Football Union (RFU) as a vice-director of the national team department and in September 2009 joined the CSKA coaching staff.

Ari Hjelm, the former Finland forward, then 49, was the first player from the Nordic nation to reach three figures in terms of international appearances, and told delegates at the annual Football Association of Finland gala: "To win 100 caps requires you to have been fit and in good shape all of the time. I spent several years in the national team, 13 in all. Few of the squad nowadays enjoy as many."

Goce Sedloski started a new chapter in his career when he sat in the Former Yugoslav Republic of Macedonia dugout for the first time in his role as assistant coach to John Toshack in November 2011. Before the goalless draw with Albania in Prilep, Sedloski — who played 100 times at the heart of the Macedonia defence — he received his medal and cap from Football Federation of Macedonia president Haralampie Hadzi-Risteski. "Every match I played for Macedonia was a source of great pleasure for me," said Sedloski, then 37. "I always represented my country with all of my heart and I'll continue to work the same way in my coaching career."

Current Ukrainian internationals Anatoliy Tymoshchuk and Andriy Shevchenko and coach Oleh Blokhin were each given a commemorative cap and medal by Oleksandr Bandurko, the Football Federation of Ukraine first vice-president, to recognise their years of service before the Euro 2012 co-hosts' 3-3 friendly draw with Germany in Kyiv.

Shevchenko, Ukraine's all-time leading scorer with 46 goals at that point, said: "I am delighted to receive this prestigious award from UEFA. I have been playing for Ukraine for more than 15 years and had a lot of memorable games. I hope the team will achieve the best result possible during the forthcoming European Championship."

Tymoshchuk earned his 100th cap in a friendly defeat by Brazil 13 months earlier – three days after Shevchenko became the first Ukrainian to reach the milestone. "This is a great idea that recognises the significant contribution of players from different national teams to the development of European football," added Tymoshchuk. "I am pleased to be among the first players in the history of Ukrainian football to receive the UEFA centurion award and I hope that, over time, there will be more such players in Ukraine." Blokhin – in his second spell as Ukraine coach – scored 42 goals in 112 outings for the Soviet Union between 1972 and 1988, both records.

Four Netherlands greats picked up awards, with Edwin van der Sar, Frank de Boer, Giovanni van Bronckhorst and Phillip Cocu receiving them from Royal Netherlands Football Association president and UEFA Executive Committee member Michael van Praag before the Oranje's 0-0 draw with Switzerland. "This is a reward for years and years of sportsmanship and an ambassadorial role for the nation," said Van Praag. "As a representative of the KNVB I am extremely proud that we have no less then four players who are getting this award."

Also honoured was the late József Bozsik, a midfielder for the great Hungary side of the 1950s, who died aged 52 in 1978. His son, former national coach Péter Bozsik, was present at the Ferenc Puskás Stadium in Budapest for Hungary's game against Sweden to accept the award on his father's behalf. "It was an unexpected award but I can say that it brought special joy to the whole family," he said. "I am really glad that my father's name is still known all over Europe. I am also proud that he was the second to gain 101 caps in an era when Hungarian football was amongst the best in the entire world. I am thankful to UEFA for remembering my father and I acknowledge UEFA's very positive commitments to all parts of the game."

Born in 1925 in the Kispest area of Budapest, Bozsik learned the game on local pitches, playing with best friend and neighbour Ferenc Puskás. After Kispesti AC – who became known as Budapest Honvéd during their 1950s heyday – signed him as a youth, he made his first-team debut in 1943. Bozsik took his bow with Hungary's national side against Bulgaria in 1947 and proceeded to win 101 caps, scoring 11 goals, culminating in his farewell appearance against Uruguay in 1962, the year he retired from playing. A fundamental part of the Mighty Magyars team, he was an Olympic gold medallist in Helsinki in 1952 – at Yugoslavia's expense – and a World Cup finalist two years later when Hungary lost the title to West Germany in Berne. He also featured at the 1958 tournament in Sweden. The side built around Bozsik, Puskás, Sándor Kocsis, Nándor Hidegkuti, Zoltán Czibor and Gyula Grosics scored notable victories against world powers Brazil, Uruguay, the USSR and, famously, England. Operating as a right half (defensive midfielder) in coach Gusztáv Sebes's extremely flexible attacking formation, Bozsik scored one of the goals in the 6-3 Wembley victory over England on 25 November 1953 – the hosts' first home defeat by opponents from outside the British Isles. Bozsik and company repeated the dose by beating England 7-1 at the Népstadion (now the Ferenc Puskás stadium) in Budapest on 23 May 1954. Considered Hungary's most intelligent midfield creator, he played a total of 447 first-class matches for the eye-catching Honvéd side, scoring 33 goals, and winning the Mitropa Cup in 1959 as well as five Hungarian championships. Bozsik later had a spell in charge of Honvéd and coached the national team for a single match, against Austria in 1974, before retiring because of illness. He died four years later aged 52.

Four days after turning 20 in February 1997, Yiannis Okkas made his debut for Cyprus in a 3-2 friendly defeat by Poland. He scored his first goal two months later against Bulgaria, while his effort in a 2-1 home loss to France in Euro 2004 qualifying – a delicate chip over goalkeeper Grégory Coupet – is regarded as arguably Cyprus's greatest. The Mediterranean island's most-capped player, he marked his 100th outing with a goal – his 26th at international level – in a 2-1 home reverse against Norway on 8 October 2010. Aside from his strike versus France, Okkas famously equalised with a volley when Cyprus drew 1-1 with Germany during Euro 2008 qualifying.

Okkas never looked back after breaking into the Nea Salamis first team at the age of 16. In 1997, he took his striking talent across town to Anorthosis and quickly established himself as a key player in a side which won three successive Cypriot league titles during his time at the club. He left Anorthosis in 2000 and spent the next seven seasons in Greece, winning the cup with PAOK in his first campaign and again in 2002/03, and consecutive domestic doubles at Olympiacos. In 2007, he made history by becoming the first Cypriot to sign a professional contract with a Spanish club when he joined Celta. In his sole season in Galicia, Okkas scored six goals in 24 Liga appearances. Returning home in

2008 he joined Omonia but his stint with the Nicosia side lasted only one season as he rejoined Anorthosis – where he remains to this day – the following summer.

Former Austria playmaker Andreas Herzog, who represented his nation 103 times before retiring in 2004, collected his cap and medal from UEFA President Michel Platini. "It's a great honour to get the award from Michel Platini. He was my idol when I started playing, and to get the UEFA award from him is very exciting". It shows that it is something special to play more than 100 games for your country. The award will have a special place in my house."

Sami Hyypiä, hung up his boots last May with 105 Finland caps to his name. "Of course it is nice to receive this kind of award," he said. "Looking back, 100 matches is a big number and I feel honoured to belong to a club of this kind. There are many happy memories from the many years I played for Finland. They are something I will never forget."

It was against Finland that former Estonia forward Indrek Zelinski made the last of his 103 national-team appearances in May 2010. "I was happy to see old friends and ex team-mates. It's fantastic UEFA has started this award for players who gave a lot to their national teams."

Romania's Dorinel Munteanu gave long national service, spanning 134 caps, between 1991 and 2007 and welcomed the UEFA initiative. "This has been a very nice surprise for me," the ex-midfielder said. "We talk a lot about money and bonuses in football, but recognition of this kind, especially coming from the highest European football authority, is worth much more. I am deeply honoured that my work and efforts are so highly valued."

Theodoros Zagorakis was a combative, industrious defensive midfielder with a powerful right-foot shot, who achieved footballing immortality by captaining Greece to a fairy-tale triumph at Euro 2004 in Portugal. He made a sensational major international tournament debut, playing every minute of the team's unlikely triumph and was voted Player of the Tournament by UEFA and finished fifth in the 2004 Ballon d'Or poll. He became the first Greek footballer to achieve a century of international caps, reaching the milestone on 17 November 2004 in a World Cup qualifier at home to Kazakhstan. His first international goal did not arrive until his 101st appearance − in a 2-1 World Cup qualifying win over Denmark in February 2005; he would add two more before winning his 120th and final cap for Greece in a special farewell appearance against Spain in Salonika in August 2007 − three months after he had retired to become president of PAOK. He started his career with local club Kavala before joining top-flight PAOK in 1992 and became a Greek international two years later; he would go on to start each of Greece's next 28 internationals.

Zagorakis made 155 league appearances for PAOK before moving to Leicester City in January 1998 to became a cult figure during a successful period for the club under manager Martin O'Neill. He returned to Greece in summer 2000, joining AEK, to win the Greek Cup at the end of his second season, defeating Olympiacos FC 2-1 in the Athens final. He joined Italian outfit Bologna but a year later he was back in

Greece following the club's relegation to Serie B, rejoining PAOK on a two-year contract.

Angelos Basinas won his 100th cap for Greece while at Portsmouth in a 2010 World Cup qualifier against Israel; it proved to be his final appearance. He became a pivotal member of the Greek national side under Otto Rehhagel, shining in the team's extraordinary Euro 2004 triumph in Portugal, where he scored a penalty in the opening 2-1 triumph over the hosts, then provided the assist for Angelos Charisteas's winning goal against the same opponents in the final. Over the next four years he missed just one competitive international for his country and captained the side at Euro 2008. Basinas received a commemorative cap and medal from UEFA to mark his century of international appearances on 7 October 2011, before Greece's 2-0 victory against Croatia in European Championship qualifying. "It's a great honour for me to be presented with this award by UEFA. It's a tough task to reach 100 caps with the national team and I want to thank my family for always standing by my side."

Basinas won his first cap for Greece in an August 1999 friendly against El Salvador in Kavala, then scored his first international goal two days later – against the same opposition and at the same venue. Born in Karditsa in central Greece, he began his career in Athens with Panathinaikos, moving out of defence to establish himself as a holding midfielder.

He increased his profile internationally by starring for Panathinaikos in the 2000/01 and 2001/02 Champions League, playing 12 matches and scoring two goals in each campaign and reaching the quarter-finals of the latter, in which he scored the winning penalty in the first leg at home to Barcelona. A Greek double winner in 2003/04, he left Panathinaikos a year later for Spanish club Mallorca, where he became a key midfielder. In July 2008 he signed a three-year contract with AEK but left after just six months for Portsmouth. Following Portsmouth's relegation he had a brief spell in France with Ligue 1 newcomers Arles before returning to Greece to see out his career in the lower leagues.

Current captain Giorgos Karagounis, were among those honoured before Euro 2012 qualifiers. Karagounis, who earned his 111th cap in Greece's 2-0 win against Croatia on 7 October 2011, had double cause for celebration, admitting it had been a "special night". "The awards made it special and then came this victory after a hard-fought match. We are all happy and proud." The captain of the Greece side that finished runners–up to Spain at the 1998 European Under-21 Championship, he made his senior debut the following year, against El Salvador, and soon became a regular in Otto Rehhagel's side. He scored the opening goal of Euro 2004 with a low drive as Greece upset hosts Portugal 2-1, but was suspended for the final against the same opponents three weeks later as Greece captured the European title in Lisbon.

A consistent performer for his country, he started every one of Greece's 12 qualifying matches for Euro 2008, scoring both goals in a March 2008 friendly against Portugal (2-1) and featuring prominently at the finals in Austria. A legendary figure at Athens club Panathinaikos, where he has spent the bulk of his career – interspersed with spells abroad in Italy and Portugal, Karagounis reached 100 international caps during the Euro 2012 qualifying campaign. He joined Panathinaikos in his teens and though he did not win a major domestic honour with the Greens over the next five years, he shone for the club in Europe, notably in 2000/01 and 2001/02 when the Athens outfit had lengthy runs in the Champions League. Joining Inter from Panathinaikos in 2003, he became only the second Greek to play for the Italian club (after Grigoris Georgatos) but despite winning his first club trophy — the Coppa Italia, in his second season — he featured only intermittently for the Nerazzurri. He moved to Benfica in 2005 and thrived under coach Fernando Santos in 2006/07, helping the team reach the UEFA Cup quarter-finals. Back at Panathinaikos, he skippered the club to a Greek double in 2009/10 prior to making his World Cup bow at the finals in South Africa, where he was the team captain and started all three matches. Karagounis retained his place as national team skipper under new coach Fernando Santos, his former boss at Benfica, and won his 100th cap in a Euro 2012 qualifying victory over Latvia in Piraeus on 8 October 2010.

Speaking after captaining Armenia to a 4-1 victory against former Yugoslav Republic of Macedonia which kept their hopes of reaching the Euro 2012 play-offs alive, Sargis Hovsepyan said: "I'm really happy that I've played 124 matches for the national team. I would like to thank the coaches who believed in me and allowed me to play. When you pull on your national team shirt you feel real pride. Can you imagine how many times I've had this feeling? I never strived to set any record. My main goal was always to help the team perform well and try to win, but I'm glad I was lucky to reach 100 caps for the national team." Hovsepyan received a commemorative cap and medal from UEFA to mark his century of international appearances on 7 October, before taking the field.

His long international career began in 1992 with a home friendly against Moldova. His first goal came from the penalty spot during a 2-1 victory in Kazakhstan on 2 June 2007, with his 100th cap being won 14 months later as Armenia lost 4-0 to Spain in a 2010 World Cup qualifier.

A central defender, Hovsepyan made his debut for local side Malatia Yerevan as a teenager in 1990 but after just one season in the first team he joined Lori Kirovakan. He was already at the club that became Pyunik following the break-up of the Soviet Union. He won three league titles, the Armenian Cup and was twice voted Armenian player of the year while with the capital outfit. After moving to Zenit in 1998 Hovsepyan made 153 appearances in a five-year stay which yielded the Russian Cup in 1999 and a third-place Premier-Liga finish two years later. A spell with Torpedo-Metallurg followed in 2003 but after only a handful of games he returned to Pyunik. In 2008, he was again recognised as Armenia's best player, while two years later he won his tenth league championship with the Yerevan club.

Unlike Hovsepyan, the road to Poland or Ukraine came to an end for Miroslav Karhan as Slovakia lost 1-0 at home against Russia – a defeat which brought an end the 35-year-old's international career. "It wasn't a spontaneous decision," he said. "I said before qualifying that while the team had a chance to advance to the championship I would be available; now that's over along with my secret dream to say farewell next year." On receiving his commemorative cap and medal from UEFA before that qualifier, Karhan added: "One hundred games for the national team is a nice number, but statistics have never been important to me."

The midfielder endured a debut to remember for Slovakia when he turned out against Israel in Kosice on 6 September 1995. He required four stitches to a cut he received above his eyebrow in the first half, but remained on the field for the duration as Slovakia won 1-0. He helped Slovakia qualify for the 2010 World Cup – their first major tournament as an independent nation – but an Achilles injury ruled him out of the squad and thereby prevented him from earning his 100th cap at the tournament. Slovakia's most-capped player brought up his century of international appearances during a 1-1 draw with the Republic of Ireland on 12 October 2010 in Zilina. "He was our best player, for sure," said coach Vladimír Weiss after the Euro 2012 qualifier.

A Slovakian Cup winner with Spartak Trnava in 1998, Karhan spent a single season with Betis and Besiktas – for whom he featured in a 3-0 Champions League group stage defeat of Barcelona – prior to signing for Wolfsburg in 2001 when he was voted Slovakian footballer of the year in 2002. In six seasons, Karhan amassed 173 Bundesliga appearances and nine goals. He remained in Germany after leaving Wolfsburg in 2007, joining Mainz, who he helped win promotion to the Bundesliga in his second season. After 109 league games for the Rhineland side, he returned to Spartak Trnava for the start of the 2011/12 campaign.

Rütü Reçber was the finest Turkish goalkeeper of all time, peaking at the 2002 World Cup, where he performed wonders to help Turkey surpass expectations and finish third. He started all seven matches for Turkey at the 2002 World Cup, where his consistent excellence earned him a place in FIFA's All-Star Squad. He also appeared in three European Championship final tournaments. Recber became the second Turkish international to reach 100 caps, after Bülent Korkmaz, celebrating the landmark with a clean sheet in a 2-0 win against Albania on 26 March 2005. He retired from the international arena after earning a record 118th cap in the Euro 2008 semi-final against Germany but returned for a one-minute farewell appearance in a World Cup qualifier against Armenia in October 2009.

Rüstü received a commemorative cap and medal from UEFA to mark his century of international appearances on 11 October 2011, before Turkey's 1-0 victory against Azerbaijan in European Championship qualifying. "To be remembered and not forgotten is a big honour," he said. "These presents will take pride of place in my house."

Discovered by coach Fatih Terim at Antalyaspor, Recber joined Fenerbahçe in 1994 and went on to replace Engin Ipekoglu as No. 1 at club and international level, making his Turkey debut in a Euro '96 qualifier against Iceland on 12 October 1994. He won the league title with Fenerbahçe in 1995/96 before achieving his first major international exposure at Euro '96, where he was an ever-present; repeated the feat at Euro 2000, where Turkey reached the quarter-finals. He won further Süper Lig titles with Fenerbahçe in 2001, 2005 and 2007 and made a club-record 49 UEFA club competition appearances before a move to Istanbul rivals Besiktas in 2007. Understudy to Volkan Demirel at Euro 2008 he replaced his suspended team-mate for the quarter-final against Croatia, making a decisive save in the penalty shoot-out. A double winner with Besiktas in 2009, he claimed the Turkish Cup again two years later, playing 120 minutes (plus penalty shoot-out) in the final against Istanbul BB SK, the day after his 38th birthday.

Centre-back Bülent Korkmaz, a Galatasaray legend, became the first player to win 100 international caps for Turkey – a feat he achieved in August 2004. He made his first appearance for the national team in a 5-0 defeat by the Republic of Ireland in the team's opening Euro '92 qualifier on 17 October 1990 and made his major tournament bow for Turkey at Euro '96; he reappeared at the 2002 World Cup, starting six of the seven games and scoring in a 3-0 group stage defeat of China en route to a third-place finish. Korkmaz made 102 appearances in UEFA club competitions for Galatasaray and ended his career on the same number of caps for Turkey after a final, post-retirement farewell appearance against Bulgaria in Sofia on 17 August 2005.

Bülent received a commemorative cap and medal to mark his century of international appearances on 11 October 2011, before Turkey's 1-0 win against Azerbaijan in European Championship qualifier. "When I reached 100 games for Galatasaray, UEFA gave me a nice painting," he said. "Like I did with that award, I'll give this gift pride of place in my house. I would like to thank UEFA very much." He joined Galatasaray at the age of 11, initially as a goalkeeper before switching to a defensive midfielder then a central defender. Promoted to the first-team squad during the 1988/89 season and became a stalwart of the back four, winning his first trophy in 1991 – the Turkish Cup – followed by a league and cup double two years later. Appointed as Galatasaray captain in 1995 he went on to hold on to the position for the next decade until his retirement, leading the Istanbul giants to five Turkish titles, four Turkish Cup wins and the UEFA Cup against Arsenal FC on penalties in the final and Super Cup (2-1 against Real Madrid CF) in 2000; he also helped Cim bom to the quarter-finals of the 2000/01 Champions League.

Hakan Sukur is Turkey's all-time record scorer with 51 goals in 112 international appearances, the 'Bull of the Bosphorus' was immensely prolific for Galatasaray, where he had three spells and won 14 major honours, including the 2000 UEFA Cup. First capped by Turkey in March 1992 while a Bursaspor player, he became the team's resident centre-forward, appearing at the European Championships of 1996 and 2000 and scored the fastest goal in World Cup finals history (timed at 11 seconds) in the third-place play-off against co-hosts South Korea in 2002. Twelve months later he was voted by UEFA as Turkey's Golden Player of the previous 50 years.

Sukur brought up a half-century of international goals when he scored four times in a 5-0 defeat of Moldova on 11 October 2006 and closed his account the following June with his 51st goal as Turkey lost 3-2 to Bosnia-Herzegovina in a Euro 2008 qualifier. He retired in 2008 as the Turkish top flight's all-time record marksman with 249 goals. He also found the net a Galatasaray-record 38 times in UEFA club competition. Hakan received a commemorative cap and medal from UEFA to mark his century of international appearances on 7 October 2011, before Turkey's 1-0 victory against Azerbaijan in European Championship qualifying. "There's no doubt that every game I played for the national team holds a very special place in my heart," he said. "I'm deeply honoured that my international career, filled with significant memories, is recognised by UEFA." He won the Turkish Cup with Sakaryaspor before moving in 1990 to Bursaspor and joining Galatasaray for the first time in 1992, landing the title in his first two seasons. A move to Italy followed in 1995 but Sukur failed to settle at Torino and made a quick return to Galatasaray, winning the Turkish Süper Lig golden boot for three successive seasons (1996/97 to 1998/99), all of which brought further titles. He scored six goals in nine games – including one in each of the quarter-final and semi-final ties – as Galatasaray won the 1999/2000 UEFA Cup, becoming the first Turkish team to win a European club trophy. Spells abroad between 2000 and 2003 – at Inter, Parma and Blackburn – led him back to the home comforts of Galatasaray, where he won the Turkish Cup for the sixth time before sealing his seventh and eighth league titles.

Karel Poborský won his first cap in the Czech Republic's first match as an independent nation, a friendly against Turkey in Istanbul on 23 February 1994, but was not a regular in the team that reached Euro '96, making just one start in the qualifying competition. He came of age at Euro '96, starting all six games for Dušan Uhrin's unsung side as they reached the final; his first international goal – a spectacular impromptu lob – defeated Portugal 1-0 in the quarter-final at Villa Park. He remained in England after his Euro exploits, joining Manchester United, but after 18 months at Old Trafford

– in which he earned a 1996/97 Premier League winners' medal – he left for Benfica in January 1998, before a spell with Lazio, and then returned home to win two league titles and the Czech Cup with Sparta. He remained a consistent performer for his country, appearing at Euro 2000 and Euro 2004. A few months before the latter tournament he became the most-capped Czech international when he made his 91st international appearance, bypassing Zdenk Nehoda. Fittingly, he ended his international career at the 2006 World Cup, when he made his 118th appearance in the group encounter against eventual champions Italy. A native of Trebon in southern Bohemia, Poborský was encouraged to pursue a footballing career by his father, a former professional, and joined local team Eské Budjovice at the age of 12. Made his senior debut for the club at 18 and helped them reach the Czechoslovakian top flight before joining Viktoria Žižkov. He left Žižkov for Slavia at the start of the 1995/96 season and starred in the club's first championship success in 49 years, scoring 11 goals in 26 appearances.

Dejan Stankovic played all three games for Serbia & Montenegro at the 2006 and 2010 World Cups, the latter purely under the guise of Serbia. He made his 100th international appearance in a 3-1 defeat of the Faroe Islands, a European Championship qualifier on 6 September 2011. "This moment is one I'll never forget," said Stankovic after receiving a commemorative cap and medal from UEFA for reaching the appearance milestone. "I remember very well each of those 100 games, they made me richer."

Stankovic joined Crvena Zvezda aged 14 and won the Yugoslavian league title at 16, making seven appearances in 1994/95; he helped the Belgrade club to two domestic cup wins in the next two seasons and was captain as he scored 15 goals in 1997/98. He scored twice – both headers – on his international debut against South Korea on 22 April 1998 and made it into Yugoslavia's World Cup squad in France, making three appearances; he joined Lazio after the tournament and won the Cup Winners' Cup and Super Cup the following year. A double winner with Lazio in 1999/2000, he remained in Rome for the next three-and-a-half years, scoring 22 goals in 137 Serie A games, before transferring to Inter in January 2004. A fundamental player in Inter's five successive Scudetto wins from 2005/06 onwards, Stankovic reached 100 appearances in UEFA club competition in a 2-0 defeat at Barcelona in the 2009/10 Champions League. He came on as a second-half substitute during the Nerazzurri's Champions League final victory later that season against Bayern as Inter completed an historic treble and scored one of the best goals in the 2010/11 Champions League when he volleyed in from near the halfway line after 25 seconds against FC Schalke 04.

Fernando Couto was the first Portuguese footballer to reach a century of international caps. A highly accomplished central defender who won major club honours, including league titles in Portugal, Italy and Spain, Couto pipped Luís Figo to become Portugal's first centurion on 11 October 2003 in a friendly against Albania, receiving a commemorative cap and medal from UEFA to mark his century of international appearances on 7 October 2011, before Portugal's 5-3 win against Iceland in European Championship qualifying. "It was fantastic," said Couto. "It was a very important tribute for me. It's the recognition of a career, and that is fantastic." An ever-present again for Portugal at Euro 2000, where they reached the semi-finals, he also represented his country at the 2002 World Cup. He retired from international football after Euro 2004 with 110 caps and eight goals to his name. He started out at Porto but had two seasons away at Famalicão and Académica before establishing himself as a defensive linchpin with the Dragons.

Having helped Portugal win the 1989 U-20 World Cup in Saudi Arabia and graduated to the senior national side in December of the following year, Couto made his debut in a friendly against the United States. He became a prominent figure for both club and country in the early 1990s, winning two Liga titles and two Portuguese Cups with Porto before he moved abroad, at the age of 25, to join Parma. A superb debut season in Italy brought him four Serie A goals and victory in the UEFA Cup as Parma defeated Juventus 2-1 on aggregate in the final. He left Parma for Barcelona in 1996 after an impressive performance at Euro '96, where he played every minute for Portugal and scored the winning goal in a group game against Turkey. He collected six trophies during his two-year stint with Barça, including the Cup Winners' Cup and the Liga title, before returning to Italy to join Lazio, where he enjoyed further success, winning the Cup Winners' Cup (again) in his first season and a Serie A/Coppa Italia double in his second.

Luis Figo is the holder of a Portuguese record 127 caps and the legendary winger had double cause for celebration as

Paulo Bento's side booked their place at Euro 2012 with an emphatic 6–2 defeat of Bosnia and Herzegovina at the Estádio do Sport Lisboa e Benfica. "I was fortunate and happy to receive an ovation on an unforgettable day for Portugal," the then 39-year-old said. "We qualified with a big result in a stadium I don't visit often but where I made many appearances for my country."

A mainstay of the Portuguese national side for 15 years, his international career incorporated three European Championships and two World Cups, peaking with a dazzling performance at Euro 2000, after which he won the Ballon d'Or as European footballer of the year. He collected the World Player of the Year crown a year later and went on to collect a total of 127 international caps – a Portuguese record – after captaining his country to fourth place at the 2006 World Cup in Germany. On 15 November 2011 Figo was given a commemorative cap and medal by UEFA to mark his century of international appearances.

Luis Figo came to prominence in his teens, notably at international level, where he helped Portugal to victory in the 1989 European U16 Championship in Denmark and to the U-20 World Cup crown two years later on home soil. After six years at Sporting, during which he won his first major club trophy, the 1995 Portuguese Cup, he moved to Barcelona where he enjoyed five fabulous seasons winning the Copa del Rey and Cup Winners' Cup in 1997, followed by the Spanish league and cup double in 1998 and a further Liga title in 1999. He left Barça for arch-rivals Real Madrid in 2000 in a world-record transfer and maintained his world-class form at the Santiago Bernabéu, winning two Liga titles plus the 2002 Champions League during a five-year spell. He ended his career at Inter, where he won the Scudetto in each of his four seasons at the club.

WORLD CENTURIONS

MARCOS EVANGELISTA DE MORAE, better known as Cafu, won an incredible 142 caps for Brazil; he never tired, never slowed down and never stopped and is arguably the greatest full back to ever play the game. He won the World Cup twice, in 1994 and 2002 and was also victorious in 15 of his 18 World Cup appearances, beginning with a 3-2 win over the Netherlands in the USA. He has also appeared in the 1998 and 2006 finals, before retiring in 2008 aged 38.

Born in 1970, the right-back was one of the most skilful, successful and widely respected attacking full-backs in the modern game. During a long career at club level he has achieved success in South America and Europe as well as making history in a record breaking international career. Cafu began his career with his hometown club São Paulo in the late 1980s, as they enjoyed great success in the early part of the 1990s. In six years with the club, he won a Brazilian League Championship in 1991, the Copa Libertadores and the Intercontinental Cup in each of the next two years, becoming established in the national team.

Cafu played in the Copa America in both 1991 and 1993

before making his World Cup debut in the U.S.A. in 1994, playing three matches as Brazil won their first title since 1970. After that tournament, he left Brazil to move to Real Zaragoza in Spain, but returned home after just one season to join Palmeiras. In 1997, Cafu captained his country to success in the Copa America and his performances were rewarded with a move to Italy and AS Roma.

In his second World Cup in 1998, he helped Brazil to the final again where they were beaten by host nation France, but further international success came a year later with a successful defence of the Copa America. In 2001, Cafu picked up his first club honour in Europe when he helped Roma to the Serie A championship.

The 2002 World Cup in Japan and South Korea saw Cafu become the first player in the competition's history to play in three finals, lifting the trophy after captaining Brazil to victory over Germany in the final. He moved to AC Milan a year later, winning another Serie A title in his first season and a first European Champions League in 2007, having seen his international career end in disappointment with a World Cup quarter final defeat in 2006.

Brazil and Argentina are, of course fierce rivals, and also have players of enormous international distinction. Argentina defender Roberto Ayala became a centurion in June 2006 in a friendly against Angola in a warm-up match for the 2006 World Cup. The man they call El Ratón (The Mouse) made his 100th appearance in the famous blue and white stripes as Maxi Rodriguez's strike and an own goal from Angola's Andre Mateus secured a 2-0 win for Jose Pekerman's team.

In completing his century, Ayala joined a select band of players that includes Diego Simeone (106) and Javier Zanetti (102). The Valencia man made the libero position his own back in 1994 and was an undisputed first choice in the Albiceleste back line ever since. As well as being a key component of the side that took silver at the 1996 Olympics in Atlanta, Ayala featured in all five of his country's games at the 1998 World Cup in France. It was an entirely different story at Korea/Japan 2002, though, when he was struck down with injury while warming up for the opening game against Nigeria, and was forced to sit out the rest of the tournament.

The tough-tackling centre-back began his career with Ferro Carril Oeste and enjoyed a spell with River Plate before embarking for Europe, where his first port of call was Italy. After turning out for Napoli and AC Milan, he signed on the dotted line for an upwardly mobile Valencia in 2000. Ayala announced his international retirement days after his country's defeat against Brazil in the final of the Copa America Venezuela 2007. However, neither the resounding 3-0 scoreline or the decisive own goal he scored appear to have been factors: "I took this decision a long time ago and it doesn't have anything to do with what happened against Brazil. I just think that every cycle comes to an end and my time with the national team is no different." His departure left a void at the back that Argentina were sure to find difficult to fill.

Ayala was born in Parana, in the region of Entre Rios, on 14 April 1973. Curiously enough, the young Roberto was not overly keen on the beautiful game: "My friends used to play football all the time, but I didn't think it was much fun" he remarks. Despite this initial lack of enthusiasm, by the age of 15 he was playing alongside his father in defence for Atletico Parana, where he would take the first steps in his professional career. In 1990, the gifted defender enjoyed a successful trial at Ferro Carril Oeste, going on to make his top flight debut two years later under the tutelage of Carlos Timoteo Griguol. He quickly showed the aptitudes that made him such a superb libero: pace, impeccable defensive timing and outstanding aerial ability, despite measuring just 5ft 10. In 1994 his path would cross with that of Daniel Alberto Passarella, then coach of River Plate, changing his career for ever. It was El Gran Capitan who brought Ayala to Los Millonarios and who, after taking the national team reins, would give him his first international call-up. On 16 November 1994, the emerging defender made his debut for Argentina in a friendly match against fellow South Americans Chile.

Ayala soon became an integral member of Passarella's Albiceleste set-up. That Olympic silver medal was followed by inclusion in the 1998 World Cup squad. However, that tournament would bring with it one of Roberto's most painful experiences in the blue-and-white of Argentina. Ayala was the man left floundering as Dutch maestro Dennis Bergkamp scored the goal that gave Netherlands a 2-1 quarter-final win. Yet the France 1998 exit paled in comparison to the losses of both his mother and sister that very same year. Showing incredible strength of character, Ayala redoubled his efforts to win a regular starting place at AC Milan, who had signed him for 7.3 million euros from Napoli. Though first-team minutes continued to elude him at the Rossoneri, Ayala was delighted to receive the call from Marcelo Bielsa, Passarella's successor in the Argentina hot seat.

Further disappointment followed at the Copa America Paraguay 1999, where Argentina were knocked out at the quarter-final stage by eternal rivals Brazil, Ayala having a late penalty saved by Dida. Worse was to come at the 2002 FIFA World Cup Korea/Japan, Ayala falling injured in the warm-up prior to his side's opener against Nigeria and having to watch the team's first-round exit from the sidelines. The rugged defender, however, proved one of the under-fire Bielsa's staunchest supporters: "You can see that the job means absolutely everything to him. I think that he should carry on."

Thus, El Loco Bielsa earned a stay of execution at the helm of the Albiceleste, contributing to a rollercoaster 2004 for Ayala and his team-mates. After a series of outstanding displays at that year's Copa America in Peru, old foes Brazil once more undid Argentina. Leading the final 2-1 with just moments remaining, Auriverde striker Adriano outmanoeuvred Ayala to grab a last-gasp equaliser, which preceded the Brazilians emerging triumphant after extra-time and penalties. The Men's Olympic Football Tournament at Athens 2004 would bring some measure of relief, Bielsa inviting the experienced defender to take part in his second Olympic Games. The decision paid off, Ayala captaining Argentina to the gold medal. "It's the happiest moment of my international career," he said afterwards.

Bielsa's subsequent departure came as something of a shock, and was followed by Ayala spending a lengthy spell out of action through injury. Under new national team coach Jose Pekerman, he recovered his rightful place at the heart of the Argentinian defence, although he was no longer team captain. He continued to lead by example, however, opening the scoring against the host nation in the quarter-finals of Germany 2006. He was less precise with his spot-kick after the tie had gone to penalties, his effort one of two saved by Germany keeper Jens Lehmann. After yet another last eight exit, a dejected Ayala vowed that: "I'll only stop dreaming of (being successful with) the national team on the day I retire from football." One year on, at the age of 34 and still a regular under current Argentina supremo Alfio Basile, Real Zaragoza's new signing has had a change of heart. Despite having never won a title with the senior side, he has left an indelible stamp on Argentinian football. His 115 caps are a national record (43 under Passarella, 48 under Bielsa, 14 under Pekerman and ten under Alfio Basile), while he has played a record 40 FIFA World Cup qualifiers and ten matches at the finals themselves. Nor has anybody worn the captain's armband on more occasions, Ayala's tally of 64 even higher than Diego Armando Maradona's total of 57. "It's an honour, a real pleasure and very moving to know that I've accumulated those kinds of numbers. But my heart tells me that I'd change any record or individual landmark for a trophy. Even so, I know that over time, when I look back on my experiences with the national team, I can't fail to be thrilled with those statistics."

Incredibly for a player with nearly 145 caps, Javier Zanetti played in just two World Cups. Coach Diego Maradona left a then 37-year-old Zanetti out of the 2010 squad having taken the captain's armband from him prior to the finals. A year later, he was still going strong for Inter and country under new boss Alejandro Sabella and played in the 2011 Copa America. England fans, though, probably remember him for his craftiness in the 1998 World Cup...

His landmark game arrived on Sunday 26 June 2005. Helping Argentina win their Confederations Cup Germany 2005 semi-final over Mexico, the veteran right-back was taking part in his 100th match for Argentina. The new centurion marked the event in the best possible way. Not only did his side claw their way through to a showpiece final with Brazil after a tense penalty shoot-out, but FIFA's Technical Study Group named him the Man of the Match award. Outstanding for the full 120 minutes, Zanetti was not only a rock in defence; he provided constant support for the strikers, especially with his marauding runs down the right flank.

At Milan, he won the Inter captaincy, and he has long been an idol of the tifosi, who have affectionately baptised him Il trattore (The tractor) for his incomparable work-rate. At 32 years of age, the full-back became the second most-capped player in the history of Argentinian football, behind former Inter star Diego Simeone (106 appearances). He is also the 112th player to join exclusive century club, and the 13th South American to do so.

Cameroon's captain Rigobert Song reached the milestone of 100 caps marking a new achievement for African football.

There had been only six African footballers who had passed the 100-cap total before Song and all hail from north Africa countries. Hossam Hassan of Egypt lead a list of four other compatriots ahead of Noureddine Naybet of Morocco.

Song became the first player from sub-Saharan Africa to join the exclusive club. The tenacious defender, whose club career has seen him play in several of the world's top leagues, made his debut as a 17-year-old for the Indomitable Lions in 1993. His aggressive style and strong leadership qualities marked him out as one of the continent's most charismatic players over the decades. That he is known as "The General" by his Cameroon team mates is no coincidence. "I love Cameroon and I love being a symbol for the country. It is a great honour. It is for that reason I have always honoured call-ups to play for the team and why I have been able to captain a side like the Indomitable Lions of Cameroon. I'm always content to be with the national team. It has a really great ambiance and we form one big, happy family."

Born in Nkengilock, Song played at Red Star Bangou and then Tonnerre Yaoundé before moving to Metz in France after the 1994 World Cup finals in the USA. His club career took him to Salernitana in Italy, Liverpool and West Ham in England, FC Cologne in Germany, back to France with Lens and Galatasaray. His honours include captaining Cameroon to two African Nations Cup titles and playing in the Champions League with Lens. Africa's failure to deliver more players to the century club often arose from a scarcity of fixtures. Two decades ago, few teams played matches outside of those which served as qualifiers for the World Cup, the Nations Cup or the Olympic Games, which prior to 1992 were played at full international level in Africa and Asia. The qualifiers were also knockout affairs, meaning that many countries played just two matches before being eliminated and then had to wait an age before returning to action. When African footballers started playing at professional clubs in Europe, they were infrequently back home for national team duty. Up until 1988, the Nations Cup finals did not allow European-based footballers to feature at the tournament.

As of July 2012, the most capped international footballer of all is Egypt's pocket dynamo Ahmed Hassan who made his 184th appearance for his country in a friendly against Kenya in March 2012. He overtook Egypt's previous record holder Hossam Hassan of 170 on 25th January 2010 in the Africa Cup of Nations quarter final against Cameroon before overtaking former Saudi Arabia goalkeeper Mohamed Al-Deayea in 2012.

Hossam Hassan ended his Egypt career with 170 caps. For a while, he was the world's most capped international, receiving a special armband from FIFA president Sepp Blatter when he won his 151st cap in Cairo, eclipsing Lothar Matthaus of Germany's old record of 150. Mexico's Claudio Suárez later claimed the record with 172 caps while the other African centurions are Ibrahim Hassan, Hani Ramzy and Nader El Sayed, all of Egypt.

Hassan equalled Matthaus' record against the United Arab Emirates in Cairo. Egypt won 2-1 but was unable to add to the occasion with another of his signature goals with his twin brother Ibrahim, also a centurion, ironically scored the winning goal against Henri Michel's team. A member of the Egyptian squad at the World Cup in Italy in 1990 where the Pharaohs put up an impressive showing but narrowly failed to get past the first round in a tough group with England, Ireland and the Netherlands, Hassan had made his debut as a teenage starter in the friendly against Norway in Oslo but had to wait for a further two years before gaining a regular berth in the national side.

He played at the African Nations Cup finals in 1986 which Egypt won on home soil and again in 1988, 1992 and 1998, when he scored seven goals as the north Africans again took the continental title. But he could have had many more caps had he not been dropped during the era of Dutch coach Ruud Krol, who left him out for the 1996 finals in South Africa.

Winning his 100th cap, Ecuador's number 10, Alex Aguinaga, also ended proceedings on a high note by scoring a penalty in his side's 2-2 draw at home to Costa Rica in November 2002.

Cobi Jones attained his 100th cap in probably the USA's most astonishing victory, beating the mighty Brazil 1-0 in the semi-finals of the Concacaf Gold Cup. Alexi Lalas only managed 96 caps for his country.

Tony Meola earned 100 caps for the United States between 1988 and 2006. The agile shot-stopper, who was the American No. 1 at the World Cup at Italy 1990 and USA 1994, is recognised as the man who opened doors for the likes of Kasey Keller, Tim Howard and Brad Friedel - to whom he acted as No. 2 in the 2002 World Cup. Meola made the transition into manager with Major Indoor Soccer League outfit the New Jersey Ironmen. He wore his own gloves for the last five games with the Ironmen in their inaugural season.

Meola once tried out to be place kicker for the gridiron side New York Jets and starred in an off-Broadway play and even fronted his own mortgage firm. Meola is a native of Kearny, New Jersey, the iconic 'soccer town' from where national teammates John Harkes and Tab Ramos both hailed. His career spanned nearly 20 years and saw him play briefly in England and win an MLS Cup with Kansas City Wizards in 2000. He was originally planning to retire from playing in 2006 after finishing up his contract with the MetroStars (now the New York Red Bulls), but that was until he received an offer he just couldn't refuse. "I was contacted by the Ironmen. At first I didn't have any interest in playing indoor soccer again (he played the fast-paced American version of indoor early on in his career), but they came up with a plan where I could get involved in the front office and learn the ropes of that side of the game... and I jumped at the opportunity."

Meola points to qualifying for Italy 1990 – and putting an end to a 40-year finals drought for the USA – as his proudest moment. "The highlight had to be 1990, when we got back to the World Cup," he said. "It wasn't like it is today. We had no pro league and no money and in the end we did it. When we reached Italy, everything kind of flowed out of that. Doors opened for the players of today and we ended up with a top-tier league and now it's all taken for granted."

Kasey Keller's international career spans 17 years, four

World Cups, over 100 caps and his club life has seen him line up in four countries on two continents with eight different clubs. Keller earned the silver ball as second-best player at the U-20 World Championship in Saudi Arabia in 1989. He received the biggest compliment of all in the form of a much-publicised quotation from Romario, the Brazilian goalscoring legend. In 1998 when the Seleção lost to Keller and the USA 1-0 in a famous upset at the Rose Bowl, the diminutive Brazilian remarked: "That was, quite simply, the best performance I have ever seen by a goalkeeper in my life."

Few players have had such a major and sustained impact on Mexican football as Rafael Marquez, his country's only representative in Europe for several years. A born leader, he won every possible domestic and continental honour during his time with Barcelona, as well as captaining Mexico at three World Cups. A number of club teams that have earned a very special place in the centre-half's heart. Though he has turned out for four different club sides, Marquez has never hidden his depth of feeling for first club Atlas, where he came up through the youth system before breaking into the first team, and Barça, where he made his name as a world-class performer. Bridging the gap between those two clubs were Ligue 1 outfit Monaco. He made 12 World Cup appearances, a Mexican record. He is also the only man to captain El Tri three times at the global showpiece. Marquez notched two goals on the biggest stage of all, one against Argentina at Germany 2006 and another versus hosts South Africa in 2010.

With Monaco he won Ligue 1 and the French Supercup

in 2000, the 2003 League Cup, then a staggering 12 titles at Barcelona, including four La Liga triumphs, two Champions Leagues, and Club World Cup success in 2009. On the international scene he has claimed two pieces of silverware with Mexico – Confederations Cup 1999 and CONCACAF Gold Cup 2003.

At 17, the versatile defender made his full debut for Mexico against Ecuador, initially subject to some confusion after the youngster was mistakenly selected instead of his cousin and fellow Atlas player, Cesar Marquez. However, both Rafael and Cesar ended up appearing in the match. Having just become only the eighth player to win a century of caps for Mexico, he joined an exclusive club featuring such luminaries of the Azteca game as Claudio Suarez, Pavel Pardo and Ramon Ramirez.

INDEX

AC Milan 110, 121, 125

Adams, Tony 42

Adidas xx

Agius, Gilbert 186, 187

Aguinaga, Alex 222

Aitken, Roy 143

Allison, Malcolm 43

Alonso, Xabi 168

Ancelotti, Carlo 110

Anderson, Viv 79

Anelka, Nicolas 109

Aragonés, Luis 172

Armfield, Jimmy 36

Armstrong, Joe 19

Arsenal 100

Ayala, Roberto 214, 215, 216, 217

Baggio, Roberto 161

Bahramov, Tofiq 37

Baker, Joe 11, 22

Baldini, Franco 126, 128

Ball, Alan 39, 44

Banks, Gordon xvi, 31, 39, 42, 63, 64, 68, 69, 70, 77

Barmby, Nicky 92

Barnes, John 79

Basinas, Angelos 199

Bates, Ken 48, 49, 50

Beckenbauer 7, 27, 40, 46, 53, 55, 143, 151, 152, 153, 154

Beckham, David x, xiii, xiv, xvi, xviii, xxi, xxii, 2, 24, 25, 28, 29, 31, 42, 45, 54, 57, 73, 85, 114, 123, 137, 138
  - *100th cap 88*
  - *role at London 2012 134*
  - *debut as captain (2000) 96*
  - *debut v Moldova (1996) 85, 90*
  - *dropped (2006) 98, 101*

- *dropped from Team GB 130*
- *on move to AC Milan 111*
- *on reaching 100 caps 106*
- *ruled out of 2010 World Cup 126*

Beckham, Victoria 113, 123
Bellamy, Craig 131
Bentley, David 99, 109
Benzema, Karim 169
Berg, Henning 163
Bernstein, David 85, 133
Best, Clyde 59
Best, George 1, 2, 18, 22, 44, 87, 114, 145
Beverley, Joy 5
Blanchflower, Danny 60
Bobby Charlton's Soccer Schools 28
Bobby Moore Fund, The xiii, 54, 116, 119
Bonetti, Peter xiii, xiv, 70
Bonner, Packie 148
Bozsik, Jozsef 194, 195
Brady, Liam 44
Brehme, Andreas 149
Breitner, Paul 153
Brincat, Joe 186, 189
Brooking, Sir Trevor 57
Brown, Gordon 105
Buckley, Major Frank 8

Buffon, Gianluigi 140, 179, 180
Busby, Sir Matt 17, 43, 60
Busby Babes, The 18
Busuttil, Carmel 186, 188
Butcher, Terry 103

Cafu 122, 213, 214
Caine, Michael 48
Calderon, Ramon 111
Campbell, Bobby 44, 45
Campbell, Sol 95
Cannavaro, Fabio 121, 179, 181, 182
Cap, History of the xv
Capello, Fabio xix, 41, 73, 98, 99, 100, 101, 102, 103, 105, 106, 108, 109, 114, 118, 121, 122, 125, 126, 127, 128
Carabott, David 186, 188
Carbajal, Antonio 122
Casillas, Iker 167, 168
Chapuisat, Stéphane 190, 191
Charlton xvii, xviii, xix, xx, xxii, 2, 40, 74, 85, 108, 117
Charlton, Jack 118
Charlton, Lady Norma xiii

Charlton, Sir Bobby 17, 29, 30, 42
- *100th cap 19*

- *debut v Scotland (1958) 18-21*

- *early life 19*

- *Footballer of the Year (1966) 19*

- *England's leading goalscorer 18*

- *managerial career 27*

- *on Ramsey 23*

Chinaglia, Giorgio 41

Clemence, Ray xviii, 66, 68, 70, 71, 76, 80

Clough, Brian 40, 67, 71, 76

Cocu, Phillip 194

Cohen, George 26, 117

Cole, Ashley xi, xix, 94, 137, 139

Cole, Joe 99, 109

Compton, Denis 43

Cooke, Charlie 43

Corrigan, Joe xviii

Couto, Fernando 209, 210

Crerand, Paddy 22

Crisp, Dr Tom 127

Crouch, Peter 109

Cruyff, Johann xv, 7, 158

Dalglish, Kenny 67, 141, 143, 144

de Boer, Frank 194

Del Bosque, Vicente 169

Derby County 72

Derwall, Jupp 154

Desailly, Marcel 165

Deschamps, Didier 165

Dewis, George 63

Di Stefano, Alfredo 7, 22

Domenech, Raymond 166

Donovan, Landon 113

Dörner, Dixie 184, 185

Downing, Stewart 120

Duff, Damien 146, 147

Eastham, George 22

England

- *v Argentina (1998) 95*

- *v Brazil (1970) 39*

- *v Hungary (1953) 5*

- *v Poland (1973) 70*

- *v Spain (1965) 22*

- *v USA (1950) 7*

- *v West Germany (1990) 67*

- *v W Germany (1966) 37*

- *v W Germany (1970) 39*

Eriksson, Sven–Goran 24, 25, 96, 100, 102, 106

European Cup Final (1968) 20

Eusebio xv

FA, The xvi
Ferdinand, Rio 99, 128, 132, 137
Ferguson, Bob 58
Ferguson, Sir Alex 10, 143
Figo, Luis 183, 210, 211
Finlayson, Malcolm 12
Finney, Tom ix, 7, 21, 42
Football Writers' Player of the Year (1995) 150
Foster, Ben 81

Gale, Tony 54
Gascoigne, Paul 42, 90, 91
Gattuso, Gennaro 96, 110
Gento, Francisco 6
Gerrard, Steven xi, xix, 25, 94, 99, 137, 141
Giggs, Ryan 131, 134
Given, Shay 148
Glanville, Brian 158
Gough, Richard 143
Gray, Andy 13, 14
Greaves, Jimmy 28, 40, 42, 100
Green, Geoffrey 6
Greenwood, Ron 7, 40, 66, 71, 76

Hagi, Gheorghe 160, 161

Hansen, Alan 109
Hargreaves, Owen 99
Hart, Joe 81
Hart, Michael xx
Hassan, Ahmed 221
Hassan, Hossan 221
Herzog, Andreas 162, 197
Hidegkuti, Nandor 5
Hinchcliffe, Andy 91
Hjelm, Ari 193
Hoddle, Glenn 84, 86, 90, 92, 96, 107
Hodgson, Roy xvi, 138
Hovsepyan, Sargis 201, 202
Hungarian National Team 6
Hungary v England (1954) 7
Hunt, Andy 133
Hurst, Sir Geoff xxi, 22, 37, 57, 119
Hyypiä, Sami 197

Ince, Paul xxii, 90
Inzaghi, Pipo 112

James, David 109
Jenkins, Rob 58
Jennings, Pat 78, 143, 144, 145
John, Sir Elton 10
Jones, Cobi 222

Jordaan, Danny 125

Kaka 110
Karagounis, Giorgos 200
Karhan, Miroslav 202, 203
Keane, Robbie 146, 147
Keegan, Kevin xxiii, 42, 60, 96, 106
Kelly, Mike 31
Kidd, Brian 22
Kirsten, Ulf 185, 186
Kirton, Glen 32
Klinsmann, Jurgen 61, 149, 150
Klose, Miroslav 150, 151
Kobiashvili, Levan 174, 175, 176
Kohler, Jurgen 156
Korkmaz, Bülent 205

LA Galaxy 108, 113, 117, 120
Lampard, Frank xix, 25, 94, 99, 132, 137
Lampard senior, Frank 59
Langley, Mike 43
Lato, Grzegorz 173, 174
Laudrup, Brian 160
Laudrup, Michael 158, 159, 183
Law, Denis 18, 22, 144

Leicester City 9, 69, 72, 77
Lennon, Aaron 99
Leonardo 126
Leyton Orient 73
Lineker, Gary xii, 18, 29, 42, 83, 100, 142
Lofthouse, Nat 42
London 2012 Olympics 28
Lord, Bob 58
Lord Coe 133
Lord Triesman 60
Los Angeles Galaxy 99
Low, Joachim 151

Maier, Sepp 153
Maldini, Cesare 179
Maldini, Paolo 112, 122, 177, 179, 180
Maldini. Cesare 181
Manchester United 28, 29, 42, 54
Mandela, Nelson 125
Maradona, Diego xv, 7, 68, 72, 81, 94, 122, 218
Marquez 225
Marquez, Rafael 224
Marsh, Rodney 46
Mason, Bobby 12
Matthäus, Lothar 122, 149, 151, 155

Matthews, Sir Stanley ix, 42
Maxwell, Robert 50, 51
McCarthy, Mick 148
McCartney, Sir Paul 10
McClaren, Steve 25, 98, 101, 103, 107
McGarry, Bill 3
McLintock, Frank 11
Meola, Tony 222, 223
Messi, Lionel 60
Mihaylov, Borislav 173
Mills, Danny 139
Montgomery, Jim 78

Moore, Bobby ix, xvi, xvii, xxii, 16, 32, 43, 74, 93, 108, 110, 114, 115, 123, 137
- *100th cap 41*
- *accused of theft (1970) 39*
- *and knighthood 46*
- *death of 53*
- *managerial career 46*
- *move to Fulham 44*
- *successive Wembley victories 41*
- *WHU career 44*
- *manager of Southend 47*

Moore, Stephanie 116, 119
Mourinho, Jose 158
Mullen, James 7
Mullen, Jimmy 9

Muller, Gerd 27, 40, 153
Mullery, Alan 55
Munich Air Disaster 20
Munteanu, Dorinel 197

Neville, Gary 90, 92, 137
New York Cosmos 153
Nottingham Forest 63, 72, 75, 76
Notts County 9

Okkas, Yiannis 196
Olsen, Egil 163
Olympics Games (2012) 130
Onopko, Viktor 191, 192
Orava, Dr Sakari 127
Overath, Wolfgang 153
Owen, Michael xii, 18, 42, 83

Pallister, Gary 91
Pardo, Pavel 225
Pato, Alexandre 110
Pearce, Jonathan 56
Pearce, Stuart 91, 130, 131
Pele xv, xvii, xxi, 7, 35, 36, 39, 46, 63, 151
Peters, Martin xxi, 22, 37, 57
Platini, Michel xv, 85, 173
Poborský, Karel 207
Podolski, Lucas 149

Potts, Harry 58
Puskás, Ferenc xv, 5, 6, 7, 195

Ramirez, Ramon 225
Ramsey, Sir Alf 7, 22, 23, 24, 25, 36, 38, 43, 63, 66, 69
Raúl 172, 183
Reçber, Rütü 203
Redknapp, Harry 132
Regis, Cyrille 79
Revie, Don 66
Ribery, Franck 109
Richards, Micah 131
Riise, John Arne 164
Rivera, Gianni 122
Robson, Bryan 30, 32, 42
Robson, Sir Bobby 67, 94
Romario 158, 161
Rommedahl, Dennis 158
Ronaldinho 110, 112
Ronaldo 151
Ronaldo, Cristiano 169
Rooney, Wayne xi, xix, 83, 137, 141
Rüstu 204

Schmeichel, Peter 78, 157, 158
Scholes, Paul 25

Schön, Helmut 27
Seaman, David xxii, 79, 91
Sedloski, Goce 193
Seedorf, Clarence 111, 112
Seeler, Uwe 27, 122
Shankly, Bill 60
Shaw, Jim 145
Shearer, Alan xvi, xxii, 42, 83, 92, 132
Sheringham, Teddy 61

Shilton, Peter x, xiii, xvi, xviii, 31, 85, 103, 110, 112, 117, 138
  - *100th cap 68*
  - *debut (1970) 66*
  - *last international 72*
  - *manager of Plymouth Argyle 73*
  - *on Joe Hart 82*
  - *retired from international football (1976) 71*

Showell, George 12
Simeone, Diego 92
Simpson, Mr 9
Slater, Bill 12
Song, Rigobert 219
Song, Rogobert 220
Souness, Graeme 143
Southampton 72, 76

Southgate, Gareth 91
Stankovic, Dejan 208, 209
Stiles, Nobby 23, 24
Stoichkov, Hristo 161
Streich, Joachim 183
Suarez, Claudio 225
Sukur, Hakan 206
Svenssen, Ole Thorbjørn 162
Swinbourne, Roy 12
Swindin, George 11

Taylor, Graham 100, 109
Taylor, Peter 96
Team GB 94, 130, 131, 133
Terry, John 99, 124, 141
Thuram, Lillian 165
Torres, Fernando 169
Trapattoni, Giovanni 146
Trautmann, Bert 65, 78
Tymoshchuk, Anatoliy 193, 194

UEFA xiii
 - Century of Caps
Presentations 154
Upson, Matthew 54
Ure, Ian 11

van Basten, Marco 68
van Bronckhorst, Giovanni 194

van der Sar, Edwin 194
Venables, Terry 44
Vieira, Patrick 165

Walcott, Theo 140
Warner, Jack 110
Weber, Wolfgang 37
West Bromwich Albion 9
West Ham United 40, 42
Williams, Bert 7
Wilson, Bob 11, 63, 75
Wilson, Ray 118
Winterbottom, Sir Walter 3, 4, 21, 22, 36
Wolstenholme, Kenneth 37
Wolverhampton Wanderers xvii, 3, 9
World Cup (1958) 3, 21
World Cup (1962) 21, 22
World Cup (1966) 19, 26
World Cup (1970) 38
World Cup (1974) 70
World Cup (1982) 32, 70, 71
World Cup (1990) 72
World Cup (2010) 89, 125

Wright, Billy ix, xiii, xvi, xvii, xviii, xxiii, 1, 7, 27, 41, 60, 75
 - early career 9

Wright, Kelly 12
Wright, Vicky 12
Wright – Arsenal manager 11
Wright – captain of Wolves
10
Wright – early life 8
Wright – Footballer of the
Year (1952) 4
Wright – funeral 12
Wright – Midlands Today 8
Wright-Phillips, Shaun 99
Wright – retirement 10
Wright at ATV 11
Wright awarded C.B.E. 10

Xavi Hernández 167, 170,
171, 172

Young, Ashley 140

Zagorakis, Theodoros 198
Zamorano, Ivan 158
Zanetti, Javier 95, 218
Zelinski, Indrek 197
Zewłakow, Michal 174
Zidane, Zinédine 165, 166
Zmuda, Wladyslaw 122
Zoff, Dino 176, 177, 178,
179, 181
Zola, Gianfranco 112
Zubizarreta, Andoni 167, 168

STATISTICS:

ENGLAND'S CENTURIONS

BILLY WRIGHT

SIR BOBBY CHARLTON

BOBBY MOORE

PETER SHILTON

DAVID BECKHAM

BILLY WRIGHT - 105 CAPS, 3 GOALS

CAPS	DATE	VENUE	OPPONENT	SCORE	GOALS	COMP.
1	28/9/46	Belfast	N. IRELAND	7-2		BC
2	30/9/46	Dublin	IRELAND	1-0		
3	13/11/46	Manchester	WALES	3-0		BC
4	27/11/46	Huddersfield	NETHERLANDS	8-2		
5	12/4/47	London	SCOTLAND	1-1		BC
6	3/5/47	London	FRANCE	3-0		
7	18/5/47	Zürich	SWITZERLAND	0-1		
8	25/5/47	Lisboa	PORTUGAL	10-0		
9	21/9/47	Brussels	BELGIUM	5-2		
10	18/10/47	Cardiff	WALES	3-0		BC
11	5/11/47	Liverpool	N. IRELAND	2-2		BC
12	19/11/47	London	SWEDEN	4-2		
13	10/4/48	Glasgow	SCOTLAND	2-0		BC
14	16/5/48	Torino	ITALY	4-0		
15	26/9/48	København	DENMARK	0-0		
16	9/10/48	Belfast	N. IRELAND	6-2		BC
17	11/10/48	Birmingham	WALES	1-0		BC
18	2/12/48	London	SWITZERLAND	6-0		
19	9/4/48	London	SCOTLAND	1-3		BC
20	15/5/49	Stockholm	SWEDEN	1-3		
21	18/5/49	Oslo	NORWAY	4-1	1	
22	22/5/49	Paris	FRANCE	3-1		
23	21/9/49	Liverpool	IRELAND	0-2		
24	15/10/49	Cardiff	WALES	4-1		WCQ
25	16/11/49	Manchester	N. IRELAND	9-2		WCQ
26	30/11/49	London	ITALY	2-0	1	
27	15/4/50	Glasgow	SCOTLAND	1-0		WCQ
28	14/5/50	Lisboa	PORTUGAL	5-3		
29	18/5/50	Brussel	BELGIUM	4-1		
30	25/6/50	Rio de Janeiro	CHILE	2-0		World Cup
31	26/6/50	Belo Horizonte	UNITED STATES	0-1		World Cup
32	2/7/50	Rio de Janeiro	SPAIN	0-1		World Cup
33	7/10/50	Belfast	N. IRELAND	4-1	1	BC
34	14/4/51	London	SCOTLAND	2-3		BC
35	9/5/51	London	ARGENTINA	2-1		
36	3/10/51	London	FRANCE	2-2		
37	20/10/51	Cardiff	WALES	1-1		BC
38	14/11/51	Birmingham	N. IRELAND	2-0		BC
39	28/11/51	London	AUSTRIA	2-2		
40	5/4/52	Glasgow	SCOTLAND	2-1		BC
41	18/5/52	Firenze	ITALY	1-1		
42	25/5/52	Wien	AUSTRIA	3-2		
43	28/5/52	Zürich	SWITZERLAND	3-0		
44	4/10/52	Belfast	N. IRELAND	2-2		BC
45	12/11/52	London	WALES	5-2		BC
46	26/11/52	London	BELGIUM	5-0		

47	18/4/53	London	SCOTLAND	2-2	BC
48	17/5/53	Buenos Aires	ARGENTINA	0-0 (1)	
49	24/5/53	Santiago	CHILE	2-1	
50	31/5/53	Montevideo	URUGUAY	1-2	
51	8/6/53	New York	UNITED STATES	6-3	
52	10/10/53	Cardiff	WALES	4-1	WCQ
53	21/10/53	London	FIFA	4-4	FA 90th
54	11/11/53	Liverpool	N. IRELAND	3-1	WCQ
55	25/11/53	London	HUNGARY	3-6	
56	3/4/54	Glasgow	SCOTLAND	4-2	WCQ
57	16/5/54	Beograd	YUGOSLAVIA	0-1	
58	23/5/54	Budapest	HUNGARY	1-7	
59	17/6/54	Basel	BELGIUM	4-4	World Cup
60	20/6/54	Bern	SWITZERLAND	2-0	World Cup
61	26/6/54	Basel	URUGUAY	2-4	World Cup
62	2/10/54	Belfast	N. IRELAND	2-0	BC
63	10/11/54	London	WALES	3-2	BC
64	1/12/54	London	WEST GERMANY	3-1	
65	2/4/55	London	SCOTLAND	7-2	BC
66	15/5/55	Paris	FRANCE	0-1	
67	18/5/55	Madrid	SPAIN	1-1	
68	22/5/55	Porto	PORTUGAL	1-3	
69	2/10/55	København	DENMARK	5-1	
70	22/10/55	Cardiff	WALES	1-2	BC
71	2/11/55	London	N. IRELAND	3-0	BC
72	30/11/55	London	SPAIN	4-1	
73	14/4/56	Glasgow	SCOTLAND	1-1	BC
74	9/5/56	London	BRAZIL	4-2	
75	16/5/56	Stockholm	SWEDEN	0-0	
76	20/5/56	Helsinki	FINLAND	5-1	
77	26/5/56	West Berlin	WEST GERMANY	3-1	
78	6/10/56	Belfast	N. IRELAND	1-1	BC
79	14/11/56	London	WALES	3-1	BC
80	28/11/56	London	YUGOSLAVIA	3-0	
81	5/12/56	Wolverhampton	DENMARK	5-2	WCQ
82	6/4/57	London	SCOTLAND	2-1	BC
83	8/5/57	London	IRELAND	5-1	WCQ
84	15/5/57	København	DENMARK	4-1	WCQ
85	19/5/57	Dublin	IRELAND	1-1	WCQ
86	19/10/57	Cardiff	WALES	4-0	BC
87	6/11/57	London	N. IRELAND	2-3	BC
88	27/11/57	London	FRANCE	4-0	
89	19/4/58	Glasgow	SCOTLAND	4-0	BC
90	7/5/58	London	PORTUGAL	2-1	
91	11/5/58	Beograd	YUGOSLAVIA	0-5	
92	18/5/58	Moskva	SOVIET UNION	1-1	
93	8/6/58	Göteborg	SOVIET UNION	2-2	World Cup
94	11/6/58	Göteborg	BRAZIL	0-0	World Cup
95	15/6/58	Borås	AUSTRIA	2-2	World Cup
96	17/6/58	Göteborg	SOVIET UNION	0-1	World Cup

97	4/10/58	Belfast	N. IRELAND	3-3	BC
98	22/10/58	London	SOVIET UNION	5-0	
99	26/11/58	Birmingham	WALES	2-2	BC
100	11/4/59	London	SCOTLAND	1-0	BC
101	6/5/59	London	ITALY	2-2	
102	13/5/59	Rio de Janeiro	BRAZIL	0-2	
103	17/5/59	Lima	PERU	1-4	
104	24/5/59	Cd. de México	MEXICO	1-2	
105	28/5/59	Los Angeles	UNITED STATES	8-1	

SIR BOBBY CHARLTON - 106 CAPS, 49 GOALS

Caps	Date	Venue	Opponent	Score	Goals	Comp.
1	19/4/58	Glasgow	SCOTLAND	4-0	1	BC
2	7/5/58	London	PORTUGAL	2-1	2	
3	11/5/58	Beograd	YUGOSLAVIA	0-5		
4	4/10/58	Belfast	N. IRELAND	3-3	2	BC
5	22/10/58	London	SOVIET UNION	5-0	1	
6	11/4/58	London	SCOTLAND	1-0	1	BC
7	6/5/59	London	ITALY	2-2	1	
8	13/5/59	Rio de Janeiro	BRAZIL	0-2		
9	17/5/59	Lima	PERU	1-4		
10	24/5/59	Cd. de México	MEXICO	1-2		
11	28/5/59	Los Angeles	UNITED STATES	8-1	3	
12	17/10/59	Cardiff	WALES	1-1		BC
13	28/10/59	London	SWEDEN	2-3	1	
14	9/4/60	Glasgow	SCOTLAND	1-1	1	BC
15	11/5/60	London	YUGOSLAVIA	3-3		
16	15/5/60	Madrid	SPAIN	0-3		
17	22/5/60	Budapest	HUNGARY	0-2		
18	8/10/60	Belfast	N. IRELAND	5-2	1	BC
19	19/10/60	Luxembourg	LUXEMBOURG	9-0	3	WCQ
20	26/10/60	London	SPAIN	4-2		
21	23/11/60	London	WALES	5-1	1	BC
22	15/4/61	London	SCOTLAND	9-3		BC
23	10/5/61	London	MEXICO	8-0	3	
24	21/5/61	Lisboa	PORTUGAL	1-1		WCQ
25	24/5/61	Roma	ITALY	3-2		
26	27/5/61	Wien	AUSTRIA	1-3		
27	28/9/61	London	LUXEMBOURG	4-1	2	WCQ
28	14/10/61	Cardiff	WALES	1-1		BC
29	25/10/61	London	PORTUGAL	2-0		WCQ
30	22/11/61	London	N. IRELAND	1-1	1	BC
31	4/4/62	London	AUSTRIA	3-1		
32	14/4/62	Glasgow	SCOTLAND	0-2		BC
33	9/5/62	London	SWITZERLAND	3-1		
34	20/5/62	Lima	PERU	4-0		
35	31/5/62	Rancagua	HUNGARY	1-2		World Cup
36	2/6/62	Rancagua	ARGENTINA	3-1	1	World Cup
37	7/6/62	Rancagua	BULGARIA	0-0		World Cup
38	10/6/62	Viña del Mar	BRAZIL	1-3		World Cup
39	27/2/63	Paris	FRANCE	2-5		ECQ
40	6/4/63	London	SCOTLAND	1-2		BC
41	8/5/63	London	BRAZIL	1-1		
42	29/5/63	Bratislava	CZECHOSLOVAKIA	4-2	1	
43	2/6/63	Leipzig	EAST GERMANY	2-1	1	
44	5/6/63	Basel	SWITZERLAND	8-1	3	
45	12/10/63	Cardiff	WALES	4-0	1	BC
46	23/10/63	London	FIFA	2-1		
47	20/11/63	London	N. IRELAND	8-3		BC

48	11/4/63	Glasgow	SCOTLAND	0-1		BC
49	6/5/64	London	URUGUAY	2-1		
50	17/5/64	Lisboa	PORTUGAL	4-3	1	
51	24/5/64	Dublin	IRELAND	3-1		
52	27/5/64	New York	UNITED STATES	10-0	1	
53	30/5/64	Rio de Janeiro	BRAZIL	1-5		Nations Cup
54	6/6/64	Rio de Janeiro	ARGENTINA	0-1		Nations Cup
55	3/10/64	Belfast	N. IRELAND	4-3		BC
56	9/12/64	Amsterdam	NETHERLANDS	1-1		
57	10/4/65	London	SCOTLAND	2-2	1	BC
58	2/10/65	Cardiff	WALES	0-0		BC
59	20/10/65	London	AUSTRIA	2-3	1	
60	10/11/65	London	N. IRELAND	2-1		BC
61	8/12/65	Madrid	SPAIN	2-0		
62	23/2/66	London	WEST GERMANY	1-0		
63	2/4/66	Glasgow	SCOTLAND	4-3	1	BC
64	4/5/66	London	YUGOSLAVIA	2-0	1	
65	26/6/66	Helsinki	FINLAND	3-0		
66	29/6/66	Oslo	NORWAY	6-1		
67	5/7/66	Chorzów	POLAND	1-0		
68	11/7/66	London	URUGUAY	0-0		World Cup
69	16/7/66	London	MEXICO	2-0	1	World Cup
70	20/7/66	London	FRANCE	2-0		World Cup
71	23/7/66	London	ARGENTINA	1-0		World Cup
72	26/7/66	London	PORTUGAL	2-1	2	World Cup
73	30/7/66	London	WEST GERMANY	4-2		World Cup
74	22/10/66	Belfast	N. IRELAND	2-0		ECQ
75	2/11/66	London	CZECHOSLOVAKIA	0-0		
76	16/11/66	London	WALES	5-1	1	ECQ
77	15/4/67	London	SCOTLAND	2-3		ECQ
78	21/10/67	Cardiff	WALES	3-0	1	ECQ
79	22/11/67	London	N. IRELAND	2-0	1	ECQ
80	6/12/67	London	SOVIET UNION	2-2		
81	24/2/68	Glasgow	SCOTLAND	1-1		ECQ
82	3/4/68	London	SPAIN	1-0	1	ECQ
83	8/5/68	Madrid	SPAIN	2-1		ECQ
84	22/5/68	London	SWEDEN	3-1	1	
85	5/6/68	Firenze	YUGOSLAVIA	0-1		EC
86	8/6/68	Roma	SOVIET UNION	2-0	1	EC
87	6/11/68	Bucuresti	ROMANIA	0-0		
88	11/12/68	London	BULGARIA	1-1		
89	15/1/69	London	ROMANIA	1-1		
90	3/5/69	Belfast	N. IRELAND	3-1		BC
91	7/5/69	London	WALES	2-1	1	BC
92	10/5/69	London	SCOTLAND	4-1		BC
93	1/6/69	Cd. de México	MEXICO	0-0		
94	8/6/69	Montevideo	URUGUAY	2-1		
95	12/6/69	Rio de Janeiro	BRAZIL	1-2		
96	5/11/69	Amsterdam	NETHERLANDS	1-0		
97	10/12/69	London	PORTUGAL	1-0		
98	14/1/70	London	NETHERLANDS	0-0		

99	18/4/70	Cardiff	WALES	1-1		BC
100	21/4/70	London	N. IRELAND	3-1	1	BC
101	20/5/70	Bogotá	COLOMBIA	4-0	1	
102	24/5/70	Quito	ECUADOR	2-0		
103	2/6/70	Guadalajara	ROMANIA	1-0		World Cup
104	7/6/70	Guadalajara	BRAZIL	0-1		World Cup
105	11/6/70	Guadalajara	CZECHOSLOVAKIA	1-0		World Cup
106	14/6/70	León	WEST GERMANY	2-3		World Cup

BOBBY MOORE – 108 CAPS, 2 GOALS

CAPS	DATE	VENUE	OPPONENT	SCORE	GOALS	COMP.
1	20/5/62	Lima	PERU	4-0		
2	31/5/62	Rancagua	HUNGARY	1-2		World Cup
3	2/6/62	Rancagua	ARGENTINA	3-1		World Cup
4	7/6/62	Rancagua	BULGARIA	0-0		World Cup
5	10/6/62	Viña del Mar	BRAZIL	1-3		World Cup
6	3/10/62	Sheffield	FRANCE	1-1		ECQ
7	20/10/62	Belfast	N. IRELAND	3-1		BC
8	21/11/62	London	WALES	4-0		BC
9	27/2/63	Paris	FRANCE	2-5		ECQ
10	6/4/63	London	SCOTLAND	1-2		BC
11	8/5/63	London	BRAZIL	1-1		
12	29/5/63	Bratislava	CZECHOSLOVAKIA	4-2		
13	2/6/63	Leipzig	EAST GERMANY	2-1		
14	5/6/63	Basel	SWITZERLAND	8-1		
15	12/10/63	Cardiff	WALES	4-0		BC
16	23/10/63	London	FIFA	2-1		
17	20/11/63	London	N. IRELAND	8-3		BC
18	11/4/64	Glasgow	SCOTLAND	0-1		BC
19	6/5/64	London	URUGUAY	2-1		
20	17/5/64	Lisboa	PORTUGAL	4-3		
21	24/5/64	Dublin	IRELAND	3-1		
22	30/5/64	Rio de Janeiro	BRAZIL	1-5		Nations Cup
23	4/6/64	São Paulo	PORTUGAL	1-1		Nations Cup
24	6/6/64	Rio de Janeiro	ARGENTINA	0-1		Nations Cup
25	3/10/64	Belfast	N. IRELAND	4-3		BC
26	21/10/64	London	BELGIUM	2-2		
27	10/4/65	London	SCOTLAND	2-2		BC
28	5/5/65	London	HUNGARY	1-0		
29	9/5/65	Beograd	YUGOSLAVIA	1-1		
30	12/5/65	Nürnberg	WEST GERMANY	1-0		
31	16/5/65	Göteborg	SWEDEN	2-1		
32	2/10/65	Cardiff	WALES	0-0		BC
33	20/10/65	London	AUSTRIA	2-3		
34	10/11/65	London	N. IRELAND	2-1		BC
35	8/12/65	Madrid	SPAIN	2-0		
36	5/1/66	Liverpool	POLAND	1-1	1	
37	23/2/66	London	WEST GERMANY	1-0		
38	2/4/66	Glasgow	SCOTLAND	4-3		BC
39	29/6/66	Oslo	NORWAY	6-1	1	
40	3/7/66	København	DENMARK	2-0		
41	5/7/66	Chorzów	POLAND	1-0		
42	11/7/66	London	URUGUAY	0-0		World Cup
43	16/7/66	London	MEXICO	2-0		World Cup
44	20/7/66	London	FRANCE	2-0		World Cup
45	23/7/66	London	ARGENTINA	1-0		World Cup
46	26/7/66	London	PORTUGAL	2-1		World Cup
47	30/7/66	London	WEST GERMANY	4-2		World Cup

48	22/10/66	Belfast	N. IRELAND	2-0	ECQ
49	2/11/66	London	CZECHOSLOVAKIA	0-0	
50	16/11/66	London	WALES	5-1	ECQ
51	15/4/67	London	SCOTLAND	2-3	ECQ
52	24/5/67	London	SPAIN	2-0	
53	27/5/67	Wien	AUSTRIA	1-0	
54	21/10/67	Cardiff	WALES	3-0	ECQ
55	22/11/67	London	N. IRELAND	2-0	ECQ
56	6/12/67	London	SOVIET UNION	2-2	
57	24/2/68	Glasgow	SCOTLAND	1-1	ECQ
58	3/4/68	London	SPAIN	1-0	ECQ
59	8/5/68	Madrid	SPAIN	2 1	ECQ
60	22/5/68	London	SWEDEN	3-1	
61	1/6/68	Hannover	WEST GERMANY	0-1	
62	5/6/68	Firenze	YUGOSLAVIA	0-1	EC
63	8/6/68	Roma	SOVIET UNION	2-0	EC
64	6/11/68	Bucuresti	ROMANIA	0-0	
65	11/12/68	London	BULGARIA	1-1	
66	12/3/69	London	FRANCE	5-0	
67	3/5/69	Belfast	N. IRELAND	3-1	BC
68	7/5/69	London	WALES	2-1	BC
69	10/5/69	London	SCOTLAND	4-1	BC
70	1/6/69	Cd. de México	MEXICO	0-0	
71	8/6/69	Montevideo	URUGUAY	2-1	
72	12/6/69	Rio de Janeiro	BRAZIL	1-2	
73	5/11/69	Amsterdam	NETHERLANDS	1-0	
74	10/12/69	London	PORTUGAL	1-0	
75	25/2/70	Brussel	BELGIUM	3-1	
76	18/4/70	Cardiff	WALES	1-1	BC
77	21/4/70	London	N. IRELAND	3-1	BC
78	25/4/70	Glasgow	SCOTLAND	0-0	BC
79	20/5/70	Bogotá	COLOMBIA	4-0	
80	24/5/70	Quito	ECUADOR	2-0	
81	2/6/70	Guadalajara	ROMANIA	1-0	World Cup
82	7/6/70	Guadalajara	BRAZIL	0-1	World Cup
83	11/6/70	Guadalajara	CZECHOSLOVAKIA	1-0	World Cup
84	14/6/70	Leon	WEST GERMANY	2-3	World Cup
85	25/11/70	London	EAST GERMANY	3-1	
86	21/4/71	London	GREECE	3-0	ECQ
87	12/5/71	London	MALTA	5-0	ECQ
88	15/5/71	Belfast	N. IRELAND	1-0	BC
89	22/5/71	London	SCOTLAND	3-1	BC
90	13/10/71	Basel	SWITZERLAND	3-2	ECQ
91	10/11/71	London	SWITZERLAND	1-1	ECQ
92	1/12/71	Piraeus	GREECE	2-0	ECQ
93	29/4/72	London	WEST GERMANY	1-3	ECQ
94	13/5/72	West Berlin	WEST GERMANY	0-0	ECQ
95	20/5/72	Cardiff	WALES	3-0	BC
96	27/5/72	Glasgow	SCOTLAND	1-0	BC
97	11/10/72	London	YUGOSLAVIA	1-1	

98	15/11/72	Cardiff	WALES	1-0	WCQ
99	24/1/73	London	WALES	1-1	WCQ
100	14/2/73	Glasgow	SCOTLAND	5-0	
101	12/5/73	Liverpool	N. IRELAND	2-1	BC
102	15/5/73	London	WALES	3-0	BC
103	19/5/73	London	SCOTLAND	1-0	BC
104	27/5/73	Praha	CZECHOSLOVAKIA	1-1	
105	6/6/73	Chorzów	POLAND	0-2	WCQ
106	10/6/73	Moskva	SOVIET UNION	2-1	
107	14/6/73	Torino	ITALY	0-2	
108	14/11/73	London	ITALY	0-1	

PETER SHILTON - 125 CAPS, 0 GOALS

Caps	Date	Venue	OPPONENT	Score	Comp
1	25/11/70	London	EAST GERMANY	3-1	
2	19/5/71	London	WALES	0-0	BC
3	10/11/71	London	SWITZERLAND	1-1	ECQ
4	23/5/72	London	N. IRELAND	0-1	BC
5	11/10/72	London	YUGOSLAVIA	1-1	
6	14/2/73	Glasgow	SCOTLAND	5-0	
7	12/5/73	Liverpool	N. IRELAND	2-1	BC
8	15/5/73	London	WALES	3-0	BC
9	19/5/73	London	SCOTLAND	1-0	BC
10	27/5/73	Praha	CZECHOSLOVAKIA	1-1	
11	6/6/73	Chorzów	POLAND	0-2	WCQ
12	10/6/73	Moskva	SOVIET UNION	2-1	
13	14/6/73	Torino	ITALY	0-2	
14	26/9/73	London	AUSTRIA	7-0	
15	17/10/73	London	POLAND	1-1	WCQ
16	14/11/73	London	ITALY	0-1	
17	11/5/74	Cardiff	WALES	2-0	BC
18	15/5/74	London	N. IRELAND	1-0	BC
19	18/5/74	Glasgow	SCOTLAND	0-2	BC
20	22/5/74	London	ARGENTINA	2-2	
21	16/4/75	London	CYPRUS	5-0	ECQ
22	28/5/77	Belfast	N. IRELAND	2-1	BC
23	31/5/77	London	WALES	0-1	BC
24	13/5/78	Cardiff	WALES	3-1	BC
25	24/5/78	London	HUNGARY	4-1	
26	29/11/78	London	CZECHOSLOVAKIA	1-0	
27	10/6/79	Stockholm	SWEDEN	0-0	
28	13/6/79	Wien	AUSTRIA	3-4	
29	17/10/79	Belfast	N. IRELAND	5-1	ECQ
30	26/3/80	Barcelona	SPAIN	2-0	
31	15/6/80	Torino	ITALY	0-1	EC
32	10/9/80	London	NORWAY	4-0	WCQ
33	19/11/80	London	SWITZERLAND	2-1	WCQ
34	29/4/81	London	ROMANIA	0-0	WCQ
35	18/11/81	London	HUNGARY	1-0	WCQ
36	25/5/82	London	NETHERLANDS	2-0	
37	29/5/82	Glasgow	SCOTLAND	1-0	BC
38	16/6/82	Bilbao	FRANCE	3-1	World Cup
39	20/6/82	Bilbao	CZECHOSLOVAKIA	2-0	World Cup
40	25/6/82	Bilbao	KUWAIT	1-0	World Cup
41	29/6/82	Madrid	WEST GERMANY	0-0	World Cup
42	5/7/82	Madrid	SPAIN	0-0	World Cup
43	22/9/82	København	DENMARK	2-2	ECQ
44	13/10/82	London	WEST GERMANY	1-2	
45	17/11/82	Thessaloniki	GREECE	3-0	ECQ
46	23/2/83	London	WALES	2-1	BC
47	30/3/83	London	GREECE	0-0	ECQ
48	27/4/83	London	HUNGARY	2-0	ECQ

49	28/5/83	Belfast	N. IRELAND	0-0	BC
50	1/6/83	London	SCOTLAND	2-0	BC
51	12/6/83	Sydney	AUSTRALIA	0-0	
52	15/6/83	Brisbane	AUSTRALIA	1-0	
53	19/6/83	Melbourne	AUSTRALIA	1-1	
54	21/9/83	London	DENMARK	0-1	ECQ
55	12/10/83	Budapest	HUNGARY	3-0	ECQ
56	29/2/84	Paris	FRANCE	0-2	
57	4/4/84	London	N. IRELAND	1-0	BC
58	2/5/84	Wrexham	WALES	0-1	BC
59	26/5/84	Glasgow	SCOTLAND	1-1	BC
60	2/6/84	London	SOVIET UNION	0-2	
61	10/6/84	Rio de Janeiro	BRAZIL	2-0	
62	13/6/84	Montevideo	URUGUAY	0-2	
63	17/6/84	Santiago	CHILE	0-0	
64	12/9/84	London	EAST GERMANY	1-0	
65	17/10/84	London	FINLAND	5-0	WCQ
66	14/11/84	Istanbul	TURKEY	8-0	WCQ
67	27/2/85	Belfast	N. IRELAND	1-0	WCQ
68	1/5/85	Bucuresti	ROMANIA	0-0	WCQ
69	22/5/85	Helsinki	FINLAND	1-1	WCQ
70	25/5/85	Glasgow	SCOTLAND	0-1	
71	6/6/85	Cd. de México	ITALY	1-2	City Tournament
72	12/6/85	Cd. de México	WEST GERMANY	3-0	City Tournament
73	11/9/85	London	ROMANIA	1-1	WCQ
74	16/10/85	London	TURKEY	5-0	WCQ
75	13/11/85	London	N. IRELAND	0-0	WCQ
76	29/1/86	Cairo	EGYPT	4-0	
77	26/2/86	Tel Aviv	ISRAEL	2-1	
78	26/3/86	Tbilisi	SOVIET UNION	1-0	
79	23/4/86	London	SCOTLAND	2-1	
80	17/5/86	Los Angeles	MEXICO	3-0	
81	24/5/86	Burnaby	CANADA	1-0	
82	3/6/86	Monterrey	PORTUGAL	0-1	World Cup
83	6/6/86	Monterrey	MOROCCO	0-0	World Cup
84	11/6/86	Monterrey	POLAND	3-0	World Cup
85	18/6/86	Cd. de México	PARAGUAY	3-0	World Cup
86	22/6/86	Cd. de México	ARGENTINA	1-2	World Cup
87	10/9/86	Stockholm	SWEDEN	0-1	
88	15/10/86	London	N. IRELAND	3-0	ECQ
89	18/2/87	Madrid	SPAIN	4-2	
90	1/4/87	Belfast	N. IRELAND	2-0	ECQ
91	19/5/87	London	BRAZIL	1-1	Rous Cup
92	9/9/87	Düsseldorf	WEST GERMANY	1-3	
93	14/10/87	London	TURKEY	8-0	ECQ
94	11/11/87	Beograd	YUGOSLAVIA	4-1	ECQ
95	23/3/88	London	NETHERLANDS	2-2	
96	21/5/88	London	SCOTLAND	1-0	Rous Cup
97	24/5/88	London	COLOMBIA	1-1	Rous Cup
98	28/5/88	Lausanne	SWITZERLAND	1-0	
99	12/6/88	Stuttgart	IRELAND	0-1	EC

100	15/6/88	Düsseldorf	NETHERLANDS	1-3	EC
101	14/9/88	London	DENMARK	1-0	
102	19/10/88	London	SWEDEN	0-0	WCQ
103	8/2/89	Athinai	GREECE	2-1	
104	8/3/89	Tiranë	ALBANIA	2-0	WCQ
105	26/4/89	London	ALBANIA	5-0	WCQ
106	23/5/89	London	CHILE	0-0	Rous Cup
107	27/5/89	Glasgow	SCOTLAND	2-0	Rous Cup
108	3/6/89	London	POLAND	3-0	WCQ
109	7/6/89	København	DENMARK	1-1	
110	6/9/89	Stockholm	SWEDEN	0-0	WCQ
111	11/10/89	Chorzów	POLAND	0-0	WCQ
112	15/11/89	London	ITALY	0-0	
113	23/12/89	London	YUGOSLAVIA	2-1	
114	28/ 3/90	London	BRAZIL	1-0	
115	25/ 4/90	London	CZECHOSLOVAKIA	4-2	
116	15/ 5/90	London	DENMARK	1-0	
117	22/ 5/90	London	URUGUAY	1-2	
118	2/6/90	Tunis	TUNISIA	1-1	
119	11/ 6/90	Cagliari	IRELAND	1-1	World Cup
120	16/ 6/90	Cagliari	NETHERLANDS	0-0	World Cup
121	21/ 6/90	Cagliari	EGYPT	1-0	World Cup
122	26/ 6/90	Bologna	BELGIUM	1-0	World Cup
123	1/7/90	Napoli	CAMEROON	3-2	World Cup
124	4/7/90	Torino	WEST GERMANY	1-1	World Cup
125	7/7/90	Bari	ITALY	1-2	

DAVID BECKHAM - 115 CAPS, 17 GOALS

CAPS	DATE	VENUE	OPPONENT	SCORE	GLS	COMP.
1	1- 9-96	Chisinau	MOLDOVA	3-0		WCQ
2	9-10-96	London	POLAND	2-1		WCQ
3	9-11-96	Tbilisi	GEORGIA	2-0		WCQ
4	12- 2-97	London	ITALY	0-1		WCQ
5	30- 4-97	London	GEORGIA	2-0		WCQ
6	24- 5-97	Manchester	SOUTH AFRICA	2-1		
7	31- 5-97	Chorzów	POLAND	2-0		WCQ
8	4- 6-97	Nantes	ITALY	2-0		Le Tournoi
9	7- 6-97	Montpellier	FRANCE	1-0		Le Tournoi
10	10- 9-97	London	MOLDOVA	4-0		WCQ
11	11-10-97	Roma	ITALY	0-0		WCQ
12	15-11-97	London	CAMEROON	2-0		
13	22- 4-98	London	PORTUGAL	3-0		
14	23- 5-98	London	SAUDI ARABIA	0-0		
15	29- 5-98	Casablanca	BELGIUM	0-0		Int. Tourn.
16	22- 6-98	Toulouse	ROMANIA	1-2		World Cup
17	26- 6-98	Lens	COLOMBIA	2-0	1	World Cup
18	30- 6-98	Saint-Etienne	ARGENTINA	2-2		World Cup
19	14-10-98	Luxembourg	LUXEMBOURG	3-0		ECQ
20	19-11-98	London	CZECH REPUBLIC	2-0		
21	10- 2-99	London	FRANCE	0-2		
22	27- 3-99	London	POLAND	3-1		ECQ
23	5- 6-99	London	SWEDEN	0-0		ECQ
24	4- 9-99	London	LUXEMBOURG	6-0		ECQ
25	8- 9-99	Warszawa	POLAND	0-0		ECQ
26	13-11-99	Glasgow	SCOTLAND	2-0		ECQ
27	17-11-99	London	SCOTLAND	0-1		ECQ
28	23- 2-00	London	ARGENTINA	0-0		
29	27- 5-00	London	BRAZIL	1-1		
30	31- 5-00	London	UKRAINE	2-0		
31	3- 6-00	La Valletta	MALTA	2-1		
32	12- 6-00	Eindhoven	PORTUGAL	2-3		EURO
33	17- 6-00	Charleroi	GERMANY	1-0		EURO
34	20- 6-00	Charleroi	ROMANIA	2-3		EURO
35	2- 9-00	Saint-Denis	FRANCE	1-1		
36	7-10-00	London	GERMANY	0-1		WCQ
37	15-11-00	Torino	ITALY	0-1		
38	28- 2-01	Birmingham	SPAIN	3-0		
39	24- 3-01	Liverpool	FINLAND	2-1	1	WCQ
40	28- 3-01	Tirana	ALBANIA	3-1		WCQ
41	25- 5-01	Derby	MEXICO	4-0	1	
42	6- 6-01	Athinai	GREECE	2-0	1	WCQ
43	15- 8-01	London	NETHERLANDS	0-2		
44	1- 9-01	München	GERMANY	5-1		WCQ
45	5- 9-01	Newcastle	ALBANIA	2-0		WCQ
46	6-10-01	Manchester	GREECE	2-2	1	WCQ
47	10-11-01	Manchester	SWEDEN	1-1	1	

48	13- 2-02	Amsterdam	NETHERLANDS	1-1		
49	27- 3-02	Leeds	ITALY	1-2		
50	2- 6-02	Saitama	SWEDEN	1-1		World Cup
51	7- 6-02	Sapporo	ARGENTINA	1-0	1	World Cup
52	12- 6-02	Osaka	NIGERIA	0-0		World Cup
53	15- 6-02	Niigata	DENMARK	3-0		World Cup
54	21- 6-02	Shizuoka	BRAZIL	1-2		World Cup
55	12-10-02	Bratislava	SLOVAKIA	2-1	1	ECQ
56	16-10-02	Southampton	MACEDONIA	2-2	1	ECQ
57	12- 2-03	London	AUSTRALIA	1-3		
58	29- 3-03	Vaduz	LIECHTENSTEIN	2-0	1	ECQ
59	2- 4-03	Sunderland	TURKEY	2-0	1	ECQ
60	22- 5-03	Durban	SOUTH AFRICA	2-1		
61	20- 8-03	Ipswich	CROATIA	3-1	1	
62	6- 9-03	Skopje	MACEDONIA	2-1	1	ECQ
63	10- 9-03	Manchester	LIECHTENSTEIN	2-0		ECQ
64	11-10-03	Istanbul	TURKEY	0-0		ECQ
65	16-11-03	Manchester	DENMARK	2-3		
66	18- 2-04	Loulé	PORTUGAL	1-1		
67	1- 6-04	Manchester	JAPAN	1-1		Inter. Tourn.
68	5- 6-04	Manchester	ICELAND	6-1		Inter. Tourn.
69	13- 6-04	Lisboa	FRANCE	1-2		EURO
70	17- 6-04	Coimbra	SWITZERLAND	3-0		EURO
71	21- 6-04	Lisboa	CROATIA	4-2		EURO
72	24- 6-04	Lisboa	PORTUGAL	2-2		EURO
73	18- 8-04	Newcastle	UKRAINE	3-0	1	
74	4- 9-04	Wien	AUSTRIA	2-2		WCQ
75	8- 9-04	Chorzów	POLAND	2-1		WCQ
76	9-10-04	Manchester	WALES	2-0	1	WCQ
77	17-11-04	Madrid	SPAIN	0-1		
78	9- 2-05	Birmingham	NETHERLANDS	0-0		
79	26- 3-05	Manchester	N. IRELAND	4-0		WCQ
80	30- 3-05	Newcastle	AZERBAIJAN	2-0	1	WCQ
81	31- 5-05	East Rutherford	COLOMBIA	3-2		
82	17- 8-05	København	DENMARK	1-4		
83	3- 9-05	Cardiff	WALES	1-0		WCQ
84	7- 9-05	Belfast	N. IRELAND	0-1		WCQ
85	8-10-05	Manchester	AUSTRIA	1-0		WCQ
86	12-11-05	Genève	ARGENTINA	3-2		
87	1- 3-06	Liverpool	URUGUAY	2-1		
88	30- 5-06	Manchester	HUNGARY	3-1		
89	3- 6-06	Manchester	JAMAICA	6-0		
90	10- 6-06	Frankfurt	PARAGUAY	1-0		World Cup
91	15- 6-06	Nürnberg	TRIN & TOB.	2-0		World Cup
92	20- 6-06	Koln	SWEDEN	2-2		World Cup
93	25- 6-06	Stuttgart	ECUADOR	1-0	1	World Cup
94	1- 7-06	Gelsenkirchen	PORTUGAL	0-0		World Cup
95	1- 6-07	London	BRAZIL	1-1		
96	6- 6-07	Tallinn	ESTONIA	3-0		ECQ
97	22- 8-07	London	GERMANY	1-2		

98	16–11–07	Wien	AUSTRIA	1–0	
99	21–11–07	London	CROATIA	2–3	ECQ
100	26– 3–08	Saint-Denis	FRANCE	0–1	
101	28– 5–08	London	UNITED STATES	2–0	
102	1– 6–08	Port of Spain	TRIN & TOB.	3–0	
103	20– 8–08	London	CZECH REPUBLIC	2–2	
104	6– 9–08	Barcelona	ANDORRA	2–0	WCQ
105	10– 9–08	Zagreb	CROATIA	4–1	WCQ
106	11–10–08	London	KAZAKHSTAN	5–1	WCQ
107	15–10–08	Minsk	BELARUS	3–1	WCQ
108	11– 2–09	Sevilla	SPAIN	0–2	
109	28– 3–09	London	SLOVAKIA	4–0	
110	1– 4–09	London	UKRAINE	2–1	WCQ
111	6– 6–09	Almaty	KAZAKHSTAN	4–0	WCQ
112	10– 6–09	London	ANDORRA	6–0	WCQ
113	12– 8–09	Amsterdam	NETHERLANDS	2–2	
114	9– 9–09	London	CROATIA	5–1	
115	14–10–09	London	BELARUS	3–0	

STATISTICS:

THE 100 CLUB

EVERY PLAYER TO HAVE REACHED 100 CAPS
AS OF JULY 31ST 2012

	NAME	NATION	CAPS	FIRST	LAST	DURATION
1	Ahmed Hassan	Egypt	184	29 December 1995	1 June 2012	16 years, 155days
2	Mohamed Al-Deayea	Saudi Arabia	178	24 September 1993	11 May 2006	12 years, 229 days
3	Claudio Suárez	Mexico	178*	25 July 1992	1 June 2006	13 years, 311 days
=	Hossam Hassan	Egypt	169	10 September 1985	23 June 2006	20 years, 150 days
5	Iván Hurtado	Ecuador	167	24 May 1992	16 May 2010	17 years, 357 days
=	Vitālijs Astafjevs	Latvia	167	26 August 1992	17 November 2010	18 years, 83 days
7	Adnan Al-Talyani	UAE	164	27 March 1983	17 December 1997	13 years, 282 days
=	Cobi Jones	USA	164	3 September 1992	9 October 2004	12 years, 36 days
9	Sami Al-Jaber	Saudi Arabia	163	15 October 1992	7 February 2006	13 years, 251 days
10	Martin Reim	Estonia	157	3 June 1992	6 June 2009	17 years, 3 days
11	Lothar Matthäus	FRG/Germany	150	14 June 1980	20 June 2000	20 years, 6 days
12	Ali Daei	Iran	149	6 June 1993	21 June 2006	13 years, 15 days
13	Pável Pardo	Mexico	148*	31 August 1996	11 April 2009	12 years, 223 days
14	Tawan Sripan	Thailand	145	11 October 1992	14 November 2008	16 years, 34 days
=	Javier Zanetti	Argentina	145	16 November 1994	16 July 2011	16 years, 242 days
16	Marko Kristal	Estonia	143	3 June 1992	20 April 2005	12 years, 321 days
=	Thomas Ravelli	Sweden	143	15 February 1981	11 October 1997	16 years, 238 days
=	Landon Donovan	United States	143*	25 October 2000	12 June 2012	11 years, 231 days
19	Moh. Al-Khilaiwi	Saudi Arabia	142	24 September 1990	5 October 2001	11 years, 11 days
=	Cafu	Brazil	142	12 September 1990	1 July 2006	15 years, 292 days
=	Lilian Thuram	France	142	17 August 1994	13 June 2008	13 years, 301 days
22	Majed Abdullah	Saudi Arabia	139	4 May 1978	29 June 1994	16 years, 56 days
23	Rigobert Song	Cameroon	138	22 September 1993	24 June 2010	16 years, 275 days
24	Amado Guevara	Honduras	137	5 May 1994	21 June 2010	16 years, 47 days
=	Jari Litmanen	Finland	137	22 October 1989	17 November 2010	21 years, 26 days
=	Walter Centeno	Costa Rica	137	27 September 1995	18 November 2009	14 years, 52 days
27	Fabio Cannavaro	Italy	136	22 January 1997	24 June 2010	13 years, 153 days
=	Hong Myung-Bo	South Korea	136	4 February 1990	20 November 2002	12 years, 289 days

29	Gerardo Torrado	Mexico	135	9 June 1999	25 June 2011	12 years, 16 days
=	Iker Casillas	Spain	135	3 June 2000	23 June 2012	12 years, 20 days
30	Bashar Abdullah	Kuwait	134	16 March 1996	12 June 2007	11 years, 88 days
=	Jeff Agcos	United States	134	10 January 1988	26 May 2003	15 years, 136 days
=	Dorinel Munteanu	Romania	134	23 May 1991	12 September 2007	16 years, 112 days
=	Essam El-Hadary	Egypt	134	1 September 1996	15 June 2012	15 years, 283 days
35	Lee Woon-Jae	South Korea	132	5 March 1994	11 August 2010	16 years, 159 days
36	Kiatisuk Senamuang	Thailand	130	8 April 1993	3 October 2007	14 years, 178 days
=	Edwin van der Sar	Netherlands	130	7 June 1995	15 October 2008	13 years, 130 days
=	Luis Marín	Costa Rica	130	23 June 1993	21 November 2007	14 years, 151 days
=	Anders Svensson	Sweden	130	12 November 1999	19 June 2012	12 years, 220 days
40	Piyapong Pue-on	Thailand	129	20 June 1981	12 September 1997	16 years, 84 days
=	Peter Schmeichel	Denmark	129	10 May 1988	25 April 2001	12 years, 350 days
=	Jorge Campos	Mexico	129★	20 November 1991	19 November 2003	11 years, 364 days
43	Marcelo Balboa	United States	128	10 January 1988	16 January 2000	12 years, 6 days
=	Roberto Palacios	Peru	128	25 November 1992	14 October 2009	16 years, 323 days
=	Sargis Hovsepyan	Armenia	128	14 October 1992	31 May 2012	19 years, 230 days
=	Javad Nekounam	Iran	128	24 May 2000	27 May 2012	12 years, 3 days
47	Luís Figo	Portugal	127	12 October 1991	8 July 2006	14 years, 269 days
=	Lee Young-Pyo	South Korea	127	12 June 1999	25 January 2011	11 years, 227 days
49	Hussein Saeed	Iraq	126	17 July 1977	3 March 1990	12 years, 229 days
=	Paolo Maldini	Italy	126	31 March 1988	18 June 2002	14 years, 79 days
=	Andoni Zubizarreta	Spain	126	23 January 1985	24 June 1998	13 years, 152 days
52	Gheorghe Hagi	Romania	125	10 August 1983	24 June 2000	16 years, 319 days
=	Ibrahim Hassan	Egypt	125	14 March 1989	6 January 2002	12 years, 298 days
=	Roberto Carlos	Brazil	125	26 February 1992	1 July 2006	14 years, 125 days
=	Peter Shilton	England	125	25 November 1970	7 July 1990	19 years, 224 days
=	Shay Given	Ireland	125	27 June 1996	18 June 2012	15 years, 357 days
57	Hany Ramzy	Egypt	124	16 November 1988	12 February 2003	14 years, 88 days

	Name	Country	Caps			
=	Dusit Chalermsan	Thailand	124	27 June 1996	28 June 2004	8 years, 1 day
=	Andres Oper	Estonia	124	19 May 1995	5 June 2012	17 years, 17 days
60	Thierry Henry	France	123	11 October 1997	1 April 2009	11 years, 172 days
=	Ali Karimi	Iran	123	13 October 1998	13 March 2010	11 years, 151 days
62	Yoo Sang-Chul	South Korea	122	5 March 1994	3 June 2005	11 years, 90 days
=	Masami Ihara	Japan	122	27 January 1988	5 July 1999	11 years, 159 days
=	Abdullah Zubromawi	Saudi Arabia	122	17 September 1993	11 June 2002	8 years, 267 days
=	David Carabott	Malta	122	15 November 1987	9 February 2005	17 years, 86 days
66	Cha Bum-Kun	South Korea	121	7 May 1972	10 June 1986	14 years, 34 days
=	Aide Iskandar	Singapore	121	21 February 1995	12 September 2007	12 years, 203 days
=	Ramón Ramírez	Mexico	121	4 December 1991	15 November 2000	8 years, 347 days
69	Ian Goodison	Jamaica	120★	3 March 1996	23 May 2009	12 years, 330 days
=	Rüştü Reçber	Turkey	120	12 October 1994	25 June 2008	13 years, 257 days
=	Theodoros Zagorakis	Greece	120	7 September 1994	22 August 2007	12 years, 349 days
=	Mart Poom	Estonia	120	3 June 1992	10 June 2009	17 years, 7 day
=	Giorgos Karagounis	Greece	120	20 August 1999	16 June 2012	12 years, 301 days
=	Robbie Keane	Ireland	120	20 March 1998	18 June 2012	14 years, 90 days
=	Miroslav Klose	Germany	120	24 March 2001	22 June 2012	11 years, 85 days
76	Pat Jennings	N. Ireland	119	15 April 1964	12 June 1986	22 years, 58 days
=	Gilbert Agius	Malta	119	7 November 1993	18 November 2009	16 years, 11 days
=	Anatoliy Tymoshchuk	Ukraine	119	26 April 2000	19 June 2012	12 years, 54 days
79	Karel Poborský	Czech Rep.	118	23 February 1994	22 June 2006	12 years, 119 days
=	Geremi	Cameroon	118	6 October 1996	14 October 2010	14 years, 109 days
=	Yasuhito Endō	Japan	118	20 November 2002	29 February 2012	8 years, 325 days
=	Dennis Rommedahl	Denmark	118	16 August 2000	13 June 2012	11 years, 302 days
83	Heinz Hermann	Switzerland	117	6 September 1978	13 November 1991	13 years, 68 days
=	Andrejs Rubins	Latvia	117	10 November 1998	11 October 2011	12 years, 335 days
=	Angus Eve	Trin. & Tob	117	12 April 1994	12 July 2005	11 years, 91 days
=	Gianluigi Buffon	Italy	117	29 October 1997	18 June 2012	14 years, 235 days

	Name	Country		Caps		Age
=	Olof Mellberg	Sweden	23 February 2000	117	19 June 2012	12 years, 117 days
88	Abdulrahim Jumaa	UAE	25 November 1998	116	1 April 2009	10 years, 127 days
=	Marcel Desailly	France	22 August 1993	116	17 June 2004	10 years, 300 days
=	Yoshikatsu Kawaguchi	Japan	13 February 1997	116	19 November 2008	11 years, 280 days
=	Roland Nilsson	Sweden	1 May 1986	116	11 October 2000	14 years, 163 days
92	Roberto Ayala	Argentina	16 November 1994	115	15 July 2007	12 years, 241 days
=	David Beckham	England	1 September 1996	115	14 September 2009	13 years, 13 days
=	Hao Haidong	China PR	22 August 1992	115	17 November 2004	12 years, 87 day
=	Noureddine Naybet	Morocco	9 August 1990	115	28 January 2006	15 years, 172 days
=	Gheorghe Popescu	Romania	20 September 1988	115	29 March 2003	14 years, 190 days
=	S. Subramani	Singapore	27 June 1996	115	4 February 2007	10 years, 222 days
=	Björn Nordqvist	Sweden	4 May 1963	115	4 October 1978	15 years, 153 days
99	Stern John	Trin. & Tob	15 February 1995	114	6 September 2011	16 years, 203 days
=	Kristen Viikmäe	Estonia	26 January 1997	114	30 December 2009	12 years, 338 days
=	Li Weifeng	China PR	22 November 1998	114	22 June 2008	9 years, 213 days
102	Carmel Busuttil	Malta	5 June 1982	113★	25 April 2001	18 years, 324 days
=	Bashar Bani Yaseen	Jordan	16 August 1999	113	3 June 2012	12 years, 292 days
=	Xavi	Spain	15 November 2000	113	23 June 2012	11 years, 221 days
=	Viktor Onopko[1]	CIS/Russia	29 April 1992	113	18 August 2004	12 years, 111 days
105	Zuhair Bakhit	UAE	23 January 1988	112	16 December 2002	14 years, 327 days
=	Frank de Boer	Netherlands	26 September 1990	112	26 June 2004	13 years, 274 days
=	Alain Geiger	Switzerland	19 November 1980	112	8 June 1996	15 years, 202 day
=	Hakan Şükür	Turkey	25 March 1992	112	17 October 2007	15 years, 206 days
=	Jon Dahl Tomasson	Denmark	29 March 1997	112	24 June 2010	13 years, 362 days
=	Dino Zoff	Italy	20 April 1968	112	29 May 1983	15 years, 39 days
112	Abdulsalaam Jumaa	UAE	19 March 1997	111	6 January 2010	12 years, 283 days
=	Claudio Reyna	United States	15 January 1994	111★	22 June 2006	12 years, 158 days
=	Carlos Valderrama	Colombia	27 October 1985	111	26 June 1998	12 years, 242 days
=	Mehdi Mahdavikia	Iran	5 December 1996	111	17 June 2009	12 years, 194 days

	Name	Country	Caps			
=	José Manuel Rey	Venezuela	111	8 June 1997	6 September 2011	14 years, 90 days
=	Rafael Márquez	Mexico	111	5 February 1997	4 September 2011	14 years, 211 days
=	Andriy Shevchenko	Ukraine	111	25 March 1995	19 June 2012	17 years, 86 days
119	Nohair Al-Shammari	Kuwait	110	27 June 1996	14 January 2009	12 years, 201 days
=	Paul Caligiuri	United States	110	9 October 1984	16 November 1997	13 years, 38 days
=	Nader El-Sayed	Egypt	110	8 September 1992	19 June 2005	12 years, 284 days
=	Fernando Couto	Portugal	110	19 December 1990	8 June 2005	14 years, 171 days
=	Carlos Gamarra	Paraguay	110	3 March 1993	7 October 2006	13 years, 218 days
=	Yuji Nakazawa	Japan	110	8 September 1999	4 September 2010	14 years, 69 days
=	Rolando Fonseca	Costa Rica	110★	27 May 1992	14 June 2008	16 years, 18 days
=	Kevin Kilbane	Rep. of Ireland	110	6 September 1997	12 October 2010	13 years, 36 days
=	Mauricio Solís	Costa Rica	110	23 September 1993	20 June 2006	12 years, 270 days
128	Álex Aguinaga	Ecuador	109	5 March 1987	13 July 2004	17 years, 130 days
=	Sulaiman Al-Habashi	Kuwait	109	1 January 1986	18 December 1996	10 years, 352 days
=	Niclas Alexandersson	Sweden	109	10 November 1993	10 June 2008	14 years, 213 days
=	Abdel-Zaher El-Saqua	Egypt	109	1 September 1997	28 January 2010	12 years, 149 days
=	Samuel Eto'o	Cameroon	109	9 March 1997	7 October 2011	14 years, 212 days
=	Alberto García Aspe	Mexico	109	26 April 1988	17 June 2002	14 years, 52 days
=	Raio Piiroja	Estonia	109	21 November 1998	29 February 2012	13 years, 100 days
=	Hatem Aqel	Jordan	109	16 August 1999	18 May 2012	12 years, 276 days
=	Amer Deeb	Jordan	109	30 August 2002	3 June 2012	9 years, 278 days
=	Fan Zhiyi	China PR	109	22 August 1992	4 June 2002	9 years, 286 days
138	Jürgen Klinsmann	FRG/Germany	108	12 December 1987	4 July 1998	10 years, 204 days
=	Juris Laizāns	Latvia	108	14 October 1999	12 October 2010	10 years, 363 days
=	Jamal Mubarak	Kuwait	108	13 November 1994	10 January 2004	9 years, 58 days
=	Ioannis Okkas	Cyprus	108	16 July 1997	11 October 2011	14 years, 106 days
=	Hussein Sulaimani	Saudi Arabia	108	22 September 1996	12 December 2009	13 years, 173 days
=	Zinedine Zidane	France	108	17 August 1994	9 July 2006	11 years, 326 days
=	Thomas Helveg	Denmark	108★	20 April 1994	17 October 2007	13 years, 180 days

	Name	Country	Caps	First	Last	Span
=	Bobby Moore	England	108	20 May 1962	14 November 1973	11 years, 178 days
=	László Bölöni	Romania	108	24 September 1975	1 June 1988	12 years, 251 days
147	Baichung Bhutia	India	107	10 March 1995	18 January 2011	15 years, 314 days
=	Miroslav Karhan	Slovakia	107	6 September 1995	6 September 2011	16 years, 0 days
=	Aaron Mokoena	South Africa	107	20 February 1999	10 October 2010	11 years, 232 days
=	Patrick Vieira	France	107	26 February 1997	2 June 2009	12 years, 96 days
=	Nashat Akram	Iraq	107	5 October 2001	29 February 2012	10 years, 147 days
=	Eric Wynalda	United States	107	2 February 1990	19 February 2000	10 years, 17 days
153	Imants Bleidelis	Latvia	106	19 May 1995	21 November 2007	12 years, 186 days
=	Mulla Mohammed	Iraq	106	5 October 2001	29 February 2012	10 years, 147 days
=	Diego Pablo Simeone	Argentina	106	14 July 1988	7 June 2002	13 years, 328 days
=	van Bronckhorst	Netherlands	106	31 August 1996	6 July 2010	13 years, 309 days
=	Wael Gomaa	Egypt	106	26 April 2001	5 June 2011	10 years, 40 days
=	Bobby Charlton	England	106	19 April 1958	14 June 1970	12 years, 56 days
=	Henrik Larsson	Sweden	106	13 October 1993	6 June 2009	15 years, 236 days
=	Stiliyan Petrov	Bulgaria	106	13 December 1998	11 October 2011	12 years, 302 days
=	Édison Méndez	Ecuador	106	8 March 2000	10 June 2012	12 years, 94 days
=	Carlos Bocanegra	United States	106	9 December 2001	12 June 2012	10 years, 186 days
=	Juan Arango	Venezuela	106	15 April 1999	9 June 2012	13 years, 55 days
164	Héctor Chumpitaz	Peru	105	3 April 1965	6 September 1981	16 years, 156 days
=	Vithoon Kijmongkolsak	Thailand	105	23 March 1985	16 December 1995	10 years, 268 days
=	Sami Hyypiä	Finland	105	7 December 1992	12 October 2010	17 years, 339 days
=	Jonatan Johansson	Finland	105	16 March 1996	7 September 2010	14 years, 175 days
=	Jürgen Kohler	FRG/Germany	105	24 September 1986	4 July 1998	11 years, 283 days
=	Lúcio	Brazil	105	15 November 2000	5 September 2011	10 years, 294 days
=	Muhsin Musabah	UAE	105	17 March 1988	27 August 1999	11 years, 163 days
=	Mario Frick	Liechtenstein	105	26 October 1993	8 October 2011	17 years, 347 days
=	Kim Tae-Young	South Korea	105	21 October 1992	19 July 2004	11 years, 272 day
=	Billy Wright	England	105	28 September 1946	28 May 1959	12 years, 242 days

	Name	Country	Caps	First cap	Last cap	Span
=	Mihails Zemļinskis	Latvia	105	8 April 1992	8 September 2005	13 years, 153 days
=	Theodore Whitmore	Jamaica	105	7 November 1993	17 November 2004	11 years, 10 days
176	Michael Laudrup	Denmark	104	15 June 1982	3 July 1998	16 years, 18 days
=	Franz Beckenbauer	West Germany	103	26 September 1965	23 February 1977	11 years, 150 days
=	Joe Brincat	Malta	103★	14 October 1987	14 February 2004	16 years, 123 days
=	Stéphane Chapuisat	Switzerland	103	21 June 1989	17 June 2004	14 years, 362 days
=	Didier Deschamps	France	103	29 April 1989	2 September 2000	11 years, 126 days
=	Andreas Herzog	Austria	103	6 April 1988	30 April 2003	15 years, 24 days
=	Hwang Sun-Hong	South Korea	103	6 December 1988	20 November 2002	13 years, 349 days
=	Indrek Zelinski	Estonia	103	7 May 1994	21 May 2010	16 years, 14 days
=	Emad Mohammed	Iraq	103	12 November 2000	15 November 2011	11 years, 3 days
=	Daniel Bennett	Singapore	103	11 December 2002	11 November 2011	9 years, 336 days
=	John Arne Riise	Norway	103	31 January 2000	12 November 2011	11 years, 285 days
187	Kenny Dalglish	Scotland	102	10 November 1971	12 November 1986	15 years, 2 days
=	Borislav Mikhailov	Bulgaria	102	May 4, 1983	5 July 1998	15 years, 62 days
=	Martin Jørgensen	Denmark	102	25 March 1998	14 November 2011	13 years, 234 days
=	Bülent Korkmaz	Turkey	102	17 October 1990	17 August 2005	14 years, 304 days
=	Savo Milošević	Serbia/Yugo.	102	23 December 1994	19 November 2008	13 years, 332 days
=	Mohamed Omar	UAE	102	14 August 1996	28 January 2009	12 years, 167 days
=	Guillermo Ramírez	Guatemala	102	16 April 1997	28 March 2011	13 years, 346 days
=	Raúl	Spain	102	9 October 1996	6 September 2006	9 years, 332 days
=	Niweat Siriwong	Thailand	102	26 July 1998	29 February 2012	13 years, 218 days
=	Dejan Stanković	Serbia/Yugo.	102	9 April 1998	11 October 2010	12 years, 185 days
=	Steve Staunton	Rep. of Ireland	102	19 October 1988	16 June 2002	13 years, 240 days
=	Michał Żewłakow	Poland	102	19 June 1999	29 March 2011	11 years, 283 days
199	Leonel Álvarez	Colombia	101	14 February 1985	7 September 1997	12 years, 205 days
=	Oleg Blokhin	Soviet Union	101	16 July 1972	21 September 1988	16 years, 67 days
=	Phillip Cocu	Netherlands	101	24 April 1995	25 June 2006	11 years, 62 days
=	Thomas Häßler	FRG/Germany	101	31 August 1988	20 June 2000	11 years, 294 days

	Name	Country	Caps	First cap	Last cap	Span
=	Kasey Keller	United States	101	4 February 1990	2 July 2007	17 years, 148 days
=	Carlos Pavón	Honduras	101	17 July 1993	16 June 2010	16 years, 334 days
=	Jorge Soto	Peru	101	24 November 1992	12 October 2005	12 years, 322 days
=	Thorbjørn Svenssen	Norway	101*	11 June 1947	16 May 1962	14 years, 339 days
=	Claudio Taffarel	Brazil	101	20 September 1988	12 July 1998	9 years, 295 days
=	Thomas Sørensen	Denmark	101	18 November 1999	29 February 2012	12 years, 103 days
209	Angelos Basinas	Greece	100	18 August 1999	1 April 2009	9 years, 26 days
=	Henning Berg	Norway	100	13 May 1992	27 May 2004	12 years, 14 days
=	Denis Caniza	Paraguay	100	10 November 1996	7 September 2010	13 years, 301 days
=	Luis Capurro	Ecuador	100	6 February 1985	9 February 2003	18 years, 3 days
=	Park Ji-Sung	South Korea	100	5 April 2000	25 January 2011	10 years, 295 days
=	Ulf Kirsten[2]	DDR/Germany	100	8 May 1985	20 June 2000	15 years, 43 days
=	Levan Kobiashvili	Georgia	100	1 September 1996	11 October 2011	15 years, 40 days
=	Rúnar Kristinsson	Iceland	100	28 October 1987	18 August 2004	16 years, 295 days
=	Tony Meola	United States	100	10 June 1988	11 April 2006	17 years, 305 days
=	Joe-Max Moore	United States	100	3 September 1992	14 June 2002	9 years, 284 days
=	Nazri Nasir	Singapore	100	13 September 1990	12 July 2004	13 years, 303 days
=	Dario Šimić	Croatia	100	13 March 1996	20 August 2008	12 years, 160 days
=	Igors Stepanovs	Latvia	100	26 April 1995	10 August 2011	16 years, 106 days
=	Earnie Stewart	United States	100*	19 December 1990	18 August 2004	13 years, 243 days
=	Lukas Podolski	Germany	100	6 June 2004	17 June 2012	8 years, 11 days
=	Damien Duff	Rep. of Ireland	100	25 March 1998	18 June 2012	14 years, 90 days
=	Xabi Alorso	Spain	100	30 April 2003	23 June 2012	9 years, 54 days

OTHER EMPIRE BOOKS BY HARRY HARRIS

19 - MANCHESTER UNITED'S REMARKABLE CHAMPIONSHIP RECORD

MANCINI: DIARY OF A CHAMPION

ROMAN CONQUEST: CHELSEA FC CHAMPIONS OF EUROPE 2012

ALL THREE BOOKS ARE AVAILABLE FROM:

WWW.EMPIRE-UK.COM